The State of Magnolia

A dementia carer's diary

By Dick Durham

Dedication:

For Nancy Isabel Durham, who, in spite of all that follows, I thank God was my mother

Introduction

How I hated that robotic clock and its continuing reminder of the time I was wasting looking after my mother. Its bland face measured my valuable life with jolting, digital efficiency. I watched its red, needle-like second hand circling the dial seamlessly until it reached 12, where, with a loud click, it halted, momentarily stopping time and emancipating the large black minute hand which jerked clumsily, after its withered partner, to the next sixtieth; releasing the second hand again on its ceaseless circumnavigations. I watched the large pointer waiting patiently until its subordinate reached 12 before jumping another 60 seconds.

Another sixty seconds of my valuable life was over, another sixty of my mother's still not enough to satisfy Father Time whose scythe was not even lifted from his shoulder.

My poor, old, abandoned mother lay in her bed next to this face of infinity as it marked out her seemingly endless span and my seemingly endless duty.

The second hand symbolised my new life: ebbing away rapidly in care which I resented, while the minute hand symbolised my mother's age: she had stopped, and I was catching her up. She was insistent on not being dead and meanwhile was waiting for me. And I was catching up. I was getting old while my mother was *just* old. She couldn't get any older at least not in the sense of decrepitude, she was there: OLD. The only thing she could do next was cease and she was in no hurry to do that, not while I was around and catching up.

The ancient minute awaited the impulsive seconds as the hours became days, the days became weeks, the weeks became months. Soon, years were passing me by.

So much for time, what about space? Once you have retreated into a shell where you feel safe and happy you can be physically anywhere. An address is important only for the postman.

Her brain had been blowing fuses for some time until many things no longer added up. While intelligent she had never been an intellectual so it could be argued that perhaps it didn't matter, either to her or anyone else, because the things which she was confused about were not really all that important.

As for her identity, what's in a name? Only some sentimental dream bequeathed to a bundle of freshly delivered organism. Once you have reached a stage where you recognise someone only by their voice, you have stripped away unnecessary artifice and are dealing with the timbre of the soul. It is more essential to name a ship. Behaviour was still important as it was an act of self. Always a woman to speak her mind, she took no prisoners. And as her mind was now denying her this – the core of her being - she naturally enough tried to hang on to it for grim life. One of her last virtues to cease was her ability to scandalise. This had made her some enemies in the past, but now she was 'ill' people, who did not like to hear her version of the truth, found their discomfort mollified.

'She doesn't mean it. She doesn't really know what she's saying. She's confused, bless. She can't help it.'

Oh, but she could. This was not about the message, but the messenger. If Ma could stir things up she was still having an impact, still making a contribution. She was still relevant. She was making the wrong noises to establish herself, because making the right ones only served everyone else.

Unfortunately for me, her partner, who was soon to abandon her, did not look at my mother's altered state the same way. He had been weighing up the consequences of leaving her for some time. Would his own great age outweigh the opprobrium, which might be heaped upon him? He certainly hoped so and to that end bowed his back a little further, became ever more disagreeable and made endless requests for help. These were willingly given: after all I didn't want to get lumbered with looking after my mother, either. But the help was always wrong: the cook who made their lunch didn't warm the plates; the NHS mental health care nurses, who arrived every morning to wash and dress my mother, arrived either too early or too late; and the cleaner who came once a week didn't Hoover under the bed.

Then he started changing the dynamic of their relationship. He referred to himself as my mother's 'carer', never her partner. He told friends and neighbours that their 26 years together – following the death of my father - had been platonic. This from a man who had bought her slinky swimming costumes and badgered her to try a colour in her hair, who had taken her away regularly for weekend breaks to cottages in the country and who signed off letters to her as 'My Darling' with plenty of XXXXs. But no hair dye could add libido now and he 'wanted out' as he candidly put it.

At weddings, Christmas and Sunday lunch he would wear his old regimental tie and would speak at any given opportunity about his wartime experiences. An amateur water-colourist he had painted his close shaves in the Western Desert and hung them up in my mother's home. One Christmas my mother sat and watched one of his freshly unwrapped gifts: a video film of Nazi tanks firing rounds. She made disparaging remarks such as: 'What do we want to watch this old rubbish for?' Even then she was becoming ill and I was treating the old soldier with kid gloves, continually appeasing Ma's awkward and churlish approach. As I said the last thing I wanted was to get lumbered with mother myself. I ignored her anti-tank salvos and later told her that this man 'did a lot for her'. But being a 'character' was her way and indeed had been one of the many things, which had attracted the man to her in the first place.

Clifford's denial of a shared past with my mother was understandable, after all it was useless now she had started to forget it, but his distance appeared to exacerbate her feeling of alienation.

'I'm going home today,' she said suddenly one morning.

'You are at home,' I replied.

'Oh don't you start.'

'I'm not starting, Ma, I'm just saying you are at home'

'I want to get out of this hovel.'

'This hovel is your home. And it's not a hovel.'

'It is.'

'Look, Ma, it's nice and warm –this hovel – you're comfortable in this hovel. It's your home, this hovel. You're very lucky.'

'Oh, I know dear.'

'Some families are living out on the mountainside.'

'Dear God. Poor devils. Where?'

'In places like the Middle East.'

'Oh, them.'

'So you are really lucky. You've got your own home and it's cosy and warm and you're safe.'

'Yes, but what about the others?'

'What others?'

'The others that live here…that man.'

'That man is Clifford. The only people who live here are you and Clifford.'

'What's he doing here?'

'He's your common-law husband.'

'My what?'

'Your companion.'

'But I'm not married to him.'

'No, that's true.'

'So what's he doing here?'

'Well he's been here 25 years, he's your partner.'

'Partner? Whatever do you mean?'

'He's your lover.'
'Don't be coarse, thank-you Dicky.'
'Well anyway he's lived with you since Margaret Thatcher was running the country.'
'Really?'
'Yes he moved in after Pa died.'
'Your father's not dead.'
'He died 23 years ago, Ma.'
'Everyone's dead. Marjorie. Monty. Rhoda. Why does everyone have to die?'
'I remember you telling me once that it would be terrible to live forever.'
'Why would it?'
'Just imagine it, dragging on and on.'
I looked out of her bedroom window at the grey, estuary, at the mud-banks fissured with emerald, half-filled creeks, where Ma used to swim on summer days. Today they were spread beneath a sheet of pink-tinged, cold blue cloud, far out in the river one of the grey-hulled ferries with the company's name emblazoned on the side, was slipping from one panel of leaded glass to the next. Regular as clockwork, day and night they passed, their routine as much a virtue as mine was a vice.
'Who's paying him?' asked Ma.
'Who?'
'That man…what's his name?'
'Clifford. What do you mean "whose paying him"?'
'Well, who is paying him? He can't be doing all this work for nothing.'
'As I said he's your partner, Ma.'
'My what?'
'Your, er, the bloke you live with. The chap who's lived with you for 25 years. The fellow you took up with after

father died. The man who sold his house over the back of the town and who moved in to your house.'

'Yes, but we're not married.'

'I know you're not. He wanted to, but I talked some sense into you and said you would halve your pensions if you did.'

'I wouldn't have married HIM.'

'Maybe not but you were too casual about things and let him move in. Hang on, what do you mean you wouldn't have married HIM? You mean Clifford, so you know it's Clifford and not just a random man?'

'I want to get out of this morgue. I'm going home soon. I can't wait.'

'You know those three little boats you always like to look at?'

'Yes.'

'Well there they are.'

'Where?'

'Out of your bedroom window. Look there they are, there, well there's four of them now, but there they are all bobbing happily on the incoming tide. And you know what that means Ma?'

'What?'

'It means you are IN your home because you can see them out of the window from where you are NOW.'

'Oh yes dear.'

'And there's Kay's wall.'

'Who?'

'Kay, Frank's widow. Her wall. Your neighbour. She lives in the house next door. You can see it through your window.'

'Oh her, she's the limit.'

'She may be the limit, but that's her wall. Just outside your window. Your bedroom window which is in front of you and part of your home.'

'Is she there?'

'Not at the moment.'

'Funny girl. She wouldn't look me in the eye. But I made her say "Hello". I said "Good morning, Kay", as sweetly as possible. She had to say "Hello"'

'Well she's mad.'

'What dear?'

'She's mad, barking mad. She's not worth worrying about.'

'Oh I don't worry about her dear. I'm going bonkers anyway.'

'Well, that's true!'

'DICKEE', yelled in mock outrage.

'Well we're all a bit bonkers. You're not totally bonkers, but your memory is playing you up.'

'I may be going bonkers but there's nothing wrong with my memory.'

'Well no, not for things of long ago.'

'Well there you are then. That must be a sign of a good memory. Surely if you can remember things in the distant past then you've got a GOOD memory?'

'Can't argue with that.'

'It seems like only yesterday my mother took me to Germany.'

Maybe, I thought, early memories are bound to be more vivid because the brain was once a fresh organ, absorbing impressions like a sponge. It was young, unused, with plenty of bankable memory and so maybe earlier impressions make more impact. As we get older we are less likely to experience new sensations, but even if we do we relate them to older experiences and make them pre-conceptions almost. So what the brain absorbs later on in life is not as… well memorable…

'What seems like only yesterday is years and years ago.'

'Well it might be to you.'

'And it should be to you.'

'Why?'

'Because otherwise your reality will be different to everyone else's.'

'Are you saying I'm losing my marbles?'

'Well that's one way of putting it.'

'Charming. You wait 'til it happens to you.'

'I'm sorry Ma. I'm trying to tell you it as it is. I don't want to upset you, but surely it's important you are reminded of the truth?'

Her magnolia carpet was dented with four little square holes where the oak-veneer plywood wardrobe used to sit. I'd talked her into throwing it out to open up the room and accommodate a chair by the window so she could sit looking out. But she had no time for 'views'. Views were for parish spies and Ma was above gossip. So she sat instead looking in. Her view was the high, single bed with the commode next to it and the dark brown chest next to that on which sat her TV. A small bedside table was on the door side of the bed with a bedside lamp and a capodimonte figure of a female golfer with club raised which she'd picked up from her charity shop. Her mother, Ethel, had once been captain of the local golf team. She sat looking at the 1970s embossed wallpaper which had been painted over with magnolia emulsion. You could still see the gold and vermillion stripes in places. On this wall hung a black and white photograph of me aged six and my sister, Diana, aged three, lying down in front of me.

'Where's that bloody man? That miserable devil, what's his name?'

'Do you mean Clifford?'

'Yes, well done. That's it. Clifford. He's got a dreadful temper.'

'Has he?'

'Dreadful. He can't sit still for one minute. He's always got to be DOING something. Why doesn't he just sit down?'

'Well that's the way he is. We're all different.'

'He certainly is.'

'What?'

'Different.'

'What do you mean?'

'Well he's very kind, but the other man is a beast.'

'What other man?'

'The other one. The miserable one. The one whose always feeling sorry for himself.'

'But there is no other man, Ma. There's just Clifford.'

'It's such a silly name.'

'What is?'

'Clifford. Who's called Clifford? Fancy calling somebody that.'

'Well it's unusual, especially as a Christian name in the 1920s, but not exceptionally rare.'

'It's a pompous name. It suggests something you aren't.'

'The name is just a word. If it comes with the meaning you attach to it then that can only be bestowed on those who chose it. But once chosen you can grow into the expectations made of a name,' I said.

'Interesting thought,' said Ma.

'Anyway Clifford knows everything and yet he knows nothing.'

'What's that supposed to mean?'

'He's always right. He never stops talking. Yet he's not right he's very often wrong, wrong with such grave authority.'

'Knowledge without intelligence?'

'Precisely, dear.'

'Well whatever he is, he's looking after you.'

'Oh yes, dear, he's very good. But he wants everything done in five minutes. And then he's off. He never stops to talk anymore.'

'Well he's busy, Ma. He's got things to do.'

'What things?'

'Well cooking and washing up.'

'But no one's asked him to do the washing up. As for cooking, I taught him that. He's become quite good. If only he wouldn't lose his temper.'

'We all have our bad days, Ma.'

'Yes, but he's always doom and gloom. He worries about things before they happen, then when they don't he worries why not. How many people live in this dump?'

'Just you and Clifford, Ma.'

'But what about the other one?'

'There is no other one, just you and Clifford'

The sound of the chairlift heralded Clifford's approach. Involuntarily I counted down the revolutions of its motor, timing it to its well-known stop at the top of the steep flight of stairs. Then the clunk of the arm-rest being lifted to the vertical position. Then the click of the lock on the step as it was swung round to allow the occupant off. Next came the first creak of the floorboards, another would follow just before entry into Ma's bedroom.

The floor creaked again and Clifford entered his fine head of white hair brushed back from his boyish face. But then I noticed a glistening blob over his right ear. A smear of uncombed brilliantine? But brilliantine isn't brown. With a shock I realised it was excreta. He hadn't noticed. He must have given Ma her 'personal care' as the NHS team put it, this morning.

'Hello dear,' he said.

'Hello, who are you?'

'Who am I?'

'No, she said "How are you?"' I said ever ready to maintain the status quo for fear its change would put me in sole control.

'Oh did she? I thought she said "Who are you?"'

'I did,' said Ma, torpedoing my efforts at utilising Clifford's deafness with white spin.

'Would you like some porridge?'

'No, I don't want any damn porridge.'

'There's no need to talk like that Ma.'

'OK, dear, maybe later.'

'No, not later. I don't want any bloody porridge. It's muck.
'

'All right dear. Will you have a sip of water?'

'No, I loathe water.'

'But it is good for you, you mustn't dehydrate.'

'No, it isn't good for me and I WILL dehydrate if I want to.'

'OK, dear.'

Clifford left the room and I followed urging him to the bathroom where I washed his hair for him.

I then returned to Ma: 'You must stop berating Clifford, he's only trying to help. He's caring for you. I'm not here all the time. And he is. You are vulnerable, Ma, and need help. Clifford is providing that help and it's going to wear very thin if you keep having a go at him.'

'I'm not a fool, Dicky.'

'Well don't upset him then, if you keep going on like that you'll end up in a home.'

'Are you threatening me?'

'No, Ma, I'm just trying to make you see reason.'

'If you want me to see reason then stop being unreasonable. You're in this with him aren't you?'

'In what, Ma?'

'In this plan to keep me here.'

'Ma I don't know what to say. I'm not going to tell you you're somewhere you're not. I'm not going to tell you there are three people here when there are not. I'm your son, surely you can trust me? You have to trust me and I want you to trust me because I want to be able to reassure you.'

'Well if this is my home I want to sell it.'

'And go where?'

'Back to Leigh-on-Sea.'

'But you are in Leigh-on-Sea.'

'No, I'm not.'

'Well where do you think you are?'

'I don't know. In this dump.'

'Well give me an address in Leigh that you want to go to.'

'Sparrow's End, Woodside.'

'But Ma that's where you lived when you were a child.'

'I know.'

'It's gone now, pulled down.'

'Everything's gone, everyone's dead.'

'There's no point in worrying about it. Don't worry. It's not important. It's gone.'

'I still want to sell this place. It's too big.'

'What will you buy?'

'A nice little house in Leigh.'

'That's what this is. And if you sell it, it costs 10 grand to move and you'll only be able to afford a flat. Do you want someone living over your head? Making noise?'

'No, I do not.'

'Well there you are. You're perfectly all right here. You're warm, you're cosy. It's a nice little room. You're safe.'

'But who put all these things here?'

'What things?'

'All that stuff – that furniture.'

'Ma, you put it there. It's your furniture. You and Pa put it there when you moved here.'

'Your Pa is half baked putting it there.'

'Pa is fully baked now: he went to the crem 24 years ago.'

'DICKY.'

'Sorry, Ma, tasteless I know. You know what I thought of him. I was lucky to have a father like him. I wish I'd had another 24 years of such luck. But it was not to be and I don't want you stranded in the past.'

'Everyone's dead. But what about my rings they're not safe here. Supposing somebody sees them?'

'Whose going to see them? No one, only me and Clifford and the children.'

'What children?'

'My children.'

'Have you got children?'

'Yes.'

'My goodness you're not married are you?'

'Yes, Ma, you were at the wedding.'

'But who'd marry you?'

'Cathy.'

'Oh she's lovely. So kind, so gorgeous, so INTELLIGENT. What did she marry you for?'

'Perhaps she felt sorry for me.'

'Fancy Cathy being your wife…I can't remember anything.'

'It doesn't matter.'

'But everything's been moved round. And where does he sleep?'

'Who?'

'What's his name?'

'Clifford.'

'Yes, Clifford, that's it.'

'He sleeps in the room behind yours. That's Pa's old room. He died in there.'

Three days before Christmas, 1984, the shivering undertakers, without top-coats, turned up in the draughty alleyway between Ma's house and her next-door neighbour's. Dressed in respectful black, their heads bowed in professional sorrow at the front door, there was something pleading about their look: 'We are doing our best to seem sincere. We are treating this as your loved one not just another job.' I sympathised with their efforts at mock compassion. It reminded me of my newspaper past, door-stepping the unexpectedly bereaved. I would adopt a long-faced, fawning, forelock-touching performance to get over the threshold and snatch the family photo album.

I recognised the synthetic sympathy of the undertakers and how they rushed it to the fore, before the seams showed. Their tired, heart-on-the-sleeve routine, was like that of an end of the pier showman at the end of the evening at the end of the season. I noticed the black clothing was glossy in parts, that one of them was badly shaved, his smart shoes scuffed. The other was looking red around the features, fighting off mortality, his bread and butter, with a hangover.

Their demeanour was in complete contrast to the Asian doctor who'd turned up earlier to proclaim my father's death. He was brusque, businesslike and took one look at my father lying on his back with his mouth wide open, rammed a pillow under his chin and elbowed it violently two or three times to force its closure. Any outrage I felt, I was feeling for a corpse, I quickly rationalised.

The undertakers carried their unctuous procedure upstairs and into my father's bedroom, where, hidden behind the door, they dropped the act and got down to business. As I peeped through the gap between door and jam they quickly lifted my father into a black vinyl, zippered, body bag connected to a stretcher. Once securely sealed inside they lifted him, one each end. But the box room was tiny and they couldn't turn the stretcher from the bed towards the door. So instead they upended their charge, one of them using a knee to shunt my father lengthwise up the wall. Just before they came back through the door they dropped him from the vertical to the horizontal once more and automatically returned to pious mode, carrying him reverentially to the hearse.

'Poor man why did he have to die?'

'Been gone a long time, Ma, and you got over it a long time ago, too. Anyway I'm off now.'

'Where are you going?'

'To work.'

'Where?'

'London.'

'What do you do up there?'

'Fit formulaic journalese around glossy adverts.'

'But you used to be a reporter.'

'In the good old days.'

'So what do you do now?'

'Girl's journalism. Magazine work. Everyone wants to be a journalist now and everyone is.'

'But what about all those murders you used to like doing?'

'Murders, two a penny, these days, Anyway I was made redundant from Fleet Street when the new technology came along.'

'So you're just a threadbare typewriter ribbon?'

'Journalists are two a penny, these days. I'm told I'm lucky to have a job. Graduates are leaving college with the ability to be film producers as well as having computer skills that would enable them to run GCHQ.'

'That's a shame.'

'That's the past. I've got over it and so should you.'

I left her room and allowed the two creaks to be heard and then doubled back with my legs spread so that my feet walked the corridor immediately below the skirting board each side thereby missing the loose boards, so that I could sneak up undetected.

I peered around the doorframe to Ma's room. Her eyes were closed – almost – and her head slumped over on her pillow. Her breathing was marked. She appeared to be dozing. But then quite suddenly she started to talk.

'I can remember my home. Sparrows End. It backed on to the woods. The garden merged with the woods. It was quite magical. I would stand at the bottom of the garden looking into the wood. You could see bluebells under the dark canopy of trees. The sunlight made them glow blue in the dark. I imagined I could see fairies…

I was always hungry and went to neighbours to ask for food. My mother told me off. She used to leave me alone a lot and go and play golf, that was in the woods, too, further away where the links were. I used to stand and try and see her through the trees. I never did see her. But I stared so hard I thought I could see something…

'Everyone's dead…'

She dozed off and I went to work, but that evening returned and told her she'd told me about Sparrow's End.

'Oh, yes, dear, it's all in my diary.'

'What diary?'

'My diary back at home.'

'You are at…Oh, never mind. Where at home is it?'

'In the desk, of course.'

In a drawer of the bureau under piles of old comics I came across a pressed cardboard suitcase with reinforced plastic corners. Inside were tattered old exercise books, customised into diaries. Nancy Best's diaries. Ma's diaries. They ranged from her teenage years to her last decades with my father. Although there appeared to be a gap of many decades between.

I started to read them and found myself spying on my mother as a 19-year-old Voluntary Aid Detachment (VAD) nurse based at Shenley Military Hospital near St Albans. Here my mother was, offering care, unaware her own best years were ebbing away. And I felt ashamed.

She shared a room with three other nurses: Gene Whatling, Jean Bennett and Dorothy French and between them they grafted through tough shifts looking after wounded servicemen, but almost every night there was a dance or concert on somewhere to prepare for which they changed from their uniforms into their 'costumes' and then either cycled or hitch-hiked on American trucks to the event.

But infuriatingly Ma had scissored out whole pages – up to 10 at a time – or redacted paragraphs with daubings of ink. Perhaps, like me, she did resent spending her time in looking after people.

Her father Herbert Best was a stockbroker. He died of pneumonia aged 50 when she was just four-years-old. She has a caricature of him in fatigues drawn in 1918 in Ochey, France. He is towing a string of toy cars. Apparently he was involved with ground transport for the Royal Flying Corps. His sandy hair matches his uniform and is just a fringe around his domed, double-crowned head. It was his male pattern baldness which I resented as a teenager. It was all his fault that I had a 'high forehead' and a thinning crown when being sexy meant a Beatle mop-top.

His old airbase was very close to Nancy and may well have had some bearing on the chosen Christian name of his youngest daughter. His eldest daughter, Rhoda went to finishing school in Germany just before the next of the 'world' wars. Nancy and Rhoda's widowed mother, Ethel went out to Germany to bring Rhoda home just before World War II started. Rhoda had lodged with a family who turned their official portrait of Hitler to the wall when guests arrived. The father survived the war, but his son was lost on the Eastern Front. He just disappeared. Everyone's dead...

After the war my mother, returned to Germany to visit the family Rhoda had stayed with. Hamburg was in ruins. She told me how she remembered going through it on the train. There were piles of rubble and overturned vehicles for miles.

'I swapped cigarettes for a ruby bracelet. I didn't care. Those damn Germans. They bombed...Devon. What were they after down there? Pulverising cream teas? We had to run for cover out of the hospital at Torquay. I can see the wings now with that filthy iron cross. So when I saw Hamburg I thought serves them right. And the Great War, too. Think of all the poor men gone to their graves because of Germany.'

There was her Uncle Douglas Best cut off in his prime, she had the big penny with his name on it on the mantle-piece. Then there was her husband Dick's uncle Stanley Durham his name is hewn on the Menin Gate… blown to smithereens, buried under mud, who knows where he is… Everyone's dead.

'Dick never appreciated how lucky he was to survive. He always complained about how the war took the best years of his life away without realising the others lost all the years of their life,' she once told me.

Father knew he was no hero and maybe hated the war because of it. Maybe it underlined his shortcomings, rubbed his nose in his faint-heartedness. Yet he didn't dodge it. He did his bit, no doubt making the bit as tiny as possible. His was not a conscientious war but neither did he object to going. Not overtly anyway. His resentment for war was personified by Churchill. There was a rumour on his troop ship on route to India that the old British bulldog had a financial interest in a manufacturing company which produced nuts and bolts. Once he became wartime leader all the nuts and bolts on all the military materiel had to be changed to accommodate the Churchillian production, so it was said.

I suppose in a way there's something brave about being un-heroic in a war. There must be a 101 ways of dodging the final test, that of facing the bullets, and fudging your way through to civvy street.

Ma had thought a lot about death and loss and refused to attend funerals. She'd been to enough of them.

I returned that evening after work to find Clifford dressed in a boiler suit and wearing his old regimental beret.

Around his waist was an ancient Army issue leather belt with hooped strings to which various items could be attached, like a torch, a screwdriver or a knife. Her always wore this garb when 'going into action' whether it be blue-tacking a hook to the wall, washing up, or tending to my mother's ablutions. This time it was clearly the latter as he was wearing Marigold gloves with his name written on them in marker pen.

Ma said: 'What's wrong with me?'

Clifford, said: 'I've told you before. You've had a couple of mini-strokes. That has impaired your memory. It means your short-term memory isn't working as well as it could. It makes things very difficult for me.'

'There's nothing wrong with my memory. At least, it's better than yours.'

'I haven't had a stroke.'

'Just as well. I mean you write your name on everything, NOW. Goodness knows what you'd write it on if you had a stroke. You'd have your name hanging round your neck. And why are you wearing those gloves?'

'I've been clearing up your motion. You missed the loo again. I do wish you'd use the commode.'

'You use the DAMN COMMODE.'

'It's no good shouting at me, Nancy. I understand you don't like talking about these things, you don't like facing reality, but it just means I have to face it instead. If you use the commode, no-one's going to see it. And it can be emptied in the morning.'

'Oh do shut up. I just want to go home.'

'Well you are at home, I've told you that before, too, God knows how many times. Sometimes I think you keep doing this deliberately.'

'First of all you tell me I'm ill then you accuse me of making it up.'

'You need to take these pills and it's better if you take them with food.'

'Stop telling me what to do.'

'And you need a shower. You smell.'

'I do not.'

Clifford started to heave Ma out of bed amidst much grumbling on her part and assertive cajoling on his. They hobbled away to the bathroom. Later having both negotiated the chair lift they sat in the living room watching the anniversary of D-Day on TV. Ma sang loudly accompanying For Those in Peril on the Sea. Clifford turned the volume up louder both for his defective hearing and to try and drown out Ma.

Clifford, said: 'Oh look there's a staff officer. Wonder who that is? Oh it *is* Dannat. I think all those standards must be from the British Legion, there can't be that many veterans left. Where's that, Arrowmanches? Plenty of Airborne there, cadets anyway. Shame it's raining. I don't know if I'd have gone this time, even if I could have.'

'Oh belt up, Clifford, we all know you were there. You never stop telling us. What's stopping you, anyway?'

'I have to look after you.'

'No you do not. Is there any cake?'

'I'm not giving you any. You wouldn't eat your breakfast.'

'Bully.'

'At least it proves I'm looking after you. You need to take your 10 o'clock pills by the way.'

'I'm not taking any damn pills.'

'Nancy. You take them every day. You have to take them because you are ill. I'm your carer and it's my responsibility to see that you do take them.'

'Well I am not going to take them.'

'You are a foolish woman.'

'Oh, shut up, you ape.'

'You will take them or go without supper.'

'How dare you threaten me. I will have supper if I want and I don't need you to make it anyway.'

'Very well. I'll leave you to prepare it.'

'Where's the damn kitchen?'

'Through there. I put a sign up.'

'Put a sign up? What do you think I am a bloody motorist?'

'You are losing your mind and you keep going the wrong way. I put a sign up to help you.'

'I don't need a sign.'

'Oh, look there's Neville.'

'Who?'

'Neville, you remember. Oh you probably don't. Neville my driver. In the tank. Look he's getting wet. Shame about the weather over there. I don't suppose there'll be another one.'

'Another what?'

'Another anniversary for D Day. There's hardly anyone left. Those that Wittman left behind after Villers have grown old.'

'Well it's better than the alternative.'

'I'm not so sure. I never thought I'd end up doing this. Clearing up your motions. Getting you dressed. Making your meals.'

'Well I made your meals for long enough and at least I wasn't so damn miserable about it.'

Clifford, who once told me a doctor had described him as 'biologically young' no longer wanted my clapped-out mother. The fun woman, popular with one and all, whom he wore on his arm with pride, like his campaign medals, had gone. And unlike the medals she no longer scrubbed up well.

When she stopped making complete sense, he became impatient at first and as her condition worsened, not helped by his deafness and lack of sympathy, he became indifferent.

Undeniably he'd had a tough job. But it was one he was now resigning from.

A family crisis meeting was called. Present were Jonathan, Clifford's son, a retired school-master; Tony, Clifford's son-in-law, a social worker, myself and Cathy, my wife. It was a strange non-negotiation at which cards were not displayed openly on the table. The status quo was about to change radically and the unstated question was who's life was going to be impacted most? I didn't want Clifford to leave as my mother's care would become my responsibility. Cathy did want him to leave because, in trying to tend to my mother's needs, she had been obliged to tend to Clifford's, too. Jonathan didn't want him to leave as his father would become his responsibility. Tony held the only ace: his family were already burdened with the 24-hour care of a bed-ridden daughter and could not possibly be expected to look after Clifford as well and therefore didn't need to express a view.

Perhaps Ma's Care could be extended to help Clifford? suggested Jonathan who said his father was close to suffering a nervous breakdown. But my mother, in receipt of free Care from Mental Health nurses, was paying for extra attention from private sector meal-makers and sitters. Would Clifford or perhaps Jonathan foot the bill for even more assistance? The idea was not pursued.

When she first became ill Clifford had suggested my mother 'go into a home'. But the economics of that was complex, too. Her savings were a touch above the means tested £22,000. So should Clifford live in her house while she was dispatched to a care home for which she would pay?

Clifford unexpectedly joined the meeting. His back was bent, his face was grim. Taking sips of bottled water, he thanked Cathy for her kindness. He thanked both of us for our family's involvement in his life and then said: 'Not in weeks, but in the months ahead,' he needed to plan to leave my mother.

Jonathan, said: 'Now dad, you don't want to rush into anything, I'm not making any rash decisions.'

Tony remained silent.

Both Cathy and I put no problems in the way of this exit strategy. Nor did we express judgement on his decision. On the contrary, we all 'understood', even morality has to be suspended in allowances for the aged.

We did say that we would like to know when. We needed to work out what we were going to tell my mother: something those, whose mother she wasn't, had not considered.

Clifford, said: 'I don't think you'd better tell her I'd died.' A clinging ego. He wanted to leave a residue.

How should he behave towards her while preparing to leave? he asked. I requested he show some TLC. Even though false, it would be better that way, even for a short time, I reckoned. We could come up with something after his departure.

So it all became lovey-dovey, lips on the cheek and 'Hello darling'.

I decided to sleep at my mother's house, while the evacuation was organised. This would be no great sacrifice as she lived next door but one.

Ma knew something was up, but she combated it with a curse or parody. So, when the time came, Clifford drove away in the little Peugeot with the compass he'd glued on the dashboard which helped them locate their weekend jaunts: my mother was no navigator. The neighbours he had talked to, while carrying home the shopping alone, after my mother became house-bound, those who had sympathised, were left now with only speculative gossip. None of that mattered now, he'd gone. He'd left all his old clothes and shed-loads, two in fact, of plastic bags, broken baskets on wheels, empty ice-cream cartons and 101 other come-in-handies. His own past – apart from the medals – he dumped, too. Family photographs discarded – the ones of a couple in a broken marriage- torn in half – piles of old half finished water colours, and raincoats, hideous rubber overshoes and innumerable pairs of rubber gloves. Much of his lair looked like the tools of a serial killer's need to dispose of bodies, but was in fact simply the kit of a benign control freak. Beside his bed the built-in wall unit held two bedside cabinets covered with plate glass. Atop these, in miniature cut-glass saucers were carefully-gathered mounds of crinkly, yellow toe-nails.

The old man had shed his old skin and left my mother alone with the robot clock. There was no reassuring tick-tock coming from its mechanism, nothing which a human heart could pace itself against. No this limping time-server was digital accuracy par excellence. It was a tyrant's clock: Mussolini would have had one in every station-master's office. For there was nothing fallible about it. It would never speed up, slow down, need winding or pack up, as long as it was supplied with power it would go on indifferently until the end of… time.

And so, it seemed, would we.

So with my sister living an ocean away in New Hampshire, USA, looking after Ma was now down to me and after dinner each night I would kiss Cathy good-bye and go next door but one to sleep. And to tend my mother in the night, make her breakfast, before going to work the next morning and leaving her for the Mental Health team to wash and dress.

The robotic clock's spastic revolutions continued to mark infinity. If Wittgenstein did actually say 'Death is not a part of life' he had overlooked dying which was now the biggest part of my life.

As I continued to read through the diaries my mother kept as a young woman, I decided to start a diary of my mother as an old woman. Was it an act of self-pity? Or a testimonial of time….my time?

A diary of dementia

2009

August 31

Nobody wants the old. Why don't they just die like they are supposed to? Babies are loved, as they become children, children are cherished as they become teenagers, teenagers are admired as they turn into adults, adults are respected as they become pensioners. Pensioners are then supposed to become little old ladies or, if men, gummy, outspoken characters. And then die before becoming an encumbrance. Card signed, wreath laid, puff of smoke. Job done.

When they don't and when they just keep on keeping on, they are marginalised, because there are only so many times you can ooh and aah over their past. Memory Lane is a cul-de-sac.

When they can't talk, laugh, feed themselves, toilet themselves, read, watch TV, walk, sit up, lie down or think, they have departed, at least cognitively speaking, because they should be bloody dead. There are no greetings cards for becoming doubly incontinent, for the loss of marbles, or even for learning to drive your first cripple scooter. At this point, the cards we expect to fill in express 'sorrow for the loss of a loved one.'

I need to try and evacuate my mind. It is swimming with words uttered by my mother who was 86 in May. She has been suffering from what I am pleased to have confirmed as dementia, because it sounds more respectable than Alzheimer's, following two or perhaps more 'mini-strokes' a couple of years ago. The East of England Ambulance Service who collected her after a 'mechanical fall' marked her previous medical history as 'TIAs X 2 or more. Dementia'. And that's the first anyone knew about it. A diagnosis from an ambulance-man.

I am listening to much she says now in case more of her mind is shut-down. I am treating her words as significant because of this. But is their significance manifest only because their utterer maybe mute soon?

1st September

'Clifford?' a shout in the night.
I awoke with a start.

I ran up the stairs, naked and as quick as a flash to find Ma lying there in the pre-dawn gloaming. It's 05:15. She's awake. The commode has been used, accurately, and her 'baby pants' pulled back into place, accurately. It's as though the fairies had been in overnight.

She wants a cup of tea.

'I'll make you one in half an hour, OK? I just want to get a bit more sleep.' She's fine with that. She likes to know a time when something is going to happen even if I'm not certain she can make sense of the omnipotent clock.

Later I take round a transistor radio and leave her whistling to Radio 3.

4th September

'Clifford?' the call comes just before 6:00, she's done it again – used the commode successfully in the night. I decant it into the upstairs lavatory. 'Is the old man in any pain?' The old man in the next room, my room now, had been Clifford. I've told Ma he's gone to hospital.

'No.'

'What's wrong with him? Is it his leg or his hip?'

'No, his back, I think,' he was always bent over, after all. Although he straightened up when his son arrived by car to take him away. Clearly the burden of my mother was manifest physically.

'Oh yes, that's right, it's his back.'

Half an hour later she asks: 'Where's what's his name?'

'Who?'

'Oh, I don't know. If only everyone was called Clifford it would be so much easier,' she says then adds: 'Oh, look, there it goes again up and down.' I look out of the window and see a tree-top which keeps flickering above a roof in the wind.

'I'm so surprised when I wake up. I can't believe it,' she added.

I then tell her about my son Richard spending two days in London with our friends John and his wife Pat, who is from Thailand.

'Yes, she's lovely it's not her fault she's from a tribe. I couldn't marry someone from a tribe. I just couldn't. It's not her fault she's foreign.'

She then started talking about the opera Carmen and how she saw it in Hamburg after the war.

'We couldn't sit together, it was so popular. I sat between two wogs!' When I pulled a face she added: 'Germans!'

'Rhoda, poor Rhoda. Rhoda's dead. Why does everyone have to die?'

I tuned the TV to a children's channel which was broadcasting Pingu, a Scandinavian cartoon about a penguin which converses successfully in squawks.

Ma laughs: 'Why can't everyone talk like that? At least you can understand them!'

September 16th

Ma got up yesterday and fell. She's hurt her right leg. Toileting has just got a whole lot more tedious. After finally managing her movement to and disrobing for the commode, she only had a small wee.

'Oh that's a shame you haven't done very much,' I say.

'Oh good. I don't care. I'm not a performing idiot.'

She called me a devil who was trying to kill her off after I finally lost my patience with her continued questions about why she had to sit on the commode.

'Because otherwise you will sit in shit in your bed.'
Not good admittedly, but there's a limit to continual
waiting for her to move a few inches along the bed,
continued explanation as to why she must use the
commode and continual rudeness from her.
She asked for Clifford who would not have talked to her
like that.

September 20th

'If I'm dying I want to get on with it,' Ma exclaimed last
night to Cathy who had gone round to give her tea.
This morning the little ginger-haired nurse with freckly
arms and wide hips arrived. A conscientious and God-
fearing soul.
'How's the pain Nancy?'
'Oh it comes and goes,' said old yellow face, her big jaw
chewing on toast. Then a little later, probably through
awkwardness that I was there, Maureen, the nurse, asked
again 'Is it giving you much trouble this morning?'
Ma's yellow jaws swivelled round; her mad white hair
askew and her imperious blue eyes focusing: 'I've already
answered your question,'
she said like some ghastly spectre of Queen Victoria.
The damnable thing about age and illness is that we must
keep making allowances for it. Yet I feel mean towards
my own mother when she is so unpleasant. I want to tease
her, to 'get her back' and have to fight such a tendency by
leaving the room. Even such a departure is a 'win' for the
old crone who will say and did: 'Now go away and leave
me alone, I know what you are doing.'

This was a reference to my throwing the bed sheet over her head while I got the blankets straightened and tucked in up to her chin.

'I don't want to die,' she said pushing off the makeshift shroud. Then later I suggested she remove her cardigan or rather I remove it for her as being morning she would now be too hot. 'No!' she yelled, 'you want me to die.'

Later on Maureen, having washed and straightened Ma's clothes, left a note of instructions for tomorrow's nurse Mags, an elder statesman of nurses, practical, dour, no-nonsense. 'If she reads this she 'aint got to 'aul her about so much,' said Maureen, adding: 'I said to your mum you're only dusty, get the Pledge out!'

I left Ma on the commode after dinner while I washed up. She decided to get off it unassisted and fell. Cathy and I managed to get her up, not before Cathy asked if she was in pain. Ma knows that pain means paramedics will be called and so refused to answer, covering her face with her arm like a child.

'You're right and I'm wrong,' she said childishly.

Even Cathy, ever patient, is now getting fed up with her. 'I'm seeing another side to her, perhaps the real side,' she said.

I gave her the soft toy dog to play with before I left and made doggy noises.

'Oh go away Dicky, I might be mad but I'm not daft. I'm surprised I'm not dead yet.'

22nd September

'You must go and get Dick. Is he there? Where is he?'
'I scattered him out there,' I said pointing to the river.
'They tell me he's dead. Is he?'

'Yes, Ma. Your husband died 25 years ago at Christmas. Now how about a nice cup of tea?'

'No I'm going to have my dinner.'

'Are you hungry? I'll make you some toast.'

'No I hate toast.'

'Nice cup of tea?'

'No don't make any tea, I'm going to make dinner.'

'It's half past six in the morning. You have dinner every day at the same time when Dee makes it.'

'All right,' she said with vehemence and volume for being countermanded.

Dee is a bird-like elderly lady who dyes her hair and wears tight clothes like a teenager. She is supplied by an agency, which supplies people to cook meals. There are such agencies. As we edge away from living cadavers there are agencies, which will help us 'get back to normal.'

The Occupational Therapist nurse called today to hear a story from Cathy about Ma's continued beastliness. Cathy came in to find Ma yelling at Dee, to: 'Do what you are told!' The Occupational Therapist said Ma could be 'grieving' the loss of Clifford. Certainly she is lucid and articulate a lot of the time, as well as being confused. So she must realise the changes: Clifford gone, all the nurses in and out, me being here and her being virtually bed-ridden. She did say some weeks back when I said I was going down the pub: 'Oh that. You still do that? With a nice wife, surely you just want to sit and hold hands and talk?'

'About what, beer?' I said jokingly. But I took the point, maybe she does miss the old curmudgeon. If so we're all getting it in the neck.

24th September

An onshore gale sent exploding geysers up against the promenade wall at High Water, but after 20 minutes of ebb the sea was reduced to fingers of froth grasping at the beach, trying to hang on, like a man clinging to a cliff edge.

'I was very upset that Dick just left and didn't want to see me.'

'You mean Clifford, Ma.'

'Yes, but things like that don't affect me. I couldn't care less. I can't be bothered.'

This was the first direct reference to Clifford's departure.

'All these people are awful,' she said about the nurses.

'No they're wonderful.'

'Yes, they are but they get all giggly.'

'Well that's better than them coming in and whacking you.'

'Do you mind, I'll give them a sock on the jaw. I'm not as ill as I look.'

26th September

There's a sketch of Ma drawn in 1927, when she was aged four, by an artist calling himself 'Delino' from Victoria Arcade in Southend, which was demolished in the 1960s. Her hair is bobbed over a round face with a button nose, small down-turned mouth and sad, blue eyes. People say it's 'very Lucie Atwell' but this is no caricature, Ma's eyes hold a look of profound melancholia. It's hard to dismiss the notion that this is a little girl who knows what's coming.

It hangs downstairs in the 'front room' the exhibits room of family heirlooms.

'I want to get out of here and just walk and walk and walk until I get right across …'

I notice smears of excreta on the commode lid, so I have now hidden it hoping to ensure better accuracy. The commode doesn't need a lid. A lid is there to make it something other than a loo next to your bed.

I slept in too long, but Ma at least managed to keep the residue mostly within the bounds of her nappy.

I keep joking that I will take her soft toy dogs for a swim in Leigh Creek. 'Don't you touch my little darlings…

'I suppose I'll spend another ghastly day talking to myself because no one else will talk to me. Thank God for my wonderful films. I don't know what I'd do without them, ghastly old rubbish.'

This evening Ma is eating baked beans on toast, her false teeth clicking like knitting needles. She is watching Fred Astaire and Ginger Rogers in Swing Time and recalling how all her schoolmates at Westcliff High School For Girls, knew the tunes. I tried hard to ignore the obvious juxtaposition: my mother's old grey head and naturally useless limbs lying in bed while she watched the lustrous-haired stars of her youth dancing the night away.

13 January 1943

'Henry <u>can</u> <u>not</u> dance although he insists he can. At the end I argued about music with him, because he said there was nothing to touch Strauss. He said that when Strauss was first brought to America everyone raved and shouted, clapped and cheered so I said: "Oh, Americans" He said all the best music was to be found in America, I said it was not, but in Germany and Italy and told him it was because

*he could not understand Beethoven that he did not like it
and because Strauss was so easy and quick and jiggy that
he did. He said there was a story in everything Strauss had
written and I said there were whole legends in Rimsky-
Korsakov and advised him to expand his knowledge of
music – so the evening wasn't very pleasant.*
*'I walked off as the thought of talking utter nonsense was
not appealing when bed was waiting.'*

My mother could dance, although, in my time, I only
witnessed her swivelling to Chubby Checker's Twist
Again at a party thrown by my parents in the 1960s.
There was an oddity: my mother was an excellent hostess,
great company, good fun, the 'life and soul of the party'
and yet loathed throwing them. My father, was quiet, shy,
a bit of a dark horse, and added nothing to the knees-up yet
he loved them!

27th September

Valerie Davidson of the NHS Mental Health team talked
this morning about some of her former clients. Trained by
nuns at a charity-run care home, Nazareth House, she
recalled one woman whose body was a permanent 'S –
shape' from where her family had left her in her bed until
even that was too demanding for them and she was
transferred to the home.
'When she stood up her legs still stayed in the S-shape she
had grown into. She kept her eyes closed most of the time
and all her food was liquidised. But if anyone put parsnip
in it she spat it out.'

She told me of another patient, 'one of our ladies', who showed her carer the garden. Valerie agreed that it was lovely, the sun shining on it and all, then the patient said 'Yes but I'm worried about the elephant up the tree there. It keeps slipping down.'

She said many people in 'their last hours' choose to be alone to die. 'Not everyone wants somebody there holding their hand. I don't think I'd want to be gawped at.' She knew of people, surrounded by family and close to death, who waited until the family went to have tea or a cigarette, 'And they would die while the family were out of the room.'

Dying, unlike being born, can be timed. Both are the most intimate moments of a span. Yet privacy is only afforded to the former. Unlike the heralding of the stork, few wish to fly with the raven.

'One of my ladies asked if anyone would give her a cuddle. I used to lay with my ladies, holding them. I'm sure it's not PC but human contact is everything,' said Valerie.

She described Ma as 'feisty' but felt she might have given up trying to walk. But Ma is lazy and won't do anything physical or intellectual which requires a little effort.

When Valerie had gone Ma asked why the other people's belongings are left here.

'What things?'

'I'll get them.'

'Go on then.'

'No, I can sense there is a trap waiting for me.'

'Yes – reality.'

I am a brute, but I believe I must counter Ma's fantasies at every turn. I must keep turning her back to the truth.

Simply allowing her to build a fairy world would be just as

bad as the family who left their old mum to become a human S.

28th September

Ma fell over yesterday evening while attempting to draw the curtains. In doing so she knocked over her commode. Cleaning up I used hand tissues which I then threw down the upstairs lavatory, blocking it. So this morning before making Ma's breakfast I bailed out the water closet and unscrewed the bowl from the floorboards, disconnected it from the flush pipe and the exit waste and dragged out the large clot of tissue paper gagging the waste pipe, cursing aloud as I did so.
'My word you are angry,' Ma said from her bed.
After getting it working once more, I pushed Ma up The Broadway in her wheel-chair, at her insistence, to buy my youngest daughter Emily, an 18th birthday present – a silver 'moonstone' bracelet. It looked hideous to me, but she can always take it back, I thought.

1st October

'Look at that figure of a man becoming a huge giant isn't that clever?'
said Ma looking at a shadow of me thrown on the ceiling by her night-lamp.
I tucked her in with her soft toy dogs, bought for her by my eldest daughter, Katie. 'My little darlings. They are so pretty. Hello babies. I never knew a dog that didn't bite, but it's such a shame they don't ever lick me.'
Yet earlier she had acknowledged they can't eat because:
'They can't open their mouths'!

3rd October

Telephoned Muriel Best, the second wife of Gill Best, former pub landlord and Ma's dead cousin. She lives near Redruth, Cornwall.

'Oh I'm just packing to go away for four days in Padstow,' she said as if too busy to take my call. As it was the only time in 58 years I'd ever rung her, I was irritated by her prosaic response. Any worries I'd had about such a call distressing her momentarily, as it could only mean one thing, were therefore immediately dispersed.

She'd had a 'long emotional' letter from Clifford, which another relative had told me about and which was the point of my call.

'I suppose he feels bad about it,' she said.

She was not aware I had moved in. I also explained how things had been difficult over the last months by Clifford's point blank refusal, at first, to allow us to put in care measures and his complaining about the quality of same once we'd overcome this.

'Oh yes, I thought I could read something between the lines.'

His attempt to clear his guilt seemed underhand.

According to Clifford's re-writing of history, this was a woman he'd only had a platonic relationship with. Yet here he was writing testimonial justifications to Ma's family. It angered me.

Muriel pointed out that he was 89 and had clearly found things were 'too much for him'.

'Give Nancy my love. I was always fond of her, she was always very kind to me and was … well… Nancy, she talked sense.'

Er, but, hang on a minute, she's not dead!
And with that it was off to Padstow.
Hands washed. Job done.
One has to move on.
(I never heard from her again.)

4ᵗʰ October

Ma started saying she wanted to go home. I'd got her down
into the front room wearing her coat and covered in a
blanket: I wasn't sure if the gas fire ignition was working
and so left it off. After gently getting her to walk through
to the dining room for her lunch I then got her to walk
back to the front room both times using her walking frame.
'I hate this damn thing I'm not using it.'
'OK fall over then and go to hospital,' I said. I'd been
offish all day.
The truth is the attention now being shown to my mother
by Cathy and I has brought her back to life, and reasonable
health. The result of our care has made my responsibility
indefinite. That shouldn't be intolerable but Ma cusses
everything and refuses to make the slightest effort unless
hectored all the way.
'Can you tell the woman we're going, and say thanks for
lunch?'
'There is no woman, there's only you.'
'I want to go home.'
'You are at home. This IS your home.'
'Don't tell me lies you bastard.'
'It's language like that that drove Clifford away.'
'Good, damn you, you little beast. I want to get in the car
and go home.'

'We didn't get here by car. The only thing mechanical which transported you here is the chair-lift from your bedroom to your front room in *your* house.'

'It isn't my house you fool.'

'It is.'

'Isn't.'

'Is.'

'Isn't.'

'Is.'

Having now reduced myself to no more than a spoiled child, to my horror I was enjoying it – having a go at the ungrateful old crone that had become my mother.

Then she wanted to use the loo. So I hectored her into her walking frame and she hobbled to the downstairs loo.

'It's all right,' she announced in the hall, 'I can do it. I don't want you in here. Close the damn door at least.'

I slammed it.

Later I got her on the chair-lift and back to her room – after I'd pointed

out that she was surrounded by all her ornaments, her table, her chair, all the old long-standing parts of her home. This she saw as another trick on my part to catch her out. She wouldn't take her clothes off and get back into her nightie,

'Yes I know just what type of man you are, you want me to come crawling on all fours. Well you can go to hell unless you damn well say you're very, very sorry.'

So I left her and went home.

An hour later I returned she was now pleading for me to stay.

'I don't want to be on my own.' I cuddled her on the bed and felt a heel.

She is an old woman with senile dementia who's been abandoned by her common-law husband. I would do well to remember it. But still I hover over every cough, every rasp, with a predatory hope.

5th October

Ma's continual cussings and 'Oh my Gods' do not signify anything more than her lifetime's irritation at the slightest discomfort, real or imagined.
She asks for her 'babies', the soft toy Husky dogs to take to bed. I ask her to get off the commode and into bed first. She wants the dogs first. I give them to her. In bed, tucked up with her 'babies' she then says: 'I think they would be better off in their basket.' Infuriated at her arch gaming I leave to go to bed, but as I enter my room I hear a demanding scream of 'CLIFFORD'. I ignore her.
She didn't think much of Dame Ellen MacArthur on Desert Island Discs earlier.
'Who was that awful woman? I do hate show-offs. If she wants to go off and drown herself she'd better get on with it. Who asked her to go?'
'Well she's not sailing anymore,' I'd said, 'she's devoted her life to the environment.'
'Poor old environment.'

6h October

It's 04.15 and mother is lying on her bed with all blankets thrown off, her right leg bleeding from a scratch.
'Why have you got the bed clothes off?'

'Cos I want to get cold.'

11th October

Ma said she had a 'terrible dream' about having a pain in her head, which made her frightened. Not sure if she's hallucinating or not. She has diarrhoea, Cathy thinks she's stressed. Washing her commode out, brushing out the excreta, I thought of Candide and his fruitless expedition for gold. Am I trying to hang on to Ma's estate by keeping her in her own home rather than sending her to someone else's or am I being a dutiful son? Will I suffer the same fate as Candide whose donkey train, laden with Aztec gold tumbled off a mountain pass? All that work and pain for nought…but then again she has stated she does not want to go to 'a' home she just wants to get back to 'her' home!

14th October

She's got used to the noise of the radiator coming on in the morning. A few mornings ago she called for me to go and turn the 'pressure cooker' off before it 'boiled dry'!
She was asleep at 07.30 this morning – unusual. Didn't wake her, instead left a note for nurse to make tea.

17th October

I came in last night to find Ma tucked up in bed –my bed - complete with slippers on. I decided to sleep in her bed, mistake. At 05.30 she started calling 'Clifford' and 'Oh my God!' as per normal. I was dilatory. I dozed. She was first of all plaintive, then aggressive in her calling. Perversely I enjoyed it. Good lose your temper, again.

Have a go, again. Remind me how I loathe this responsibility, again. Eventually I went in to be confronted by a cowshed of humanity.

Sickened, I herded her along the corridor to the bathroom. Roughly, I hauled off her nightie. Forcefully I made her sit on the edge of the bath. Then, in disgust, I showered her. I have been mean this morning, swearing and making a point of emphasising the stink of Ma's shit by opening the windows. She's quite tough and is actually too selfish for it to have a lasting effect, which is a shame as I want to potty train her. Later she told me she was shocked at my language. I told her I learnt it from her swearing at Pa in bed when I was a youngster. It's true, but unfair to bring it up now. But my nastiness comes to the fore on such occasions. Would it be better to always be mean? At least that would be consistent. It's just that much of the time Ma can do rational things and, after a few minutes discourse, will even start to talk rationally. Therefore, when she goes cranky it's difficult not to hold her responsible.

23rd October

The private 'care' company sent round Kim who administered 'meds' – medication - even though this is the role of the NHS Mental Health Team. For some reason the company devised a new care plan without consulting us. When Cathy rang and cancelled them they did not seem overly concerned. Two days after cancellation Kim let herself in the house and administered 'meds' again. We called Social Services and the police. It's probably a cock-up but it's still disturbing to think that a care company can be so dangerously out of control.

So on the day Ma slept in the wrong bed and messed herself it was more than likely because she'd had two doses of 'meds'. And I'd taken it out on her.

Ma called out the other night. I went in, she was lying – stupid face to the ceiling: 'Where's Rosie?' a family pet dog from the 1960s. Later: 'Is that you Diana?' her daughter who lives in America.

6th November

'Please help me, please help me. Oh God, help me, please help me. Dear God please help me. I must go, please help me to go. I can't stay here, please help me,' and so it goes on for a burst of several minutes, several times in the night.

'Clifford?' she screamed at 2 am.

I dashed in.

'For God's sake get rid of it.'

'What?'

'The spider.'

Her night-light, which I'd set up beneath her bedside table to act as a shade, has thrown a giant shadow of the table's legs over the ceiling.

Ma was cowering under the bed-clothes.

I realised the table's shadow was like a tarantula and Ma the fly beneath the beastie's legs.

'It's only a shadow, Ma.' I moved the lamp.

In the morning I asked her about her continual pleading.

'Oh, I'm talking to God, dear.'

'What are you asking for?'

'Just to help me.'

'That's good, that's a comfort, but I didn't think you believed in God?'

'Oh, I do. Well you've got to help someone.'

A novel thought, that she's assisting the Almighty with his piety by offering him someone to help.

7th November

I found Ma naked apart from her knickers, lying on her bed having defecated on the floor en route to the lavatory. This in broad daylight with the commode untouched. A bedside commode, with much yelling and cussing, she can still use by herself at night if she wants to. Perhaps the aberration is a pathetic attempt at 'breaking out', an act of defiance against the baby safety gate I've now fitted across her bedroom door. This is to prevent her toppling down the stairs, which she has to pass en route to the loo.

11th November

'Oh you are a duck,' Ma says as I bring in her tea.
A south-west gale is blowing across the estuary and the normally benign Sea Reach is flecked with white. Ma dislikes the tempest: 'It's something which is not alive, but which makes that awful noise. I hate it. I can't help it if it frightens me.'
As the wind howls around the eaves in invisible curls I tell Ma she should not succumb to irrational fears.
She says she's worried the chimney pots will blow down, not so irrational, as Ma lost her stacks in 1987.

16 October 1987

'About 3am a terribly strong wind thundered round the house making the whole place shudder. It went on and on in an "everlasting sweep and torment" (Dorothy L Sayers) interspersed with gigantic crashes and thuds of heavy objects falling.
Made tea and Clifford watched the lights fusing over in Canvey Island as the overhead power lines waving about kept touching each other and shorting with brilliant green flashes. I sat with fingers in my ears and broke a cup. At last it was light; Clifford listened to weather forecast at 6am said the barometer was just rising at Dover and it should ease off slightly.
Both chimney stacks were off next door and ours was leaning over on their roof – Clifford phoned Bob and told him on no account to walk round that side of his house. No trains. Schools shut. Tiles ripped off, chimneys gone, even the rendering on Frank's house collapsed on to our path. The whole road looks as though it suffered a war time blitz.'

'You only get a hurricane like that every 300 years so you've got a long time to wait.'
'I don't know why you're always so nasty to me. I haven't done anything to you.'
She does not appreciate contrary opinions.
'I wonder why Dick was always so taken with that view when he was ill?'
I knew. As father lay dying from cancer of the oesophagus he told me he was going to concentrate on Yantlet Creek a fissure on the far side of the estuary where he had spent so many youthful weekends in his sailing dinghy. I was embarrassed by the tragic delusion, he held, of thinking positively to get better.

'He wanted to focus on something that was dear to him in a bid to recover,' I said.
'Yes, I never knew him. Not really.'

2 June 1978

'Bought a ribbon china 'antique' plate with George V's face on it from bric-a-brac stall in market for £10 for Dick's birthday which he won't like but which I do.'

6 June 1978

'Gave Dick the antique ribbon plate which he said was quite nice but when told the price said he hoped it was worth it, also that an antique wasn't antique unless it was over 100 years old.'

Cathy made Ma's evening meal and we three sat around while she ate it.
Ma suddenly nudged me asking me if I wanted some.
'No it's your meal'
'Shut your trap.'
She is self-conscious about her appetite, which is underlined all the more when she is the only one eating.

16 November

I was talking to NHS nurse Val Davidson in the kitchen while Ma was in the front room. Ma shouted impatiently for me to attend. She gets jealous if I'm talking with others. I walked through to the lounge and a little while later Val came in and remarked on the bearded portrait of Ma's Welsh Uncle Louis hanging on the wall.

'He has a kind face,' she said

'Benevolent,' corrected Ma in a superior way, she then waved Val away, 'Yes, off you go,' to my fury.

I apologised on Ma's behalf much to the embarrassment of Val who is 'used to it' from dementia patients.

Ma, having been abandoned by Clifford is starting to latch onto me and she now sees other women as a threat. It is all horribly surreal.

19 November

Ma is whistling along with a video film of Top Hat, before saying: 'Oh these people who compose music, they must live in heaven. They probably do in the end.'

22 November

Ma pulls a foul face and is cold towards Maureen, the NHS nurse and she started taking against Cathy, who she now calls 'Elizabeth', possibly mistaking her for Clifford's daughter of the same name.

Because of her grotty behaviour I left her in the front room while sitting with Cathy in the dining room. She started shouting 'Dicky' for me, so I shut the front room door. Ma then started banging it violently, with her fists, and yelling for me to open it.

I did so and she walked through to the dining room without her frame, like Christ's beggar, but this one a miracle of hatred. She plumped herself down in the dining room, gave us a sickly smile and said: 'Enjoying yourselves are you?' and then gave us a two-fingered salute!

So we left her there and went into the front room. Her behaviour did not improve and so I spitefully cancelled an outing in the wheelchair.

'Oh well, yes, thank-you, I was looking forward to that, but never mind,' she said, enjoying the bitterness of martyrdom.

In the evening she refused to go up to her bed, so I told her that her 'angel pies', the soft toy dogs were waiting for her in her bedroom. She then went along without complaint until arrival in her room, where the dogs were indeed 'waiting' and then she yelled: 'Cunning bastard, beast' and 'devil,' after getting her into her nightie, as I locked her behind the gate.

She's foul. I'm foul. She has an excuse. Do I?

28 November

Our middle child, Emily, gave Ma lunch, before returning to London, inviting the question: 'Where's tweetypie gone?'

She also told Cathy that, although she loathes her bed gate, as it makes her room seem like a prison, she did not try to go through it for fear of 'My picture appearing in the newspapers.'

As a law-abiding citizen she is well conditioned to not 'breaking the law'.

The statement makes me weep.

29 November

A quiet sobbing, tearless sound, then 'Oh, please help me. God help me. I'm broken. I can't do anything. I don't want you to do everything. I can't hope.'

I reassured her. Gave her a kiss. Told her I was her son.
She brightened. She smiled. We trek on.
I watched the vicar of St Clements Church walk up the hill
in the gloom of early Sunday.
I sit with her as I read a book to myself.
'Oh you good boy. You're so handsome.'
I continue reading.
'You gorgeous boy. Lovely fur. Lovely little paws,' her
admiration of Dee's teddy bear gift, is to goad me because
I'm reading instead of conversing with her.
'May I speak?'
'Of course.'
'Well are you going to talk to me?'
'What do you want to talk about?'
'If you'd only just help me.'
'Help you do what?'
'Do something.'
'Do what?'
'I don't know.'
'Well how do **I** know?'
'I want you to tell me.'
Her eyes occasionally droop. She dozes. But her voice
when the volume's turned up could scare the stiffs in the
churchyard across the road.
So much for frailty.

4 December

Ma's at it again. Shouting at Cathy, she told her to 'shut
up' while she made supper. Then she refused to sit down
on the loo so I could change her nappies. More shouting. I
shouted back and pushed her back down on the loo seat

and threatened her with a 'home' where she would be sedated with dribbling inmates.

More faux sobbing.

'I'll give you one last chance. If you don't stop shouting and abusing people you'll go to a home.'

More tearless wailing and then: ' I'm going to get out of this country.'

I left her with her soft toy dogs. The perfect objects for her affection: they don't have common accents, they aren't black, they don't interact and enjoy themselves, they don't laugh, they don't reason.

Inanimate, stuffed, silent.

5 December

Ma has a guilt complex about eating. The one thing which her condition has not altered is her appetite which has always been healthy and if it's the case that long-term memory remains relatively unaffected, then her experience as a young woman who was 'always hungry' and the days of rationing still lurk within her mind.

Because she eats alone she becomes self-conscious at meal times and is always hectoring me to: 'Have some. Do have some, darling.'

'But I don't eat a meal at lunchtime.'

With a cup of tea at 14.30 I put out two biscuits.

'Have a biscuit.'

'I don't like biscuits.'

She ate one. Then a few minutes later: 'I might as well eat the other,' she mutters guiltily before forgetting the embarrassment by whistling at another Fred Astaire film

and describing Ginger Rogers as 'soppy.' All is well once
more.

7 December

'Where is that bugger?' Ma shouts.
I wake up, the glowing green numbers inform me it's
01.50.
Ma has switched on the main light in her bedroom.
I go in and her face is sneering.
'Do you want to use the commode?'
'No, I damn well don't.'
'Well why have you got up?'
'I'm going to the lavatory.'
'But, Ma. Your commode is beside the bed. It is there for
your convenience and it is there so that you don't have to
go far in case you take a tumble. No-one can see you using
it.'
'You use it, if you want.'
I start to react telling her that everything she utters is a
complaint, that she continually bites the hand that feeds
her. I go back to bed.
'Oh help me it's going to go all over the bed.'
I leap out of bed and manhandle Ma onto the commode.
She's yelling and cursing and flailing her arms around and
as I roughly pull off her nappy and forcibly sit her on the
seat, she topples sideways and bashes her left wrist against
the chest on which sits her TV.
I straighten her up, fortunately the commode only tilted
and the contents has not spilt.
She is now shouting blue murder and wants to call the
police.

I clean her up and put on a new nappy and get her back into bed.

'I wish I had a husband, he would sock you on the jaw. You'll go to prison. I'm going to tell everyone.'

Suddenly I realise how vulnerable I am to her charges. I have perversely enjoyed making her use the commode, and she can sense this.

I make tea and we sit talking.

'At least you're contrite,' she says with a sickly grin. She's now got this power over me, she believes. But all she wants from her new found tyranny, is someone to talk to.

'I'm trapped in this room for hours, days, months. I feel it's my right to hit that gate.'

The security gate is a red rag to a bull. It's her prison door. Perhaps without it there she might use the commode instead of insisting she go to the loo. But without it she could also fall downstairs.

She sits talking about the fields, which surround Paglesham where I drove her to the day before. She talked about how she went there as a child with Aunts May and Lucy.

And it was when she got rid of an unused cold box, years after such pic-nics that sparked off a memory of a Bertie Wooster-style day out which she recalled.

21ˢᵗ July 1978

'My aunts were skilled and practised experts at picnicking. They kept a shop together and Sundays being the only day it closed then that day must be spent out of doors whatever the weather, and the whole action became an active operation each week throughout the summer. Their car was a Morris Cowley and the front seat was all in one;

affixed to the back of it was a dropleaf flap covered in American grey and white check which could lift up into a table if the weather was inclement. Inside the car in the boot were stowed hampers and baskets, rugs and sunshades, cushions and water proofs, walking sticks, a portable cooking stove, cake tins, cups and saucers and all the crockery they used at home: table napkins and even ivory napkin rings! The only thing they didn't bring were their beaded heatproof table mats.

Rhoda and I went often with them and sat in the back seat with Buster the dog who stood between us, his front paws propped on the edge of the front seat so he could look through the windscreen.

'When at last the right field was found we drove right into it so there was no carrying to do. Out came everything and the greatest attention was given to where it should be arranged to everyone's satisfaction.

'With appetites already sharpened by the fresh air the memory of the smell of a boiling fowl with vegetables cooked and prepared and heated on the stove, of that dinner out of doors lingers still. It was followed by cold fruit tart with cream.

'Water was heated, washing up done and then came the great REST as all the party (sometimes there were other adults as well) stretched out on the rugs under the sunshades on scattered cushions. Except for us – we were told to go off with Buster and not to make a noise.

'Later came a walk to go black-berrying with baskets and the walking sticks used for pulling down the brambles.

'Finally, scratched and sunburnt we drove home. Aunty May drove and Aunty Lucy sat holding a notebook ready to jot down the numbers of other motorists going too fast or committing some driving offence according to Aunt

May: 'Look at that!! Take his number Lu!' We never heard what the consequences were or even if they were ever followed up. No one paid us much attention. We were very well brought up children – under no circumstances while the car was in motion were we allowed to speak in case the driver's attention was distracted. To this day I find it difficult to utter a word when anyone is driving.'

7 December

I tell Ma I'd read her account of the picnic and wonder what she meant by the 'right field'?
'That meant one with no cows in,' Ma said perfectly rationally.
I go to make more tea.
'And come back and talk to me. A bit more of that and I wouldn't be so bad-tempered.'
I bring more tea.
Then she says that 'Elizabeth' is trying to turn me against her, suggesting she, Elizabeth in other words Cathy, is jealous of my 'knocking around' with Ma.
The curious thing about this condition is that the paranoia is applied only to the short-term memory.

8 December

I have felt a heel all day and have offered nothing but TLC to Ma who is now as happy as a sand boy, spinning like a top and even her cackle has returned to laughter. She's even chatting happily with her competitor, Cathy.
How many times must we learn that love conquers all?

10 December

Ma has a fractured left wrist. I took her to Southend General Hospital after it kept causing her pain. It was X-rayed and a leather sleeve has been put on. The consultant asked her how it happened. She said she'd fallen. But there was no mention of how. Among all the cussing is a woman of true class. I had manhandled an old lady who happens to be my mother, because she wouldn't sit on the commode. Who can blame her for wanting to get to the loo instead of using the commode which sits there in her room a tangible reminder of corruption? I can, apparently.

She will have 'fracture management' which might mean removing the cast and manipulating the bone under anaesthetic and then re-casing it in a lightweight GRP cast. Her 'bone drink', as I describe the diluted calcium she must swallow each day, appears to have done little for her osteoporosis.

11 December

I walk, hating myself, through the London night along the South Bank from the office back to my commuter train at Fenchurch Street Station.

I had found a photo album of family pictures taken in 1953, black cardboard pages held the photographs which were glued upon them and Ma's bold, clear hand had lovingly written the captions in white ink beneath.

There she was, a 29-year-old new mum with a little tanned boy in 'reins.' In every photograph the only thing Ma is focussing on is the little boy. She has thick, brown, lustrous wavy hair, a high forehead, wide cheekbones, almost Slavic. Such broad faces can be seen in sepia photographs of Russian peasant women, but this mother's tangible intelligence removed any hint of the bovine. She has a strong, dimpled chin, wide-open, large eyes. She is handsome, rather than beautiful.

With endomorphic curves, her rounded arms, full and soft and strong are carrying the endomorphic little boy; are stretched out to help the little boy walk; are handing the little boy a dolly to wash in the sea.

She holds the little chubby, boy, willy a-dangle, as he splashes in the water. The little boy is me.

I hate myself. And I can't unwind it, can't start again, can't take it back. There is no undoing. There is only regret, an insoluble stain, a scar. Not even time can wash away a regret. Though every rock of a granite headland will, in time, be smoothed and rounded by time's tides, the wrongful act can never be undone.

'I'm sorry Ma,' I mutter into the night, saying it aloud as though by casting it into the ether it has the virtue of confession, 'I'm sorry Ma,' I shout again over the river, a passer-by glances and moves on.

The black, racing river breaks white over the buttresses of Southwark Bridge. The tide is high.

All I can be is sorry and what use is that?

23 December

Snow is frozen to the lawn and temperatures have dropped to minus 5 degrees at night. Ma has complained of the cold and I've supplied an extra counterpane. Two nights ago she thought a strange man had come into her room. I told her there was no-one there.

'Well when he comes in and cuts your head off with a knife, it will serve you right, darling.'

David, the cleaner who comes on a Thursday gives Ma the 'creepers' as she puts it. She's convinced he's making a pass at her. He's in his early 30s and probably gay, but later Cathy threw some light on Ma's thinking when she discovered he'd put his arm around her to try and comfort her after she became agitated over the bedroom security gate.

So we have now fitted a security gate over the stairway and removed the bedroom gate, so she can move around upstairs when left alone, and not feel as though she's in a prison cell.

We have discovered the Occupational Therapist is somebody who can assist Ma with the challenges she faces in daily life. This person has fitted an automatic seat to the edge of the bath which lowers the user from the lip of the bath into its trough.

Ma also now has an electronic pad under her mattress which is wired to a telephone line. The idea is that if she leaves the bed for more than 15 minutes between the hours of 6pm and 6am an alarm is sent to a monitoring centre where an operator can contact Ma over an intercom to check she is OK.

This morning was the first time the robotic pad alarm system was used in anger.

At 2am I awoke with a start to the sound of a klaxon sounding.

I leaped out of bed and dashed in to find Ma dozing on her commode, and then rushed downstairs to try and stop the harsh electronic peals of the klaxon. I pulled back the curtain to get at the monitor box which had a little window which was flashing red. There was no obvious way of

stopping it. No buttons, no switches, no dials. Its
alternating hooter sounded loud enough to be used in a
nuclear power station as it was about to go critical. The
whole neighbourhood would be at the net curtains.
'FOR FUCK'S SAKE SHUT UP,' I yelled at the box,
trying to find a plug to disconnect it.
'Are you all right, Nancy?' a disembodied voice said
calmly.
'Oh, sorry. Er, yes, she's fine. Er, obviously this isn't her,
she's upstairs on the loo. She must have dozed off. But
she's fine. Thanks for asking.'
'That's OK. Good night.'
'Thank-you. Good night.'

Christmas Eve

'Clifford?'
It's 1 a.m. I lie awake listening in hope for the sound of
Ma managing to tend to herself . Then I remember the
klaxon. I leap out of bed and enter Ma's bedroom. She's
on the commode. But I have no idea how long she's been
sitting there. So I lie on her bed next to her, to keep
pressure on the pad, as, vacated, it will set the klaxon off
again.
Two more loo calls before dawn, and I sleep in until 08.30.
Breakfast is two hours late, yet Ma is silent.
I leap up and go into her room.
She's just lying there, eyes open.
'Morning. I'll make some tea.'
'No, I want my dinner I'm starving.'
I bring her up toast, tea and her 'bone drink.'
'I don't want any of that. I want my dinner.'

'It's eight o'clock, breakfast time.'

'Oh, don't be stupid.'

'Don't eat it. I can't force you to eat your toast, drink your tea or your bone drink, but you've got a five-hour wait for dinner, or what we call lunch. I'm off to work now.'

'I don't know what I've done to deserve this. I've done nothing to you,' Ma utters some faux, tearless sobbing, then adds: 'You are a nasty, little man. I didn't realise how nasty you are.'

Christmas Day

I brought her down to her lighted Christmas tree in the lounge and she opened her few presents, which she enjoyed.

We then got her round to our house for Christmas lunch at which she mimicked Cathy's mother's Scottish accent, told Cathy's potential brother-in-law he was a fool before undergoing a bowel movement in her nappies.

She also wants to know why the portrait of a sea-faring ancestor, which once hung in her home, but which has hung in my dining room for over two decades since being given to me by my father, has been 'given away'!

I took her home, changed her, and later prepared supper while she started obsessing over her walking frames. One is kept upstairs, the other downstairs. But whichever level she is on the 'right' frame is always on the wrong floor. They are exactly the same, but being presented with the incorrect walking frame is a device to keep me there forever, as once resolved the debate is over.

'Dicky, I want you to tell me the truth,' she said apropos of nothing obvious.

'I always do, but you don't like hearing it.'

She ignores my graceless barb and adds: 'You see, I can last a long time if I think I'm going to get better.'

Boxing Day

The controversy over the portrait has continued, but Cathy managed to divert Ma's attention instead to a sepia photograph of her father at a wedding party circa 1920. This was more important than a portrait as it told a story, Cathy explained.

'Yes but the painting's worth money,' said Ma, who nevertheless has now accepted it's hanging in my house and that I have not 'given it away.'

Perhaps for the first time in her life she apologises to me.

'Do you accept my apology?'

I said nothing.

'Dicky, I need to know.'

I reassured her and told her to try and stop arguing with me – her son.

'You're not my son.'

The person she Christened Richard and who she addresses as Dicky to distinguish him from her husband of the same name, she now sees as being someone other than her son. And as I try to spell this out she then has an analysis of her husband: 'Dick never liked me and I didn't like him in the end. Never mind. No-one could work him out. But I used to hate it when he just went away and didn't talk to me.'

Then, as if she realised her part in this dysfunction, it was back to her sister: 'Poor Rhoda. She was much nicer than me. Much kinder.'

My parents' union was one, which had saddened me as a child. My mother's rages - always, she hoped, out of earshot of her children - my father's submissiveness, the loveless-ness, the never saying anything, the horrid atmospheres.

I assumed they stayed together 'for the sake of the children', yet if that's all it was, their malfunctioning relationship might have been better off terminated, for, back then, it produced insecurity in my sister and I, and now just a melancholy void.

My mother's habit of switching from grim-countenanced rant, if the telephone interrupted her fuming rhetoric, to deathly-measured polite delivery, was hideous to me. Her sweet-faced, almost mad, rictus smile, employed as another anti-husband tactic when sulking, was disturbing. And yet, Ma, once told me…just once…many years after father died, how he had announced to his young wife that he would leave her when the children had grown up. For Ma to tell me this was truly shocking because she was loyal, discreet and loathed gossip. This must have been a huge blow to a young mum and yet she understood it: Pa was almost pathologically allergic to commitment. It wasn't about his spouse it was about his fear of responsibility. Of his life being taken away from him. Taken away like the war years had taken away the best years of his life, as he saw it anyway. In the end, of course, he stuck it out. But it must have taken a toll on Ma. No-one outside their suburban home ever knew.

I can recall going to big department stores with Ma and Pa as they wandered around in a kind of catatonic distraction from their hopeless relationship. Still, to this day, I find department stores, filled with gentle muzak, to lure customers around dead islands of goods, unbearably depressing.

My parents' choice of magnolia, or sometimes mushroom - which amounts to the same thing - for decoration was a kind of mute armistice. Like some sort of tangible peace balm it was spread over all surfaces: wallpaper was painted with magnolia emulsion, carpets were laid with magnolia weave, magnolia coloured curtains were drawn across the dark.

Magnolia: neutral, passionless, inert.

2010

New Year's Day

We all had a take-away curry in Ma's front room. But as she watched Richard set up his train set on her carpet, she became disorientated again and as Cathy put it: 'Felt as though she was outstaying her welcome in her own home.' She asked to go home again, so I took her upstairs to her bedroom.

She still asked to go home. I noticed a smear of excrement on one of her fingers and took her along to the lavatory. She sat on the bath stool and I asked her to 'Wash your paws' a phrase she often used.

'You do it.'

'Do what?'

'The water.'

'The water is in the sink waiting for you,' I'd mixed it to the correct temperature.

She made a sneering face, 'Bring it here,' challenging.

So I cupped my hands and lifted some of the dripping water towards her.

She lashed out and knocked it out of my hands.

'You brute, you nasty little man.'

A further check-up at hospital has revealed the wrist needs no further attention and has knitted, but it has also been discovered she has two broken ribs – which have also fused together – which happened from historical falls before Clifford's departure. It explains the pain she was feeling in her side, which she'd complained about back in September.

Clearly her old bones are fragile.

2 January

Two yells of 'Clifford' bring me into her room around 5 a.m.

'It's a damn cheek. A wog.'

'I can't see anyone.'

'A tall man, drunk, came smashing through here.'

'There is no-one here.'

'Shut-up.'

So I shouted down the stairs: ' "Go on, off you go". There he's gone now, Ma.'

Back to bed.

At 9 a.m. I bring her breakfast.

'Oh, you angel.'

Cathy's mother had given Ma a blue cardigan for Christmas and Ma had fretted over this, as she wanted to write a thank-you letter, but was finding it difficult.

She managed to scrawl three letters: C. A. R.

Today I ask if she'd like to wear the cardigan.

'Oh, if you like,'

'No, it's if you like.'

Then she starts telling me the NHS nurses aren't going to dictate to her what she should wear.

I come down fast and hard on this telling her that they are a 'God-send', a Ma phrase, and that – deliberately rudely – I say they wash her 'old carcass' every day and dress her.
'Yeah, if they turn up.'
'They turn up every day.'
'No, they don't.'
'Yes, they do. I see their car parked outside.'
I pack the cardigan away. Anything new or novel causes such absurd turbulence.
Later at lunch I come in with Cathy to find she's wearing it.
'You're not as daft as you make out,' I say deliberately tactlessly, and deliberately trying to bate her. Am I suffering from Munchausen by proxy with the victim in her second childhood? Or is it just sadism?
'I'm not a liar,' she screams.
Now I've succeeded in stressing her out she's become loose-bowelled again.
I face the cleaning of her ghastly old rear end, hanging fleshy and unformed. A saggy maw smelling of fish has to be tackled as she stands bent forward over the commode.
As I wash her I wish the horrid orifice would stop working so efficiently. I wish her body would stop running so well and join her brain in breaking up.
I wish she would die.

3 January

Decided to fix the squeaky floorboards between my room and Ma's. Her hearing is acute and it is virtually impossible to access my bedroom without alerting her. I've tried expanding my gait and walking with my feet beneath each skirting board to avoid the loose boards, but I can sense Ma concentrating on my held breath, and she asks: 'Dicky?' at the slightest squeak.

I rolled back the carpet and peeled away the rotten underlay which immediately turned to green rubber dust before hammering in two nails on the loose board. The second emitted a hiss. I frantically pulled up the nailed board and two spouts of hot water came up with it and bounced off the ceiling. I dashed downstairs and turned off all the cocks I could find and the pressure subsided but water still pumped out. I bound the pipe with PTF tape but it still leaked and so I called a local handyman.

With floorboards up, wet carpet and a mash of soaked underlay and Martin, the handyman, puzzling how to fit collars over unbendable pipes, Ma decided to pay a visit to the lavatory and easily negotiated the pitfalls before I found her, stopped her, turned her round and walked her back to her room and the commode.

As I carried the used potty to the loo she said: 'It's nothing to do with me.'

Snow started falling outside, with the temperature plummeting, and a forecast of minus 5, Ma was very chirpy over the domestic catastrophe. Martin fortunately managed to bodge it together so we could bleed the system and get the heating on, not before darkness but before the deep cold set in.

10 January

Ma dreamed of flying in an aeroplane and 'Killing wogs, no not wogs, you know what I mean. I always knew what the swastika meant. It was wonderful. Serves them right, too. They shouldn't come over here and do it to us, we'll just do it back. I was always told I was a tomboy, but still my mother was very frightened.'

20 May 1943

'Sirens went, a shell burst nearby and shrapnel rolled and skidded down the roof. It is now 2 am and my birthday. We were all awake through the noise and they all wished me many happy returns.'

The Essex County Standard of her wartime youth was full of pictures of houses with gable ends blown out showing intimate interiors: wallpaper bare to the rain, upper storey fireplaces still standing thanks to the extra brickwork involved in chimney breasts, roof slates lifted and dropped back like a scattered deck of cards. There were photographs, too, of crushed semis: one depicted an abode untouched while its neighbour tilted surreally sideways. And the stories: the haphazard nature of dropping high explosives from the air over civilian territory or strafing roads and railways. Sixty-three patients were killed when a bomb demolished part of a mental hospital in Colchester unlikely to have been a deliberate target as by that stage of his Chancellorship, Hitler had given up on his policy of euthanasia. One Dornier attack on the Liverpool Street to Harwich train left the driver and fireman killed and carriages poking crazily skywards, but only one passenger injured. Oh, but that passenger: a 19-year-old youth 'starting out on a career as a pianist' lost all the fingers on one hand.

In Dedham a six-week-old boy and mother were killed when a bomb wrecked their bungalow. 'All arrangements had been made for the baptism of the baby the following Sunday and the christening cake was actually in the house.'

Next came the Pilotless Aircraft or PACS, better known as Doodlebugs, or flying bombs one of which killed 40, mostly factory girls, ironically from the Hoffman Manufacturing Company in Chelmsford, which made ball bearings used in aircraft manufacture. They had just finished singing Christmas carols to the accompaniment of a Salvation Army band. 'Christmas decorations, a Teddy bar, a shattered doll and part of a Christmas tree were among the pathetic assortment of articles left strewn across the road,' the paper reported.

An anthology of these news stories are gathered in one of Ma's books: Essex At War complied by staff from the Essex County Standard. All bombings and strafings were 'for security reasons' placed in 'Southern England.' Essex's role as being in the front line went largely unnoticed but as a retiring fire chief P. G. Garon commented after the war: 'Essex took a devil of a lot of Southern England.'

Rhoda's husband Frank, a Canadian airman was killed when his seaplane exploded somewhere off Northern Ireland while submarine spotting in World War Two. Why does everyone have to die?

26 February 1942

A letter in Ma's diary from Flight Lieutenant Jim Meikle on hearing the news of Frank's death:

'Dear Rhoda,

'Perhaps we men in the service develop a "queer" way of looking at life; an acceptance of some things, a refusal to accept others, yet each to normal common sense would appear equally true. We each perhaps, thinking subconsciously of the "law of averages", have deep down, to expect not too much of the tomorrows. We live on the happiness of yesterdays, seek the best of the todays. And yet almost blindly we dare hope always for the somedays.
'This war has opened our eyes to so much we could not see before. A gratitude and deeper appreciation of the countless little bounties with which life has blessed us.
'I can recall so clearly Peterborough (where I first met Frank), Cornwall, Bermuda and the infrequent interludes when our paths crossed since. Many of the chaps I've known have been "reported missing". It is impossible to think other than that, in spite of any report, we will meet again. And yet -?
'Rhoda, it was my good fortune to know and understand Frank I think better than most. (You excepted of course). I know how much you meant to him, glimpsed the deep happiness and contentment you brought to him. That happiness which between two people can defy all attempts at expression in mere words.
'You are going to have a baby. I am glad with you. God bless you both.'

'So it was good then? Killing wogs?' I asked.
'Oh wonderful, dear.'
Germans were wogs and men who killed them fascinated Ma as a young nurse. I recall her telling me, as a child,

about a hard case Cockney commando called Wallineer and then to my amazement I met him in her diary:

23 February 1943

'Pensioner David Wallineer is 26, small, and wiry and tough, with a tight-drawn smile, eyes as sharp as a weasel and black hair. He is a Ministry of Pensions patient for he has a bullet in his leg from a commando raid and has been invalided out of the Army. Therefore we can't operate on him now for the MOP won't allow it and he is just having a tulle gras dressing on his wound and sulphanilamide powder spread as well.
Dressings were finished early and I cleaned the windows on Ward 1 with vinegar and polished the lockers. I asked Sergeant Major Parry if he noticed any difference. He immediately looked at the side I hadn't done and said: 'Yes that does look cleaner now. I can see a difference in it.'
Wallineer sat bolt upright and gave a running commentary on it pointing out all the smears I'd left on the panes till I squeezed some vinegar on his head.'

27 February 1943

'Had a long chat with Wallineer this morning. I asked him how long he'd been in this state and what had actually happened. And then he came out with the whole history – eight bullets through his leg and the eighth had entered the bone and was still there. "They wanted to take the bloody thing off" he said at his former hospital. And he replied: "For God's sake do and I can get out of this joint."

'He speaks pure Cockney and says what he thinks. In the afternoon I tidied three bandage boxes whilst he and Lieutenant Corporal Allard were carrying on a conversation about blood and death and laying out German uniforms, souvenirs etc. etc.'

28 February 1943

'I did a spot of polishing while the men read the Sunday papers and shouted bits of news across to each other and listened to the wireless before the 9am news. And then Colonel Muir walked in with a new M.O. and all dressings had to be undone and he inspected them all. He was very interested in Wallineer and pinched his leg several times which made W. bite his lip hard. Finally he announced there to be pus and said he'd open it at 12 pm. What a shock!! I laid up the trolley and helped shave Wallineer's leg which has to be handled very delicately. Sister injected Wallineer and we pushed him into the anaesthetic room and I pulled down the blinds.

'When Wallineer came back into the ward he was not properly conscious and was talking his head off: "Anyone want to be a cowboy report at company office tomorrow."

'Wallineer's dressings stick as they are removed and it's very painful for him but rather then let us see him pulling faces he pulls the sheet over his face.

'Cycled into Borehamwood with a long shopping list and the gramophone shop promised to change my record of 'Harlem' because the surface was rough. Had bacon, chips and peas at the Spot café.'

12 January

Ma was dozing late afternoon, but sensed someone was there and said: 'I love you, you are beautiful. I want you,' before pursing her lips and smacking a kiss. The perversity of the libido. Surely this should be the first vice to shrivel and die?

All I could hope was that Ma, like Oedipus' mum, did not realise she was flirting with her own son.

14 January

Ma was recalling her youth today and remembered a boy who was 'always following me around.'

'I didn't like him.'

But after her father's death, her young widowed mother distracted herself with her golf allowing her daughters to do what they liked including using 'Beach No 4' where she had a box tent in which they could change to go sea bathing.

One day Ma swam out to an anchored barge with the boy she didn't like.

They climbed aboard.

'I was glad he was there with me then,' she said, 'but as we swam back to shore, as soon as my feet could touch the bottom, I walked away. I never saw him again. I was silly really because he got good results. He went into the war and he didn't come back. He would have wanted to have been brave. He must have been killed, poor devil.

'I wish I'd been nicer to him.'

At home, before her illness, I could never discuss 'what happened in the war' with Ma, or even talk about it when major events of World War II made the news in contemporary times because of revisionist histories. She could not bear even thinking about conflict. She once said: 'Isn't it terrible being a man? The things you are expected to do.'

And in her diary is a vivid account of a convoy of wounded arriving at Shenley Military Hospital, which is organised by 'Madam 1', Kathleen Cooper-Abs, the British Red Cross Commandant of the establishment:

2 August 1943

'At 8pm we were all wondering whether to have supper or wait for Madam's instructions, and then Madam entered and said: "I have heard that the convoy is here.'

We gathered our torches and set off to the King George V Hall. I was with Keay, Wills, Hunter, Gilam etc etc. Madam was a bit abashed I think because she wasn't coming, or wanted really, not being a nurse.

Outside Ward 1 I came to a full stop because there were RAMC orderlies in their positions to receive the ambulances.

'Inside the immense hall the blackout was drawn and brilliant lights were on, the canteen set with small tables with newspapers and Matron came and ordered tea to be made, for the walking cases had began to arrive in a stream, some in shorts, some in working clothes, some with arms in slings, some on crutches, each carrying whatever personal baggage they'd managed to save. A row of VAD clerks at desks received them first, for their names etc. They were given tea, cigarettes, sandwiches and then sent to an MO. We carried plates of tea and sandwiches to the stretcher cases, which were now coming in fast, first to the clerks and then to the centre of the dance floor in rows.

Some bad cases were among them, one with arms off halfway and one side of his face blown out, and another tiny, shrivelled man with bad scalds. The rest were mostly legs in plaster and they looked more scruffy and most of them very tired and sleepy. Some smoked, they all talked, there was very little excitement. Piled high on their plaster cases were their tin hats, newspaper bundles and packages and one boy had a beautiful wooden chest. The RAMC orderlies were splendid. They worked carrying stretcher after stretcher out of the tricky charabanc door, into the hall without jolting one of them. They lifted and manoeuvred and gently lowered one after the other, shirt sleeves rolled up.

A Scotsman I went with to Ward 3, was very perky with a fractured tib and fib, he came from the Black Watch, others from the 10th Gordon Highlanders.

Backwards and forwards we went and gradually it became darker and storm lanterns and extra blankets for us to carry were provided.

At last we were cleared it was past 1 am and I passed through the office door as Madam said with a beaming smile: 'Goodnight Best.'

She also recalled wandering around the lower weedy levels of Southend Pier when the tide had ebbed away with her fellow VAD nurse, Jeanette James. This was quite a hazardous pursuit for young girls.

These recollections had been sparked off by my impersonation of the classic end-of-pier Laughing Policeman, a slot-machine dummy that jerked about behind glass to that old song.

'I didn't take any notice of such common entertainments,' said Ma in mock snobbery.

24 January

'Good,' I muttered to myself as I weighed everything up. I was healthy, had a family, a job, a paid off mortgage…
'What?' Ma said.
'Oh, I don't know, life?' I said.
'I can't help it, I can't help it, I can't help it, I can't help it. Help me, help me, help me, help me. Here I am, here I am, here I am, here I am. It's gone too fast, it's gone too fast, it's gone too fast…' her voice trailed away as a moment of terrible realisation subsided.
I put down her toast beside her.
'Oh lovely, lovely,' she said. If ever there was a case of comfort food…
It seems that when I talk to her I lift her out of a sort of linguistic soup of confusion and passionately expressed babble into something half-formed and almost within comprehension. Then when I stop talking to her she descends once more into a pool of mental bedlam.
It leaves me with the daunting realisation that only by constantly stimulating her with my verbal presence can I stem her cognitive deterioration.
But I can't be at her side forever. She was at my side forever when I was a baby, but babies become independent. A second childhood leads only to dependence.
This afternoon she was sitting in her armchair by the window – wasted – because of her indifference to 'views'. A view was something her husband loved looking upon more than he liked looking at her.

She was babbling a lot of nonsense and then said suddenly:
'I hate myself. I know I'm horrible and ugly and a few other things.'
'No, you're not,' I said.
'Well that's something.'
I looked out over the mudflats watching an orange finger nail of setting sun showing itself for the first time in many days just before it slipped behind the earth.
'You kill me,' she said.
'Why?'
'Well, why are you so interested in the sky?'
'You can tell the way the weather's turning.'
'Oh, damn the weather.'
The neap tide crept slowly across the mudflats. The grey sky dominated.
Ma started a false, exaggerated cough, loud, guttural to get my attention. I grimaced.
'Oh, did you pull a face at me?'
'Yes.'
'Oh well I'm glad you said that. Now please help me.'
'Help you what?'
'Get over there,' she pointed at her bed, 'and get him off my bed. I don't want him in here.'
'Come on Mr Coat,' I said, 'you've got to leave.' Then I made my Crombie stand-up, shrug in annoyance, before laying 'him' down folded on the bed with 'his' collar on the pillow.
'It's no good, Ma,' I said, 'Mr Coat says he's staying.'
'Now, Dicky, don't do that, you know it frightens me.'

30 January

'I want to go to the chemists and get some STs,' she said. I knew what she meant as I smelt the fishy smell of her repellent, urine-soaked knickers.

'What do you mean?' I asked.

'Sanitary towels.'

'Ma, you don't need sanitary towels. You don't have a period. You stopped menstruating in 1962,' I guessed.

'No I didn't.'

I wondered how much more the planet could swallow in landfill of old ladies' disposable stinking pads.

Clifford telephoned.

He revealed the cost of his old folks' home, well almost.

'It's four figures a month. I don't mind telling you.'

He wanted to be remembered to the kids.

'After all, whatever you may feel, I consider them my grandchildren.'

It seemed grotesque, all of it, none of it anyone's fault. The far end of a span is met with someone else's sentiments on a greetings card. I said nothing.

'After all I was there before they were born.'

There was nothing to say.

'I was there before you were married.'

We talked about the political situation, neutral territory. Then he started telling me his son only had a small pension, that his daughter-in-law's supply teaching was drying up.

'It's lucky I saved and saved and saved all these years because this home, though luxurious is expensive.'

I had told Clifford in the past that had he stayed put, looked after Ma until she died, I would have left him in her home and done my best to look after him.

It was pointless mentioning that now.

'It just means that when I've gone the children won't have very much. Still it can't be helped.'

No it can't, I thought. And in case it could I'd kept hold of his bank statements and building society books, which he'd abandoned when he left my mother's house.

Any approach to my mother's estate would be met with evidence of considerable wealth.

Clifford eventually asked how Ma was.

I told him she'd improved which was partly true and he was astonished, but seemed genuinely pleased.

Finally he said to me: 'Oh, just between you and me could you ask Katie (my eldest daughter) to pay that cheque in as soon as she can, only I don't like them hanging about.'

This was flagging up the fact he'd sent her £25 for her birthday on Christmas Day, just in case she hadn't mentioned it to us.

Callously I did not acknowledge his 90th birthday on 4 January.

31 January

I'm coming to the conclusion that the more time I spend with my mother the greedier she becomes for 'quality' company. The less time I spend with her the more amenable she will be to the nurses i.e. for any company.

This afternoon she was uttering broken phrases.

'I thought I had. Perhaps I did. But maybe I didn't after all.'

She struggles with nouns. She will come out with perfectly formed phrases, but being noun-less they are meaningless. Losing a language, it would seem, is the opposite of learning one, as the first words a baby grasps are nouns. It is the grammar required to talk about them that's difficult.

There are exceptions: 'Now, let me think. I can't imagine whether it's going out or coming in.'
In this case 'it' is a reference to the tide ebbing away from the mudflats beyond her window. And in this case 'it' will suffice as a noun because of the phrasing surrounding it.
And: 'I've lost my handbag,' while inaccurate as a statement of fact, it was beside her, is a perfectly formed sentence. But then again 'handbag' is possibly one of the most deeply ingrained nouns of the female psyche and therefore one of the last to pass into cognitive history.
When I told her the handbag was hanging, as it always does, on her bedside cabinet, she said: 'Get it tout suite' jokingly, her schoolgirl French still held uselessly detached in the aspic of her long-term memory.
Ma has a strange habit of twirling food around on a fork while masticating the previous mouthful. While she chews, her denture clacking, the fork circles with the next morsel of pork pie or chicken.
It is some long-standing ritual, which offers reassurance. All part of comfort food. Of knowing where the next mouthful's coming from, unlike during rationing.
'I want to know how it works,' she said suddenly this afternoon.
'How what works?'
'That lamp beside you.'
'I've shown you a million times.'
'Why?'

1 February

A cold morning and Ma is reluctant to leave her warm bed to sit on the commode. But I manage to persuade her to do so eventually. I live in hope she will have a morning motion. Because if not she will do so later when no-one's there. That's OK except when she mis-fetches the commode and deposits in her nappy. That's OK, too, except she'll then remove the nappy; still OK. But getting a fresh nappy on is beyond her. And although she will wipe herself she'll then sit on a chair or get back into bed, paper trailing from her ghastly maw. This means that when the NHS nurse turns up to wash and dress her at sometime between 10.30 and 11.00 she has to clean the room first. I sit drumming the arms of Ma's bedroom chair and singing 'Career Opportunity' while she sits on the commode.

'What's that row?' she asks.

'Punk.'

'Punk? What's that?'

'A way of singing which died out in the 70s.'

'Thank God for that.'

I cannot persuade her to 'perform' and she's complaining of the cold, but then realising that I'm hovering to get her back off the commode and into bed she now relaxes on the depository and stops moaning about the cold. By being awkward she will get more time with her son.

Eventually I manage to coerce her back into bed.

'All I want is my mummy. I hate everyone else. All they want to do is take my clothes off and make me freeze.'

3 February

I awake to a knock at the door it is 02.30. A knock at the door? Yet I know Ma has not got out of bed. When I enter her room I see her walking stick beside the bed. It was a knock on the wall.

'I need to take Dicky to the doctor's he's got measles,' she says.

'No he hasn't.'

'Yes he has.'

'No he hasn't. I'm Dicky and I'm 58, you're thinking about when I was a child.'

'Have you got spots on your face?'

'No. Now go to sleep.'

'No. I must get up I've got shopping to do.'

'There are no shops open at 2.30 in the morning.'

She's stripped off her bed jacket and nightie.

'Everything's soaking wet,' she declares. It feels dry to me and then as I try to pull her nightdress back over her head I feel the hem is indeed wet.

'Oh, you've pissed on it,' I say pissed off myself at being woken up.

'Don't use such disgusting language.'

I pull a new nightie out of her chest of drawers.

'I'm going to cut them off,' she says, referring to the length.

'Good idea, they catch on your commode.'

I return to my bed.

At breakfast time I go back into her room and draw the curtains.

'Don't do that I don't want to see that damn black.'

'It's the winter, get over it,' I say cruelly.

7 October 1943

'There was a raid on and back in our room I got into Gene's bed and watched the firework show from her window, the air almost froze our faces. Searchlights formed a star in the centre of which was a tiny silver point, zooming along and sprays of red diamonds leapt up and vanished like shooting stars and were punctuated now and then by enormous flashes of the ack ack guns.'

6 February

The weekend. Such joy. Now I have the time to clip Ma's toe nails which poke like yellow toucan beaks from old, splayed bear-like feet.

She's pleased with the extra family time.

'You are a silly haddock,' she says affectionately, perhaps an old Cockney term of endearment used for Southend knees-ups, or alternatively 'You are a soppy date,' originating from exotic imports of Empire?

I was talking to neighbour Ron Cox this afternoon he told me he lived with is old mother for her last weeks. At the end all she could utter was a repetitive count of one to 10 continuously. Her doctor, a Pole, asked Ron: 'Do you want this to go on?' He then offered a shot of morphine which Ron agreed to and it was all over. He has never told his sister: 'Or she would hang me.'

'The doctor's probably still in Broadmoor,' he said with a bleak smile.

'God I'm going to die in a minute,' Ma suddenly announced at tea time, 'I'll never get out of here.'

She asks me to get my car to take her home. I say I prefer to catch the bus.

'OK. Will you get the bus with me?'

7 February

Today is Sunday. Ma's behaviour deteriorates if the routine alters.

She is used to weekday routine. For five days a week this is what happens:

I get up make her tea – two cups – not too hot, not too cold. I bring her toast, not too much marmalade, crusts off, and cut into mouth-sized soldiers and give her a small glass of Casit, to counteract her osteoporosis, her 'bone drink' as I call it and her 'filthy muck' as she calls it. I wait while she twirls a finger of her toast or 'biscuit' as she calls it saying 'lovely' after each mouthful.

At 0700 or 0730 I will say: 'Bye Ma, I'm off to work.'

She will say: 'Oh don't go,' or 'Blast your work can't you stay here? I don't want you to go,' depending upon her mood.

The she will say: 'What time will you be home?'

'Seven.'

'That's terrible, fancy having to do that?'

And I leave.

Between 10.30 – 11.00 the NHS Mental Health nurse will arrive, wash her, dress her, make tea and leave her in her chair watching a DVD. At 11.30 the private carer, Dee Tilbrook, arrives to prepare lunch and be an occasional companion to Ma while they watch a Fred Astaire film. Dee leaves at 15.30.

After finishing her duties as a teaching assistant Cathy comes in between 16.00 and 16.30 and makes Ma tea. Cathy or I or sometimes both prepare supper for Ma and serve it at 17.30 and Cathy, undresses her, puts her nightie on and puts her to bed shortly after that.

I then return from my house at anytime between 19.15 to 21.30, give her a kiss, turn out her bedroom light but leave the landing light on to allow some illumination and say: 'I'm going to bed now.'

This works well most of the time.

But this is Sunday and at weekends I start breakfast later. The NHS nurse still turns up at the same time, but we stand Dee down to preserve Ma's savings and either Cathy or I prepare lunch.

This means Ma sees more of me and in the way of human relations, even those expressed by a wreck, starts to take me for granted with curt, unnecessary orders and contrariness over the day's demands.

For instance yesterday, Saturday, I got her downstairs for a change of scene. Then, into her wheelchair and up to the High Street for a coffee. She accused me of stealing her coat – it was in another part of her house, not her bedroom – her domain – and therefore stolen.

Some spring sunshine was greeted by Ma as 'that damn sun', the coffee was not to her liking, the wind was too cold, the cobblestones under her wheelchair too rough a ride.

Then she notices a baby, she's obsessed with the things. She starts pulling faces, waving and making goo-goo noises at it. Babies don't ask questions, don't contradict, and use direct, guileless stares that she relates to. They can't get one over on her.

One of her earliest diary entries is a description of her sister's son, Francis, who was born after his father, Frank Smith, was killed while serving in the RAF.

20 January 1943

'Seven days leave starts hooray!
Francis is a pet now. His hair is golden and growing fast
and his bones growing hard. He has a neck now but his
chin is small and still very hard to find. He sounds like a
parrot – he squawks and draws his breath in and beats his
fists and lashes out at everything. His pig is thumped until
the squeak sounds quite breathless and he sits up and
boxes his woolly ball on a piece of elastic like a mad thing.
In his bath his aim is not so good, he tries to beat his
rubber duck and nearly always misses so the water flies
round the room and soaks everything. He very nearly
manages to sit up by himself in his cot but not quite.
'A couple of sirens and one about 1 am but nothing
happened.'

This particular blonde tot waved back at a hunched crone
in a wheelchair with white hair askew and waving snake-
skin hands. Ma makes no attempt to engage the child's
mother, just another infuriating adult, let's keep it between
ourselves.
To alleviate my mild embarrassment, I instead, engage the
young mother with a smile. Ma is not exactly a lovely,
little old lady, but I don't want her mistaken for an ogre on
wheels.
We are two parents passing in the street. One smiling with
joy at her offspring's first expressions of communication,
the other a rictus grin at the declining vocabulary of his
charge's second childhood.
Then the tot starts to whine and demand some sweetmeat
or other, and I realise we share one thing: we are both at
the mercy of raging despots. Ma's behaviour induces spite
in me. I cannot help but want to get back at her and when

we return home I sit reading because she's asked me not to leave her.

'Can't you read that tonight and talk to me?'

'All right what do you want to talk about?'

Silence.

I start reading again.

'You beast. Why are you so nasty to me? I haven't done anything to you,' this plaintive, unvarnished logic is that of a once intelligent woman reduced to a child because of a disease of the brain.

The damnable thing is it doesn't seem like any diseases I've heard about. Why isn't her brain rotting? Why is it still able to be manipulative? Why isn't it shutting down faster?

She has a point, too, I could start the 'conversation' with a loop subject: her sister, mother, father, school days and run through the subjects left to her fuse-blown mind.

To her they are all fresh. To me who has been living with her for six months they are nuance-free carcasses, old bones stripped clean of anything by continual inquiry, revisionist analysis and repetition.

So she has two weapons in her 'wind up' armoury: tuneless whistling, or a faux expression of endearment for her 'doggies', the soft toy huskies with crusty patches of food dried on their nylon fur.

'I don't know where my little darlings are,' she says.

'They're upstairs in your bedroom.'

This is another territory, which, to Ma, is one requiring a car journey to get there.

'You've all got cars, why don't you use them?'

'Don't like driving,' I say reducing myself to the same childish response from my unshakeable spite. I'm really learning something about myself. I, too, am, 'not very nice.'

But I have to get her to the living room door before she will accept that no outside journey is required to get to her bedroom and she won't move until she's got her coat. And today she wants 'both of them.'

'Ma, you've got seven coats out there, which one do you want?'

'No I haven't.'

'Well you need to tell me which coat?'

'My Macintosh.'

'There are four, which colour?'

'Oh, darkish.'

I bring through the coat she has just worn up the road and dangle it as bait to get her to the door.

Once at the door she can see the stair lift and I am able to get her on it for her 30 second ride to the next floor.

9 February

Two yells of 'Clifford' wake me. The first one at 01.00. The second at 04.00. Both times Ma is hallucinating. The first time there's 'An Indian on his back frightening me to death,' in the corner of her room.

The second time I ignore the yell as I know it is more 'injuns' or other ethnics climbing out of her dread.

The dilemma is that if I leave a low lamp on in her room the shadows it throws help her construct foreign aliens, men with knives, or Germans invading her bedroom.

These bad guys exist in her clearly still vivid imagination and have invaded that particular territory from Rupert books, probably the only picture books she ever read and still looks at. She pointed out recently a particularly sinister little hunch-back with big ears and a stiletto nose which had been giving the check-trousered teddy some grief.

But if I leave no lights on she can't see the commode. And if I leave the overhead light on she can't sleep.

She has pretended the extra covers – it's cold again, minus 1 degree Celsius – are too heavy for her to lift off in order to use the commode without waking me. But she can do it. The problem still is that she can get out of bed, remove her nappy and get on the commode. What she can't do is get a fresh nappy on, so if the existing one is full, instead of pulling it up again she wrenches it off in disgust and will trail herself wherever she goes.

'I know you don't like me,' she said early this morning. I can't pretend otherwise.

If I can't get her to 'perform' before I leave for work it's just a gamble as to whether the nurse can get to her before she goes trailing or not.

Not for the first time, but perhaps more seriously, we are discussing 'putting her in a home.'

10 February

'Clifford' yelled, with pauses, clearly at 4 am. The first time sternly, the second inquiringly the third time plaintively.

I lie in bed listening as, disturbingly, she appears to refer to herself in the third person:

'Where is she? Where has she gone?'

I get up and go into her room.

'I don't think she's very well. Oh, Dicky where is she? You are responsible for her you know.'

'Yes, Ma.'
'Are we going to take her?'
'Take who?'
'You know like we did last time.'
'What last time?'
'Perhaps I'm going mad.'
'Well at least you're back in the first person.'
Ma complained about her toast being soggy. I realised Dee had turned the control down and made some more with the heat turned back up.
'You can give that muck to the birds.'
'I can't be bothered. I've thrown it away.'
'Oh Dicky they would have eaten that muck especially in this weather. If you were a bird you'd be very grateful for that muck.'
Ma has always turned off the news, be it on TV or radio, and the only part of a newspaper she ever read was the Peterborough column in father's copy of the Daily Telegraph.
So she does not approve of the 'yapping' John Humphreys on the Today programme, which I'm listening to. Then on comes her bete noire, Sarah Montague:
'Oh it's that silly cow again. Wah,wah,wah. SHUT UP.'
After the pair report on the latest insurmountabilities of the west's relations with Afghanistan, she says: 'What rubbish are they talking about now?'
Then a promise of a magazine feature about Country singer Johnny Cash's love of Scotland!
'Johnny Cash,' I say, 'Do you remember, "I walk the line"?'
'No I don't listen to that rubbish.'
I start to sing the song and at the end of the chorus Ma joins in with: 'And walk off the end of the pier.'

I've tried watching the news on the 'idiot box' as she describes the portable TV on her sideboard, but the sight of glamorous news, or sports readers invites even more critique.

9 January 1943

'Henry said would I like to come and watch a basketball game in which he was going to play – I said I'd love to- and we walked to his camp where the Americans are.
At an earlier game there had been a phone call about an air-crash on a house but everyone was absorbed in the game.
This time I watched very clever goals scored by the "Skins", who were, it was obvious, more skilled and faster than Henry's. The captain of the Skins was known as Red. He was a beautiful athlete with really bronze hair and square head. He had a Roman nose and a white, clear skin which soon shone with sweat and every outline of his muscles showed up in the brilliant light.
Henry fouled four times and was turfed out.'

11 February

The Thames slid in over the mud, a cold, shining grey skin. She used to immerse herself in the salt water of the sea so often over the years. Now, although her room overlooks it she no longer even sees it. No woman steps into the same tide twice.
'I'm perishing,' she said lying in bed fully clothed.

'I think we're going to find you somewhere else,' I ventured, 'somewhere more suitable. Somewhere which is always warm.'

'Well you're very kind,' she said, 'especially with me as I never do anything right.'

'I think I'd like to find somewhere where you can get full time nursing. And have your own toilet in the room.'

'Lavatory, dear.'

'Yes, lavatory.'

'Well I've got that,' she said pointing at the commode.

'Somewhere where you can talk to other people – if you want to – rather than just be stuck on your own all the time.'

'Yes,' she said, 'I think I know what you mean.' She gave me a momentary look of total comprehension and I felt sickened. Like all old hacks I'd always loathed PR officers, Ma would have called them Lord Haw Haws and here I was acting as a corporate liar myself oiling the skids of her eviction.

My justification, apart from the impact the ham-fisted caring of my mother was having on my own family life, was that the NHS Mental Health care team was to be disbanded and put out to private tender. They are the one good, consistent thing in Ma's life and if they are being taken away we cannot trust a private outfit again and our delicate arrangement, already beset with jeopardy from Dee's continual absences, when we have to rely on other family members if available, will collapse.

'The thing is my sister's gone and I can't get over that,' said Ma, ' and my mother, but she's still here, she still talks to me.'

'I think that might be in your imagination, Ma.'

'It might be, but I don't think so. Will we go back to Leigh?'
'Yes, or Westcliff,' I said.
'I don't know cliff test,' said Ma, 'because we're not rich are we?'
'No, but we could rent this place out to pay for somewhere nice.'
'Yes, dear, well you do whatever you want.'

12 February

As Ma ate her toast I looked out over the salt marsh. Its edges, where it met the mud, were white with frost.
'Bit of frost out there, but it's going to get milder over the next couple of days.'
'Is it like that all over the place?'
'All over where?'
'All over the world?'
'No.'
'Oh. Why not?'
'Because it's summer or autumn in the southern hemisphere and nearly spring in the north.'
'My God I can't believe it.'
She chewed on a finger of toast, 'Lovely,' then added: 'My God I'm so frightened I can't stand it.'
'Frightened of what?'
'Frightened of being killed.'
'Who by?'
'I don't know what it is, but I can't help it. I'm frightened of what's going to happen. Of what I'm going to do.'
She ate some more toast.
'Oh dear it's awful, oh dear it's terrible, oh dear it's horrible.'

'What Ma?'
'This dreadful pink stuff.'
'What pink stuff?'
'I can't help you dear.'
'What pink stuff?'
'Please don't go on about it you're frightening me.'
Ma started belching. Then: 'Please help me, please help
me, help me stop this.'
She appears to have abandoned responsibility for the
slightest act, wants someone else to step in. The story of
her life in many respects.
She asked me for some water to wipe marmalade off her
sticky fingers.
I provided her with a damp flannel.
'Oh, you might have at least used warm water.'

13 February

The pink Ma was 'seeing' we think was imagined. Two
days before she'd said to Cathy: 'Look at all this red dust
everywhere.'
'What red dust?' said Cathy.
'Oh don't you start. This dust, you know builder's dust.'
This statement was made following a visit from a rental
agent who was shown round by Cathy and who opined in
front of Ma that her house, given a new kitchen, a new
bathroom, re-decorated and re-carpeted could fetch £1,200
a month rent. We are going to need it: care home costs are
£500 - £600 a week.
I visited one this weekend.
It was in an unfashionable part of once fashionable
Westcliff-on-Sea, a scruffy, double-fronted pair of semis

knocked into one and coated with brick red paint to make it assume the semblance of a whole.

I was shown inside by a skinny woman with bad teeth who was wearing a blue, nylon uniform with a badge on her breast declaring she was an NV2. She ran through the details of the residence, the cold air turning her fetid breath, escaping from her scrawny body into ethereal smoke and expanding into the general mustiness of the place, like a genie leaving his lamp.

We walked through dark, ante-rooms, lights switched off to save on utility bills, and into a dimly-lit lounge where six old women all in night-dresses – it was mid-morning - sat silently in armchairs. Two were dozing, one staring at her hands, none took any notice of a man in an overcoat being shown round.

I felt like apologising for violating what felt like a communal bedroom.

'We have 20 guests,' said my guide, I had a strong impulse to clean her teeth, 'all women. Half of them have dementia. They range in age from 66 to 104…' The silent six did not respond. They'd lost any sense of wonder.

One hundred and four…please God, no, I thought. Ma can't live another 18 years…

'They've all just eaten,' uttered the brush-needy bouche, by way of explaining such mute response to a stranger in their midst. 'They'll be fed again mid-afternoon,' added the zoo-keeper. I had become fixated on her plaque. It would be therapeutic chipping it away…

We continued through the dark recesses of this cavern, following badly joined carpets of mis-matching pattern through corridors and up stairways to cold rooms filled with cast-off furnishings.

'It's £550 for a standard room, or £570 with en suite… a week,' she said almost in disbelief herself.

'But we've no spare rooms at present,' her breath was drawn up, like moth vapour, towards a plastic candle-labra-style light hanging from the landing ceiling.

I explained we'd need to find somewhere fairly soon as the NHS Mental Health Care team were being cut from the local government budget.

'Well there is one resident who's being moved soon to Bedfordshire to be nearer her family,' her bat-like, carbon dioxide floated ceiling-wards.

She took notes on Ma's age, 'condition' and her home address and said she would have to be 'assessed' before being offered residence.

I was next shown the dining room where another eight or so old women were seated around a television and, off to the side of this, a downstairs lavatory with shower which smelled so strongly of freshly evacuated bowels I would happily have used my guide's reeking orifice as a gasmask. The ladies staring at daytime TV seemed oblivious to the gas.

Closing my nostrils, with the sort of gurning a hot yogi might be proud of, I felt obliged to enter the wretched cell to demonstrate concern for my mother's well-being.

I could not resist a 'Coo,' in disgust.

'I'm sorry,' my guide said, 'it's just been in use. Is there anything you want to ask me?'

'Yes. Could I see the room that may be coming up...that is if it's not occupied?'

'Oh yes, of course. It's OK there's no-one in there at present.'

We ascended another stairway, up two flights of fraying carpet treads only partly covering inexpertly stained boards.

I followed the wisps of exhaled breath to the south-west corner of the house and into a dark, cramped, L-shaped room. The reason it took the form of the alphabet's 12th letter was not some environmental conceit of the original architect for the well-being of the occupier, but of how a makeshift use of plaster-board can ensure a space for one can be converted into a space for two. Of how a day's work for a jobbing carpenter could turn £500 a week into £1,000.

It's not always been the case, but few today would consider cattle trucks, even stationary ones, are fit for anything but cattle, I thought.

No furniture fits convincingly into the long and the short of an L and the room looked like a house clearance store. Suddenly, shockingly I spotted a pair of brown, upholstered slippers lodged on a shelf of a bedside unit and was reminded this was somebody's pad.

'Well thanks so much for showing me round,' I said, retreating quickly to the stairs, adding as we descended to the ground floor of the bat cave once more, 'obviously there's a lot to weigh up…'

'So you'll get back to us?' the breath filtered through teeth which looked like splintered pieces of walnut shell.

'Yes, yes, leave it with me,' I lied thinking only how grateful I was to get out into the fresh air and how I would never inhale the dragon's breath or step inside her horror mansion ever again.

'Tell you what,' I said to Cathy, 'I would never put my mother into a fucking shit-hole like that.'

My reaction was strong. I was angry. Behind the dusty curtains of forgotten houses all over the country old people are being robbed of their savings, plonked in front of televisions and toileted in herds by overworked and underpaid human collie dogs.

14 February

A call for help was uttered in the early hours, but with less volume than normal. Less urgency than usual, so I lay there waiting for the call to stop. It didn't.
'You hate me,' she said when I eventually went in.
I didn't respond.
'Is it my birthday?' she asked herself.
Then she told me she'd lost a 'little tree'.
'Have you seen it?'
'No.'
'Oh don't be daft of course you have.'
She was comfortable so I went back to bed and returned at breakfast time with her toast.
As she lay chomping she stared out of the window and said: 'It's a shame that blue's going. Oh no, there's more over there,' she swung her arm across the sky searching for breaks in the cloud.
'Yes,' I said.
'What?' she said, then realising her response was over - peremptory for the art of conversation – something she still cares about – added: 'I'm sorry darling what did you say?'
'I was just agreeing with you.'
'Agreeing with what?'
'Whatever it was you said.'
'Oh, that's polite,' she said sarcastically.

'You can have some of these biscuits, I'm not going to wolf the lot.'

'I've got my own.'

'Oh, please yourself. I wonder if it's going to rain again?'

'I hope not.'

'I love the rain. I sat there,' she pointed at her chair by the window, 'and watched it coming down over the roofs and chimneys, it was beautiful.'

Rain washes people off the street. Scatters them indoors. And briefly creates solitude. Ma finds that comforting. At least, solitude from the public.

'Do you believe in God?' I asked.

'No. Do you?'

'I don't know.'

'Well, of course you don't know. Nor do I so it's no good talking rubbish.'

She pulled down her animal print fleece.

'I don't like these blankets made out of bears, they frighten me.'

Cathy and I visited a second care home today, this one an imposing residence looking like a smartly-turned out, exclusive hotel rather like the mansions you can find dotted throughout the pinewoods of Sandbanks in Dorset. This 1930s detached, 14-room nursing home had a sweeping gravel drive, immaculately manicured gardens and a green and white striped canvas canopy over the entrance doors.

In the lobby we were confronted by a huge wooden staircase, which tumbled down almost to the threshold. It was the sort of staircase a film star might descend while in character. I could imagine Ma's favourite, Fred Astaire, serenading her arrival from its deep pile stairs.

Each newel post anchored a helium-filled, heart-shaped, balloon heralding St Valentine's Day.

A smartly turned-out Filipino matron showed us a vast bedroom on the first floor, which was in the process of being re-decorated although it hardly appeared in need of it. The place was clean and fresh.

'We don't suffer pongs here,' she said intuitively.

On the ground floor we were led past many bedrooms, their doors open and their occupants in bed-wear: men in dressing gowns, women in nighties. It was 4pm.

She led us through to a large, bright conservatory with a tastefully erected turret roof. The windows looked out onto a garden dotted with perfectly shaped conifer bushes rather like giant chess bishops, making an impact like that of a mini Palace of Versailles.

She took us into her office.

'It's £625 a week. When would your mother be thinking of coming?'

'Oh maybe April/May.'

'You might get a room downstairs by then,' she said ominously.

'Are you expecting a vacancy?'

'Anytime soon,' she said in a matter-of-fact way. Perhaps they bumped them off early to make room for new long-termers.

As she showed us out I noticed a framed photograph of actress Peggy Mount hanging from the wall.

'Wasn't she born in Leigh?' I asked.

'Yes and she died in here,' said the matron cheerfully.

For some reason I checked this later and discovered that in fact Peggy Mount had died in an actors' care home in north London.

But why spoil the branding?

18 February

Ma lay abed, her breath crackling as she told me of a dream, which 'nearly frightened me to death.' A confused and broken narrative followed which involved Cathy's 'first' marriage and a letter written by me, which went to an incorrect location.

This held similarities to an uncanny dream Ma recounted to my father years beforehand. His parents had been over on a visit from their home in New Zealand and were returning to Auckland by ship. Their trip had included a visit to grandpa's sister, May, who lived in London's Tooting with another elderly spinster, Doris.

Ma's dream was that the telephone kept ringing; that it was Doris trying to get through to let grandpa know May had died in the night. My mother told father about the dream before he got up and went downstairs to make tea.

On the doormat was a telegram, from Doris, breaking the news of May's death in the night and the phrase 'tried ringing.' The telephone had been cut off as part of the preparations for my parent's moving house to Cornwall. The fact that she had told my father about the dream before he found the telegram gave the story a creepy authenticity, which had become part of our family lore.

As she lay there semi-dozing with a hint of ragged breath the uninitiated might think her end was near, but with the news that tea was on its way, she was up out of bed and on the commode to 'pay a visit.'

I was pleased to note that a 'number two' had been duly delivered for once.

When she was back in bed I set the tea beside her.

'Are we having any of those nice biscuits you do?'

'Yes. I'm just going to make them.'
'Good. Well hurry up and do it now. I'm starving.'
And back to life she comes.

The lunch lady, Dee, has let us down again, sending a message via David, the cleaner who flits about Hoovering the house on Tuesdays, that she can't make Thursday or Friday.

We think Dee has dropped out because she knows it's half-term and therefore also knows Ma can rely on Cathy stepping in.

But, later, perhaps anticipating our scepticism, Dee turns up with paperwork 'proving' she had to be sedated for more dental work. Dee's buccal cavity is an ongoing project rivalling the painting of the Forth Bridge for the work required to re-align her protruding teeth.

The worst aspect of being responsible, in middle life for another, is having to rely on other people. I know now what an employer must face: uncertainty, cancellation, and poor time-keeping camouflaged with the emotional conspiracies of sick children, doctor's notes, and anniversary birthdays.

Meanwhile the job still has to be done.

19 February

A thump and a yell. I leap up and rush in to find Ma lying beside her bed. It's 5am. She'd used the commode for a 'number two' then wandered around to the far side of the bed where she'd fallen over.

I got her back into bed and all is well. Her crackly breath has stopped and she's uttering sensible sentences: that's to say grammatically correct sentences rather than rational ones and the volume and the drowsiness has gone. Her condition seems to ebb and flow with the tide over the estuary mudflats.

20 February

The fall seems to have done her a power of good. Very chirpy this morning and as I listen to the Today programme, she says:
'Aren't men boring when they start yacking? They don't know what they're talking about.'
Then she turns to her soft toy dogs: 'My little babies love sleeping,' and she laughs away, 'they don't want to go for a walk, not bloody likely,' more laughter and the projection of her own loathing for physical exercise, 'they love it when I pick them up by the back of their necks,' which is what she and Pa used to do with Rosie, the family Beagle.
Then she starts whistling furiously, a habit from her 'Tomboy' past.
Then she stops suddenly.
'Oh I don't know what I'm going to do with my life, well what's left of it.'
Then back to the whistling.
I cleared away Ma's books today. She can no longer read, or rather can pick out a written word very slowly, like a shop sign or an advert on TV, even slower than a child learning to read. But rows and rows of text are now meaningless. I've tried to get her to read her old favourites including escape from Colditz yarns, Marjory Allingham and Dorothy L Sayers but she sits with the pages open and scans the sentences but they do not seem to register. It's a

sad day as she loved reading. And re-reading her favourites: Vanity Fair, Pride & Prejudice, Brideshead Revisited, The Great Gatsby.

At least she can still look at Rupert and pals.

Ironically it's Rupert, which the second-hand book-dealer who I contacted, would have deprived her of.

That's if there were any rare editions which he quickly determines there is not. He flicked through her bridge books, her books on royalty and a few collectable Penguin green-band covers and offered me £60, which seemed a pitiful amount for a 70-year-old library. What's more he left me to box up the bridge and royal family books and transport them up to the junk shop myself. But at least I know I can start dumping all this paper without fear of throwing away cash.

I used Ma's basket-on-wheels to haul them up the hill to the nearest repository, the PDSA shop, where a wrinkled woman wearing spectacles fitted with a drooping chain seemed totally disinterested, behind her glass-topped reception 'desk'.

Upon realising the buried treasure in Ma's basket comprised only books she didn't even say 'Thank-you.' But instead returned to her precious bits and bobs under glass, removing items and rubbing them with a dust cloth before replacing them lovingly back into place as though she were in her own home.

On the third book run, she finally looked up to say: 'Are there any more?'

It was pretty clear she was saving me a trip to the rubbish dump.

I kept back a few books Ma had signed, using Nancy Best, her maiden name, for the sake of sentimentality.

It seemed immoral using Ma's belongings in 'helping a vet help a pet' rather than helping a neurosurgeon prevent the breakdown of memory, but I had deliberately avoided the local Mencap shop as my mother had worked there for years. Her workmates were parochial philistines thriving on a feast of gossip and I was not going to give them the chance to turnover and analyse the remains of Ma's library.

21 February

Started to rummage through Ma's garden sheds where a collection of tin tea trolleys (two); suit-case wheels (two); plastic chairs (eight); plastic ice-cream boxes (too many to count); plastic bags (ditto); baskets on wheels (three); wally trolleys (two); oven grills (four), comprised the first layer of survival storage from folks who'd experienced austerity first time round.

The book-dealer said of Clifford's pile of water-colours: 'The trouble is the young these days just want a single print from IKEA and yet everyone of retirement age seems to be painting.'

So they went to help vets help pets, too.

NHS nurse Val Davies turned up to wash Ma.

I'd mentioned how her condition seemed to rise and fall like the mercury in a barometer, and yet how, with a disease, you expected it to be all downhill.

She said: 'One of my ladies seemed to be breathing her last, but then one day she slept for 30 hours and was as right as nine-pence after that.'

We discussed assisted suicide: I mentioned Ron's decision with his mother.

She said: 'The thing is, who's to say they haven't got quality of life? If they are clean and warm and being fed, then there's no stress. As long as they're not being abused, who's to say our reality is worth anymore than theirs?'
Another care home visit. This one had big plate glass windows so you could see in from the busy road on which it stood: no dark corners being hidden from view, nothing flashy about it, and staffed solely by Filipino men caring solely for British women. It felt friendly, bright, and enjoyed a sense of role reversal from the others we'd looked at: one old crone shouted 'Carer' at the top of her voice and was tended with great patience by a young man. A bastardised version of Greensleeves, at the wrong tempo, was floating through the PA system, but Ma would like the canary in the conservatory and we've put her name down on the 'waiting list.'
Peculiar thought: a waiting list for a waiting room…

22 February

Ma complained of the 'glare' as I opened the curtains.
'Well don't worry, Ma, we're going to find you a nice room without glare.'
'Oh no you're not. Don't find me anything.'
'Yes we have to, Ma, because the NHS Mental Health Care team are being disbanded.'
'What?'
'Sacked.'
'Why?'
'So the government can save money.'
'Oh well I feel very sorry for them.'
'Yes and we will find you a nice guest house.'
'I'm not going anywhere.'

Later I told her the guest house would be warm all the time.

'Good. That's a God-send.'

'Because it's quite cold here isn't it?'

'Oh yes the whole place is like a morgue.'

'But the place we're going to is warm all the time.'

'If that's the truth then that's different.'

'And we're also making sure they take dogs.'

'That they won't?'

'No, that they will, so you can take your doggies and they can be warm there as well.'

'I'm not leaving my pictures.'

'No, we will make sure the pictures come.'

'I wonder what will happen to this building?'

'We will rent it out to pay for the guest-house bills. So it will be self-financing.'

'Oh, I don't know what you mean.'

I have become aware of a resentment within me when talking to Ma and that this is because she should be 'getting worse', that her lack of decline is not fitting in with my preconceptions. That I want to be morally responsible but only if that has a time limit. The arts of conversation have been side-lined by me because by now she should be a gibbering wreck.

The fact she is not has brought me back to humanity and even though she talks about people who are long dead as though they are alive I have decided to communicate with more effort.

I recalled how, when I was a child, she had made a visit, with Pa, to have a last look at Aunty May, this one her own father's sister, in her coffin.

Ma suddenly looked sharp.

'Yes,' she said, 'I remember that.'

And then we talked about the wars which had taken so many men away.

'My mother was always so grateful she never had any men (sons). How dreadful just to go forward and be shot. And all for nothing, except "Oh he was a wonderful soldier who dies so bravely". What nonsense.'

11 August 1940

'Dear Rhoda,

I hate Sundays now. It's a day of reckoning. I think of childhood, school... complexes. Of things and happenings. Other worlds. Life doesn't seem real anymore. Once I was an apprentice architect...a student. What's the use! My last birthday I celebrated in the Army. In the evening I went to the village pub. I drank. Something soft...an atmosphere... seemed to embrace me. I was in a haven. So sheltered.

Training continues. I expect to go to Chesterfield at the end of this month for a further part of my course. Finally we go to Aldershot. And after that... who knows.

I've been homesick, dusty, tired and, oh, I've missed you all so terribly.

The threat of German invasion has caused considerable upheaval in the training of "rankers" as officers. Normally it requires some six months or so before a man is gazetted.

'The RASC is made up of two sections a) supply and b) transport. We are not normally a front line fighting force. Now we have threat of invasion we have got to learn advanced infantry training...

My fondest love to you all and an earnest desire that we shall meet again soon,

Yours as ever,

Percy.'

Ma has written on the envelope: 'Letters from friend of our family, Percy Butler, killed invasion of Europe. Don't throw away as it is all history.'
He enlisted in the Royal Army Service Corps, as a private in June 1940, but was later made a second lieutenant in an 'emergency commission' in the Infantry Training Corps with the 2nd Battalion, Essex Regiment for the 'duration of emergency' as stated on his service record. There's a photograph of him in his uniform on his wedding day with Ma on his right and his bride, Betty on his left. Tall, high-browed, lantern-jawed, slim; an almost handsome man revelling in masculinity.
While attached to the 2 Glosters he was killed in action in North West Europe on 13 April 1945 and is buried in Milsbeek War Cemetery, Limburg, Netherlands.

23 February

'Oh, isn't it dreadful?' the statement wakes me at 06.30. Is it a reference to the continuing cold or damp weather? Who knows, but it's quickly followed up with: 'Never mind we'll be going home soon, thank God.'
'Yes, we will find a nice place for you,' I say going in to check.
'Stop that,' she says sharply, 'I'm going to live with me mother,' deliberately using incorrect grammar as a way of

reassuring herself that her statement was prosaic as opposed to fantastic.

'She's long dead, Ma. I'll make some tea.'

26 February

'He's a fool and I can't stand the sight of him and I haven't got any bandages, I haven't got a car, I can't drive. But I don't think he's dead. He keeps hanging around me trying to attract my attention. But why should he shout out my name "Nancy"?'

This strange monologue concerns, as far as I can determine, the cleaner, David, who comes in on Tuesdays. He cried out after cutting his finger.

'He's always working with wood,' said Ma, 'but I can't stand the sight of him. I can't help it I just don't like him.'

There may be something in this as Emily does not like David either. There's something creepy about him they reckon. He has a certain campness, and maybe it's because of that: that he's not camp enough. After all modern women like gays and Ma always loved Frankie Howard, but for them their sexuality must be overt: Queer as opposed to just queer.

'I just can't bear the sight of him. Some people just give me the shudders.'

I asked why and Ma mimicked David, laying her head to one side, affecting a cheesy smile and saying: 'Are you all right, Nancy?'

I guess that is a little creepy.

27 February

A crash and a yell woke me at 06.15. Ma was lying on the floor of her bedroom threshold. She was unhurt and I heaved her onto the commode. She'd got up, drawn the curtains to see 'the blue before it goes' as the sun disappeared into cloud, then wandered aimlessly before falling.

26 January 1943

'It is 6pm and nearly blackout time but there is still a light in the sister's home in the distance. This is a very ugly building with red bricks and a blue roof but part is hidden by two large elms. The drive slopes away to the right and runs out of sight behind the cedar tree, which grows outside our window. Green lawns slope down with three fat pin-cushion bushes the last of which meets a well cut yellow green hedge. The rest of the view is a tangle of bare elms behind which acres of fields and woods are hidden in a blue mist.'

Her face was pale –perhaps a touch of shock – but she was soon back to her normal self with a litany of woe: 'I might as well be dead. Come back AT ONCE.'
This then switched to 'Lovely, gorgeous, delicious,' as she crunched her toast and marmalade, her expression changing from that of little girl lost before breakfast to imperious old monarch during it.
Her big-boned face crunched down on the toasted fingers with great deliberation. I was put in mind of those old Punch cartoons of the 1920s and earlier when great rotund

empires depicted as Tweedledum and Tweedledee-shaped bodies devoured parts of the world.

Maybe she's just projecting her own frustration at being helpless on the vulnerable soldiers of toast, holding them up, inspecting them, with all the compassion of an old lioness, before relishing a great and noisy crunch into their middles. Then a brief period of contemplation while the snap, snap of her plastic molars mash away.

'Don't forget your bone drink,' I say.

'I already have,' she says, nothing wrong, cognitively speaking, with that!

'What are they? Maniacs talking about how they got everything wrong?' she asked as we listened to the Today programme's reporting of an earthquake in Chile.

28 February

I was woken at midnight by Ma entering my room: a first.

'There's a man in my room. He's put toys out for the children and he's got a revolver.'

'Go back to bed before you fall over,' I said callously.

'Oh bugger off. I'm very frightened.'

She told me his name was Eric.

At daybreak it's raining again. Grey skies. Rivers of water in the gutters, skins of water peeling down the middle of the road. Radiators click as they expand with more water, heated this time, and the sound of poppelling overhead as rain pattered on the roof.

The brent geese have gone, perhaps there's less rain in Siberia.

On the commode Ma sits, her soiled pants discarded, not noticing an unfortunate stain on the soft furnished chair where she inadvertently sat between knicker drop and mobile loo. 'God know's what my hair's like,' she said. I did not say it would disgrace a scarecrow, a very old scarecrow, as the last bastion of female vanity comes into play. How many women can be seen, plastic teeth set in faces like greased prunes as they totter on skinny, buboe-covered legs, who have perfect helmets of painted hair ? Yet those who don't colour or sculpt the last organic part of their body, which can be quality controlled, actually come as a shock. The coiffured pass by unseen, the unkempt stand out. Both achieve the wrong result.

I wash the mud off her wheelchair spokes, in the rain, in preparation for transporting her to a 'home'.

I'm angry because she has complained about the fact her toast had included a crust, the bread had come to the end of the waxy wrapper, yet she still ate it. Then both cups of tea were too cold: they are always too hot when I place them beside her so she leaves them until they are too cold. Can't she see how sick I am of spending my time in an endless round of fine tuning over her pointless existence? 'Oh you don't like me do you? I don't like not being liked.'

'Look, Ma, I do like you. You are my mother, I love you. But you need to make yourself a bit more likeable. You don't say : "Oh that second cup wasn't much good," in a dismissive way. Pa ended up not liking you. Clifford buggered off, now you're starting on me.'

Totally unfair because of course she's never going to change. She was never going to change when she could. Now she is probably not even aware of her infuriating rudeness, which has run the course of her whole life. But I have to blow sometimes and it doesn't do her any harm to be brought up sharp now and then.

1 March

'I'm frightened. I spend my whole life being frightened.'
'It's because you spend too much time on your own,' I
said cunningly selling her the next location.
I spent yesterday clearing the tool shed. In the end after
weighing up the labour involved in picking out the non-
ferrous metal from the chaff, against what the brass could
be worth I swept it all away: screws, nails, bolts, nuts into
double plastic rubbish bags. Hoped the bin-men did not
suspect it was anything more than domestic waste. Twenty
rubbish sacks lay in wait on the pavement. Maybe they'll
think we've had a party.

2 March

The call of: 'Barbara? Barbara? Can you help me?' woke
me up at 04.45. I ignored her. It would only be help to pull
off the bed-clothes which she can manage. In the event the
pleas died away and she returned to slumber. At 06.00 I
brought her breakfast and had to remind her it was there.
'I'm not very hungry dear. I don't feel very well.'
'Well, have your tea.'
She sat up and immediately started munching toast.
A pink, full moon dropped through still, blue-grey clouds
to the west.
'Thought you said you weren't hungry? You're eating so
that's good, you're better.'
'No I'm not.'
I think I can smell her.
'Do you want to go to the lavatory?'
'No. I can't be bothered.'

Perhaps it's my punishment for ignoring her earlier pleas.
'Do you want to go in the bed then?'
'Don't be nasty. You're always asking me horrible questions.'
So, like as not, the NHS team will have a mucky time of it, I think, as I leave for the office.

3 March

Another bad day yesterday. As predicted Ma had a shit storm and the NHS team had sheets, bedding, cushions and clothing to wash. Clifford's
old reclining armchair which he'd left behind, got the worst of it. I'm sitting on it now aware that a brown stain is on the seat: scrubbed and now dry but forever disfigured.
Ma has had two falls in the last 24 hours but has refused doctors and ambulances. We think she's OK, but her left side is giving her pain and causing her to call out for assistance just to get out of bed. She is to be 'assessed' by the care home inspector in two day's time. I hope she will hold out long enough to be considered 'fit' enough to get over someone else's threshold. I've had enough.
I assume they make sure they are not taking on too much. Her condition is to be 'evaluated.' She will undergo a cost-benefit analysis.
She called for me at 2 am wanting the bedclothes pulled off so she could get onto the commode. I eventually got up and whipped the covers off, like a magician with a sheet under a glass.
'Don't do it like that,' she shouted angrily. I'm a bastard, I did it deliberately like that. I'm sick of her.
'If you're going to shout I'll leave you to it,' I said.

But I got the old carcass on the chair-lavatory. After a release of urine and the cessation of dripping, I told her to get up and pull her 'panties' up as I call them.

'Is it finished?'

'How should I know? Sounds like it,' I said in sudden disgust and self-pity for my lot.

She'd laid a stool, too, so I wiped her, hauled up her padded pants and got her back into bed.

Pink-tinged, cold blue cloud lay over the estuary this morning. And one of the grey-hulled, white-upper-worked, lorry-filled ferries which run from Dartford to the continent is slipping behind the telegraph pole which carries the tracery of the outside world to Ma's home. Regular as clockwork, day and night the ships pass.

4th March

'Please help' etc. and I've just turned in. It's 21.30. I get up and throw back her bedclothes.

'Don't do it like that,' she screams in anger. Eyes of blue blazing furiously. So I throw them back over again.

'Bastard.'

Later I find she's got out and had a pee on her own, she can still do this but continues to ask for help. Dr. Beverton called yesterday to check her left side, which was giving her pain – she'd had a couple of falls two days ago. No cracked ribs just bruising and this morning that had improved - she's more mobile and in less pain.

The doctor told Cathy Ma's got the blood pressure of a teenager.

No joy there then.

I'm off to Calais this morning on a job. So it's early breakfast for the queen, and the usual litany of 'lovely,

lovely' as she scoffs her toast. Outside the inky blue sky is supported by an inky blue estuary upon which the ship channel buoys are winking.

5th March

'I had a nice day in France yesterday.'
'Good' said Ma dismissively.
'Oh you don't want to hear about it?'
'I think all French people are barmy.'
'Why?'
'You see all I want you to do is talk, but you won't so why should I?'
Then with her right hand she started scratching the bed-clothes like a hen. Cathy thinks this is a sign of distress.
'I only asked you why you thought French people were barmy.'
'Dicky, I have been to France and I quite enjoyed myself so just leave me alone and stop going on at me. The French have got a dreadful language nobody can understand it.'
I think it's simply that a question now is like an attack, perhaps because it requires effort to form an answer. Maybe she can't form answers.

6th March

Afternoon. Outside brilliant sunshine over the cold, fissured estuary. Ma's got the curtains drawn. 'I hate that damn sun. I don't want to be burnt by it.'
I tap my cup on the radiator. 'Yes little boys like banging drums,' she says and starts whistling to drown out the tapping.

I doze. She whistles Carmen lying on her side, fully dressed, on the bed.
I turn the radiator off for the first time since October. Putting her to bed she is convinced someone is going to steal the maroon pullover I've just removed 'The amount of pinching that goes on round here is unbelievable.'

7th March

'I wish we could turn the clocks back so that we are not as we are now,' said Ma as I opened her sketch-books and autograph albums from her school days 1936-37, as Cathy continues the process of 'house clearance'.
I looked at photographs of Ma, as a toddler, yesterday as we cleared her stuff. A very plump, little, brown-skinned creature with intense, sad eyes playing in the wavelets on the seashore at Chalkwell, piggy-back riding, hugging a dog and nearly always alongside her taller, older, sleeker, sister Rhoda.
I 'have told' of Ma's superiority complex before, but that seems reserved just for behaviour or accent, about anything deeper she has in fact low self- esteem, always saying she's 'stupid' or useless and clearly someone told her this from a young age. I found her sketch-book with naïve, water-colour paintings of street scenes in Germany in 1937, and pencil sketches of various nurses she worked with in Torquay. It won a prize at Westcliff High School for Girls. Ma was annoyed I'd 'found' it though she enjoyed some of her memories briefly. But she's not over-indulgent with sentimentality and told me I could have it 'When I'm dead.' I'll give it to Emily. We also found a heart-shaped embroidered photo album containing pictures of her school friends and VAD colleagues including the

elusive Jeanette James, whom often came up in mother's chatter and who left with a husband for Australia back in the 1930s and 'never wrote.'

'I never heard of her again.'

I tried another name from her diary: Mitford.

25 March 1943

'Forgot to say that VAD Mitford died on Tues: 23 at 11.30pm over in Ward 18. She had septicemia and pneumonia. She was at pay parade last Thursday and said: "I'm still supposed to be off sick" and was about third in the queue.

She worked in the kitchens as a cook, and was a tall, thin, pale girl – with a lovely voice. She was cousin to Unity Mitford. I remember her at the New Year's dance as the Mad Hatter. She was very sweet natured – I'm not saying this because she's dead, but I took all my TAB's and vaccinations at the same time as her and we talked quite a lot during the long waits at out-patients.

What a shock for everyone. I can't realise it. There's the most frightful notice up in the PAD room "Collections for a wreath for Mitford please" and a little box with a slit in it. I can see her sitting in the armchair now looking ill always, her dark, fuzzy hair and her long legs.'

If the name meant anything, Ma did not react.

Whether it's down to the melancholy of Sunday or the nostalgia of recounting a life through memorabilia I don't know, but I could not shake off a feeling of sadness, today.

8th March

'I wonder if my babies are warm enough? No, they're not warm enough, we need to find somewhere warmer for them. Yes, it's terrible this place.'

9th March

Caring is a job for nuns; with little else to do except pray. Caring when you've got three kids battling their chances in a recession; while dancing just ahead of technology's omnipotence in a job where you are already obsolete is no joke. While baling out the viscous urine from her commode a tiny drip disgusts me as it sears my hand. In a fury of resentment I wipe it off subversively on the loo curtain and go back to bed.
'Dicky? Dicky?'
At last Clifford has died in her mind.
'Dicky? Can you come here and get this little boy? It's all right dear, Dicky?'
Oh well it's nearly 6 o'clock, might as well get up anyway. No mention of the 'child' as I bring in the toast, just 'Lovely.'
Ma tends to talk only when there's no one in the room, perhaps to make up for the isolation. To fill the void.

11th March

They are cellulose impregnated with various chemicals and will 'biodegrade in an active landfill site within 6-12 months.' They are Coochie Coo fragranced baby wipes and the cute little brown-eyed baby with suspiciously mature hair on the packet doesn't look like my mum. Incontinence is cute at one end of life but not the other.

12th March

'Dicky? Dicky? Can you get that pudding?' As it is 5 am I did not object to dealing with the figment of a fragmented mind. The little white bells of the snowdrops I'd dug from her garden were now drooped and brown, but the daffodils from the greengrocer have opened their trumpets as if to herald Ma's 'approval' for her care home. Confirmation is coming next week.

Her perfectly formed upper teeth lay on the floor this morning, which explained why her regular tirade of 'oos and ahhs' was uttered through tight lips. As I scrubbed them before re-entry I noticed that 'wallies' as they are affectionately termed in Scotland, suffer from plaque too. The sediment of nutrition forms as tough a layer on epoxy as on enamel.

She was talking today about her pre-war visit to Germany, in 1937, with her mother Ethel to see how Rhoda was settling down – her sister was there to learn German – and they went with cousin Gil and his wife Doris.

'And guess what? Gil and Doris saw old Hitler eating cakes,' she said.

'They said: "We've actually seen Hitler." I didn't want to come home, filthy old Broadway, tin cans everywhere 'cos one thing you can say the Germans are very clean.'

Clean wogs.

13th March

Cathy was told by Stephanie, the manageress of Westcliff Lodge, that Ma can move in next Thursday. Today is

Saturday. She need bring no bedding but we've decided to take her mattress in case she turns 'princess and the pea.' She does seem more tired these days, both in the morning and in the evening. It used to be the case that mornings were her worst time and she picked up speed through the day.

The creek was filling this morning, a shining snake between the mudflats; and it's a lot milder, but still grey and damp.

14th March

Once again Ma has bucked the trend – not that there is any obvious trend to buck except the elusive pattern which I keep trying to identify – she is up to full volume again with demands. Good attitude in the morning but rude as the day wears on. I'm not a carer. I want to 'get her back.' I loathe myself for it, both at the time and afterwards but seem powerless to act otherwise.

As she dropped shit all down the wrong side of the upstairs loo I made exaggerated noises of nasal disapproval. I cleaned up the mess, which by the way she denied was hers, saying it was more likely mine! At 17.20 she was 'wolfing', her word not mine, down a huge plate of cold chicken and bubble and squeak, the other half of the roast she'd had at lunchtime. This woman 'aint ailing no more. Rita the NHS nurse said this morning: 'The thing is, it's not dementia that kills them, if their heart is strong … who knows?'

This could be a long journey.

But the fact I cannot help but feel this way means it's most definitely time for mother to have someone else at her beck and call.

Take the dialectic of lunch:
I bring up the lunch.
Ma: 'What's that?'
Me: 'Lunch.'
Ma: 'I know that but what is it?'
Me: 'Meat and two veg.'
That stymies her.
She can't complain about the beast slaughtered and cooked for her appetite if she cannot identify it.
I've found myself recently, rubbing my fingers with my thumb: a sort of secular rosary, not an appeal for the Almighty's help, though that would not be spurned, but a kind of metronome for pace, a tattoo for order. It's as though chaos can be held in abeyance by ritualistic mannerism.
The old cow is now exhaling breath in noisy puffs, a suggestion of sleep.

15th March

An early, still, spring morning; the rising sun lifting colour from the exposed mudflats as though they are terra firma never drowned by salt water. And indeed the tide is so far out, that even the far away River Thames has lowered to such a degree it seems as though no power on earth could flood this area with water, and yet the tide is coming.

11 September 1995

'We took little Katie to school. In the back of the car she told me that when the tide went out it went all the way to France and then it came back again when it was in.'

Today is Monday. On Thursday she leaves her home for the last time. It seems quite shocking to think she won't be coming back. Down in her cosy front room, which she hasn't seen for weeks, large cardboard boxes are filled with books and china-ware and await freighting to my sister Diana's home in Portsmouth, New Hampshire. It has taken weeks to clear Ma's home and there is still a long way to go. The plan is to use her savings to modernise the place and get it rented to help pay for her care.
The window panes of a fishing boat out in the Ray flashed the reflected sun at me, momentarily, as the incoming tide swung the craft round.

16th March

Last night I went through the move in two days time to the 'guest house.' I explained that the time had come for Ma to have round the clock care. 'Somebody there, Ma, you do need it.'
'Yes, I hate this morgue.'
She had said to Cathy earlier that she didn't want to go to bed because she would just be left lying there for hours.
It is now probably cruel to keep her in her own home unless I give up work and live with her: her vassal 'till the end of her time.

There will be things she does not like but on the whole she will be better off, we have convinced ourselves.

About half an hour after broaching the subject of her move, with both of us in our respective beds I hear: 'But won't it cost a lot of money?'

One surprise a few days ago was that I discovered she likes the blues. I'd mentioned watching a documentary on the subject on TV the night before.

'They're not all negroes are they?'

'No, but that's where it started. Then Howlin' Wolf and others came to London in the 1950s and brought this terrific music with them. Their powerful emotion coming from the legacy of slavery.'

'Do you think there are any of them left?'

'No.'

'Shame.'

So now I know what to say when she comes across a 'negro' in the 'guest house' – I'll just say she or he is a blues performer.

That morning I put on some early Fleetwood Mac and she lay in bed, eyes closed, twirling her hand to the guitar riffs of the virtuoso Peter Green.

Later I told Rita the NHS nurse. 'Oh, your mum's so cool,' she said, without irony.

Certainly her taste in music is truly catholic; it started with classical and her occasional visits to concerts at the wartime Albert Hall, for the first one of which she still has the ticket stub stapled into her diary a three shillings and sixpenny seat in the balcony:

18 March 1943

'There was hardly a house tenanted and practically all bore overhanging signs: "To Let' or "To be Sold". Passed several buildings, which I took to be the Royal Albert in succession, until I reached the main road and it stood on my left opposite an enormous statue. There were the placards: "March 18th YEHUDI MENUHIN the world-renowned violinist."

Inside the queue moved forward and we climbed a winding staircase to the gallery. Having purchased my ticket early I was propelled into the front row next to a small foreign soldier and therefore could lean over the red, velvet edge. The building is enormous and dome-shaped like a gigantic circus arena. From the bottom row upon row of red velvet chairs nose up like tiny red squares in a pattern and above these came the boxes with curtains on either side like a dolls house. The gallery sloped up so that those in the top row looked as if they might overbalance.

The mass of people below began to grow and Red Cross nurses were busy with programmes so it resembled a swarm of brown, blue and black dotted with tiny white squares.

The whole thing looked like a stirring ant heap.

Sir Henry Wood strutted in, a red carnation in his buttonhole and a bald patch on his head. The organ joined in "God Save the King" and the Academic Overture was played.

And then Yehudi Menuhin and terrific applause. Very small and slim he shook hands with Sir Henry and stood on his right his fair shining hair making him look very young.

The first movements were Brahms violin concerto in D – Menuhin first began to sway a little with the others then he lifted his violin to his chin raised his hand and played.

He was marvellous.
After the applause subsided I went out and round the back.
I was down near the stage entrance and the corridor filled
with people in the two guinea seats. Despite the door
marked 'Private' I went in and down a slope and on the
right stood Yehudi Menuhin in the middle of a very small
room – very pale and fair. Several very smartly dressed
women in evening dress accompanied by various officers
were approaching him one by one. I pushed myself
forward and asked him if he would sign my programme.
He hesitated as though there might be a crowd of others to
follow and he said 'Well...' but I pushed my pen in his
hand and he smiled and signed. I flew out beaming.
'I left by the light of the moon found an Underground then
walked from Mark Lane to Fenchurch Street where I had
half an hour to wait for a train so I phone'd Mummy and
shrieked: "I've got his autograph!"'

It's 04.45 I can't sleep. Have made tea for us both. Out in
the river it is dark but there is moonlight and I can see
Kent clearly. And the winking buoys; three flashes of
green every 10 seconds over Canvey Island, the Chapman
Light; two flashes of red every 10 seconds further down
the river – not sure - and a continuous green flash further
down still; the West Leigh Middle. All doing their
inanimate duty to a river empty of traffic.
The silent foxes were out again last night. Up from the
cliffs and onto the rubbish sack. The Coochi Coo bag was
left uninspected and dumped on the driveway, a teabag
also and some damp tissues. Then I spotted it: a licked out
steak and kidney pie tin in the shrubs. A pink tongue
gingerly licking round the serrations for carbonised pie-

crust as my Mother dozed alone and potentially vulnerable just above. Reynard was at his work unseen as I stared at the blinking river lights. The dawn sky, coloured a vivid blue ink, is a good sign.

17th March

'I just want to be warm and go to sleep forever,' Ma announced at 04.50 this morning. It is a lot milder than of late but she felt cold after peeing on the commode.
'Well at least in the guest house it will be warm 'cos they leave the heating on all night.'
'Oh, do they? Thank God for that. I hope they like me, I don't suppose they will.'
'They'll be nicer than I am.'
'The thing is, they are all intelligent and I'm not.'
'No, you got on well with Stephanie, she liked you 'cos you've got a sense of humour and you liked her 'cos she's not soppy,' you said.
'Well I'm not going to be too clever, I'm not going to be funny.'
'Just don't be rude.'
'I hope they'll let me in to the Girl Guides.'

18th March

Took a call at work yesterday from Charlotte, one of the NHS Mental Health Care team to say that she found Ma on her back having fallen. She'd called the ambulancemen who gave Ma the all clear although they found her blood pressure a little low.
Woken at 5.00am by the 'alarmed bed' duty person, calling: 'Nancy, Nancy are you OK?' and found Ma sitting

in her chair. As the weather gets milder, she is like some creature coming out of hibernation, venturing forth from her bed more often than not only to complain of the cold. Today is the day she moves into Westcliff Lodge.

Ma, looking out over a warm, sunny estuary, said: 'Look at that sea, all glittering isn't it nice?'

Probably the final words about her 'morgue' as we hoicked her along the creaking landing to the lavatory then the stair lift and … away.

Westcliff Lodge is a double-fronted red brick pile managed by Stephanie Mirams, an attractive, flinty-eyed woman. The staff are a mix of races. The room smelled of fresh paint. The alarmed floor pad at the entry to Ma's room is not working because the carpet fitter cut through the wires. A new bed, lick of paint and new pile, all is now ready to greet the next person condemned to care.

Ma turned her bright blue eyes to me and asked: 'Where's your room?'

'I don't live here, Ma. I'll be going back to my own home.' When the penny dropped, her eyes locked mine not with condemnation or even resignation but something much worse … momentary enlightenment.

My eyes filled with tears. So did Cathy's. We both fought hard not to let the tears spill. Surface tension kept them from brimming over but blurred my vision as I tried to suppress emotion and continue in a positive patter.

We walked to the door, and looked back into the room. Ma lay on top of her bed, fully clothed, and turned to the wall; a foetus against oblivion.

Back downstairs we learned that the entry door is kept locked at all times as two residents recently tried to leave of their own accord.

'They formed the escape committee?' I said lamely, Stephanie laughed as though she'd not heard that old conker before.

I read through the contract while still fighting back my emotions. 'I feel such a heel. I cannot help but feel I'm dumping my mother,' I said to Stephanie.

'Everyone feels like this at the start. But I can tell you, knowing your Mother, she'll be as right as rain here within a fortnight.'

We, having relaxed, suddenly remembered we'd forgotten the pressure pad alarm system under Ma's bed at her own home. No-one had called Occupational Therapy to report its redundancy. Now it was too late. If we didn't do something the 'monitor' would be on the phone, shouting into an empty house to report Ma's vacancy of her bed. So round we went and lifted Clifford's Parker Knoll adjustable chair, which we'd stuffed into Ma's bedroom as a 'day chair' and which she had anointed regularly with faeces, and dumped it onto the bed to depress the alarmed pad and keep the bed in 'occupied' mode. So far we have had no calls.

19th March

She is warm, comfortable and seems happy. Moaning about the food and talking about being with 'white-haired old ladies.'

'How old do you think you are Nancy?' asked Cathy.

'I don't know dear I'm not very good at maths,' she said coyly.

'Well, you'll be 87 on your birthday.'

'Watch it!'

Clearing the house Cathy discovered a reporter's note book with the lines dated and ticks or crosses made against each date in Clifford's handwriting. An example: 'Sun 21st multiple bowel action – not diarrhoea'. He had at one time told me 'We should be prepared for the worst'.
'Oh really?' I'd enquired.
'I think Nancy may have bowel cancer.'

20th March

Spent the weekend gutting mother's house in preparation for a new kitchen/bathroom in order to receive the best rent to help pay for her care home. Down came the plywood partition Pa put up in 1983; I knew the date because fillets of folded newspaper were used as caulking between the top and the ceiling. Now the kitchen is a kitchen-diner full of light. Out went a very well constructed chipboard cupboard from the middle downstairs room, used by Chibby Thorpe, an undertaker, and the occupier before my parents, to store films. He would sit in this tiny box room watching films on a projector while his fearsome wife was fearful in another part of the bungalow-house. 84 Leigh Hill is like a dolls house for humans, with everything on a small scale, and rooms made in obvious functional shapes with no lines drawn or wasted on architectural flair. Cleaning Ma's bedroom I found a symbolic single crust of toast under her bed. We prised up the vinyl we'd screwed down under her commode rolled up the dusty and stained carpet and opened the windows.
Meanwhile, she had spent the first Sunday in her bedroom, rather than in the common lounge, which disappointed me. She had been settling in quite well even having a

'conversation' with a younger woman with one leg. However another resident who is in a more advanced stage of dementia and who wanders round asking people where her husband is, is someone Ma seems to have taken exception to.

So Ma had been confined to her room and was watching Noel Edmunds on the TV with her emergency red pull cord secured around the handles of her aluminium, walking frame, which was next to her chair. Untouched sandwiches were beside her.

She doesn't like the food, she doesn't like the bed.

'I want a space in the end of your room,' she said to Cathy and I. Our carefully expressed reassurance, mindful not to over-egg it, for fear of inviting more negativity, she responded to with a touch of resignation. Maybe she'd seen the alarm on our faces, and to be fair, when the chips are down she can be stoic, complaining only about the peripherals.

She can never come home.

The only mail received at 84 Leigh Hill now are the ceaseless cellophane brochures from the mail order factories. They will chase their quarry to the grave with 'affordable fashion on your doorstep'. The latest is from a company called Carr and Westley which uses a model of a comfortable age: neck just starting to go, bingo wings just held in check, hands coarse but still shapely. Beautifully coiffured, of course and with the wedding ring in constant view. Plenty of rouge and lip-sticked lips smiling wholesomely with no hint of coquettishness. She models hideous footwear for broadening feet with peep-toe design to accommodate talon-like nails, bras which look as though they'd hold together the staves of a broken barrel; nighties designed for the solo occupancy of a bed. The thickening model has one broad foot placed flat on the mushroom-coloured carpet pile, the other daintily lifted just ever so slightly to rest on the carefully painted toes: again just enough to show the pink, ankle-length nightie at its best, but not enough to suggest anything carnal. Copulation is just a memory for this woman, but there is no reason not to look 'nice'. It is the interregnum between sex and death.

23rd March

Cathy went with Richard to Westcliff Lodge yesterday. Ma was down in the lounge and the two women whose brains are still working, made a fuss of him. The woman with dementia asked him how old he was.
'Nearly 11.'
'Yes dear, well if you want to come with me you can come for a nice walk with me, and get away from these grey-haired old fuddy duddies.'
The woman, Cathy estimates, is in her 70s.
'No, leave him alone, he's quite happy where he is,' said Ma.
'I'm not talking to you.'
'Well I'm talking to you,'said Ma.
Meanwhile, the two with brains were winking in unison and saying 'We're old fuddy duddies,' and laughing.
Ma does not remember her home, even though she's been out of it just five days. Not the view of the weather, the room she called a morgue, the passing ships bringing in the mail order goods, nothing. It seems as though it matters not where she physically is anymore.

27th March

Ma has been at Westcliff Lodge just over a week. I have not seen her since last Sunday. Today is Saturday. Cathy hasn't been able to see her for the last three days either – she's been off sick and very busy. But the last time she was at Westcliff Lodge, Ma was performing on the Karaoke, so we take it as a sign she's 'settling in.' Stephanie has said she is complaining about her bed and we hope to take her own mattress down tomorrow. Also another consignment of nappies has been delivered to Ma's house. Two large cardboard boxes. We will take those to Westcliff Lodge and from now on it will be Stephanie's job to assess Ma's 'incontinence' and order accordingly. Meanwhile, a skip arrived at Ma's house. I've already dissembled much and torn up carpets. It will be filled in a jiffy. A local builder is to fit an Ikea kitchen, and a decorator starts today. I've taken a week's holiday to clear the house. All of this activity still cannot expunge the image I had of my mother on that first day we dropped her at Westcliff Lodge, a little old lady in her slippers, lying in the foetal position on a bed in the corner of a strange room. It was pitiful but actually I think she was simply tired.

The skip is now filled with her gutted home.

28th March

To visit. Ma in her new Velcro-strapped slippers sitting in an overheated conservatory with two other women. One is lying almost horizontal in an adjustable chair covered in a blanket and mouthing at the air. She is being fed a chocolate biscuit by an elderly man. The other woman to

my mother's left is muttering ceaselessly as she attempts to knit but can't find the end of the ball of imaginary wool.
'I can't wait to go home,' Ma says. She looks in very good shape. Dreary pop music is playing in the background, which fortunately, she seems not to be aware of.
Few agencies want to collect household goods anymore. I eventually found that Sue Ryder would: 'But we are fully booked for collections until April 6th' the woman who answered the phone told me, so I ran one bureau down there and was greeted by a peroxide blonde with mascara painted around her eyes like starbursts and heavily-ringed fingers. She asked me if I would like to 'Gift Aid' the goods.
I filled in my name and address on a form after confirming that I am a tax payer. 'It means that for every £1 we get selling the goods, we get an extra 25 pence, because we can reclaim the basic rate of tax,' she explained.
At another agency, this time for the homeless, they were less fussy. Another brassy woman also with heavily ringed fingers, impossibly French-polished nail extensions and dyed copper-coloured hair, filled in another form, this time promising me a van will turn up on Wednesday for beds, chests of drawers, old crockery.
Also, Southend Equipment Services, part of the council's arrangement with NHS, came to collect the machinery on loan to my mother to help with her disability.
A pleasant middle-aged man turned up in a small lorry with a tailgate, parked on double yellow lines and collected the bath lift with charger and handset, one of the wheeled zimmer frames, the other is still 'on loan' in the home, two commodes, one for upstairs, one for down and the bed occupancy sensor pad, which to fool it into thinking it was still supporting a human being, has been

pinned down continuously beneath Clifford's abandoned Parker Knoll chair.

As the house is cleared, even the last vestige of my mother is fading - her smell - which hangs in the air like a ghost.

1st April

Beggars can be choosers as I discovered when a one-eyed, cadaverous and unshaven removal man and his gimlet-eyed assistant dressed in a woolly hat, arrived to check out Ma's furniture.

'No, we won't take that, the arms are a bit worn,' said woolly hat about the divan, which converts into a double bed. I felt ashamed to have found the arms suitable for my own elbows. They took two beds and a mattress, three chests of drawers, but have still left me with a labour of demolishing old furniture and dump-visiting. Just before they disappeared, gimlet-eye spotted a small delicately made lamp table. 'We'll take that lamp stand.'

'No, that's not going,' I said.

Ma was watching a TV screen the size of a small bus. A children's cartoon of Dennis the Menace and his dog caused her to laugh.

When I was a child ours was the first house in the street to own a TV: a mean little wooden box with a tiny black and white screen, actually more a kind of mauve and white. On it my sister and I watched a newsflash one November evening as we sat round the 'Courtier' smokeless fire casement in the front room, toasting crumpets on a prong. President Kennedy had been shot. I went upstairs to find my parents to break the news. They were in bed, not in any attempt to produce further siblings for us, but to save on the heating.

Joyce, resident for seven years, laughed at me when I told Ma not to talk with her mouth full as she demolished a plate of sugared biscuits with her tea.

Bettine, is a tall wandering soul who drifts constantly through the rooms searching for her husband. Like the Flying Dutchman, she is doomed to search until her brain implodes further and releases her from her hopeless quest. She stands in front of the TV, unaware that Ma, Joyce and collapsed-mouth Joan are watching. Another old biddy, Connie, is dozing.

Ma tells me: 'I am never setting foot in here again, I can tell you that.' And gives me a look like thunder. Then she starts her descending whistle as a cartoon rocket on the TV, which has gone up is now coming down; no-one seems to mind.

'You see what I have to put up with,' she starts pointing at Bettine.

'Don't point Ma, it's rude.'

'Yes, that wallpaper, what colour is it?' she switches the conversation.

'Magnolia,' I say.

5th April

Easter Sunday. Took a neoprene Easter Bunny on a stand, made by Richard, and a box of Terry's Chocolates to Westcliff Lodge. Ma is in the 'living' room with Joyce, Connie, Joan as Bettine, doing her stand-up routine, is watched by two men and another woman with one leg. One man is smiling and mumbling incoherently, the other is patrician, sad-looking, and completely silent. Richard offers round the chocolates.

'I like a child with manners,' says Joyce, who also thinks Emily, 19, is my ' other half.' Ma is surrounded by small pieces of Easter Egg chocolate like sheep droppings on the carpet. She is eating bread and butter but not her chicken salad. She looks healthy, even tanned, but I'm not sure if it's the shade from a half-drawn curtain cutting out the bright sunlight so that Songs of Praise can be see on the giant TV. She seems weary, then complains about my breath; I've just had an boozy, indulgent two days with Cathy, she says she hates chocolates, boxes of that is. She likes chocolate but not the pre-arranged choice of manufacturers. She is happy to say goodbye to Richard and Emily, but horrified when I get up to say goodbye.

'Where are you going?'

'Home, but I'll be back on a warm day to take you out.'

'Oh, go away!'

The wind outside the overheated home is a bitter north-wester.

I came home for more Google diagnosis. According to one website, Ma is in stage six of dementia with stage seven, the final stage, still to come.

7th April

The house, my house, seems strangely peaceful now that the faint whizzing of the baby monitor is no longer with us. It worked even with the 'parent' part of it two doors from Ma's home. Over it we could hear her continued burst of pleading or cursing and the occasional cry for help. She was canny though, each time she started saying something which caught my ear as being interesting – throwing up some unknown fact or experience – I would call for silence and listen, but each time I did, so she, too, fell silent. Also in her house I would tip-toe up the stairs when the same thing happened, but again she would stop talking. Whether via technological device or human ear, she seemed to sense being eavesdropped.

Her smell has completely left her home and is now barely detectable on the skip filled with old carpets, bathroom tiles and chipboard partitions awaiting collection outside. This evening I visited her and she said, describing an African care worker: 'You know that black slave?'

'Er, yes.'

'He's gorgeous.'

I later discovered this was Daniel Adu-Agumang, from Ghana, who had hit it off with my mother as soon as they met. He made her laugh by being as facetious as she was trying to be and they've developed a rapport.

I suppose if food and drink is brought to your side, if you are assisted in and out of your chair, in and out of your bed, you could be forgiven for imagining that such attention is supplied by a bondsman.

15ᵗʰ April

Cathy visited yesterday and discovered Ma had been 'bowling' via a computer screen. During her visit Ma pointing, said of one resident: 'I think that woman has got one leg,' which was the case, then added: 'She's got two,' about Joyce, who indeed still has both.

When she started whistling she did so furtively, Cathy thinks she's been told to stop.

'I must see my mummy, she must be wondering where I am?'

22 September 1943

'Mummy is having her operation this morning – I have got a "compassionate night at home". At Sparrows End I found Rhoda cooking my supper. She was very worried and our phone rang and rang and rang every five minutes all enquiries about Mummy and each time it disturbed Francis and woke him up when we had just got him off with a sweetie.
At 11.30 we phoned the hospital again – Mummy was under morphia, Dr Lush had been to see her and pronounced her condition as "satisfactory".
Then the sirens went.
However we went to bed and slept.'

23 September 1943

'I was dying to see Mummy and cycled like mad to the Southend General, up the stairs, into the private wards. Poor mother was so weak she couldn't move and looked rather like a small boy, her hair is cut short and she wore a white operation jacket back to front. She was feeling ghastly but was pleased to see me...
Dr Lush was very nice and said she thought Mummy would be quite all right - a total hysterectomy was performed, a small amount of x-ray treatment later would quell all doubts.'

The last sentence was edited out with a cover of ink, but which I removed with a damp cloth. It's peculiar that illness, surgery and incapacitation are conditions to be ashamed of.

27 September 1943

The night sister is very noisy and kind – she gives Mummy an injection every night and calls her 'dearie.' The day sister is an old hag with baby curls and white bonnet. When Mother said: "I can't eat anything yet" this creature replied: "Can't is dead – can is alive." Quite, quite mad. Mummy nearly threw the flit at her but was too weak.'

18th April

Hot spring sunshine sparkled on the big spring tide. Cars glinted and shunted slowly along Southend Esplanade. Ma, out of the chill easterly wind to the west of Rossi's ice-cream parlour, lapped at one of their medium cones, closed her eyes, soaked up the sun and said 'Bliss.'
I had wheeled her there from Westcliff Lodge. Jackie, one of the carers, had got her ready, coat on and toileted, and in her chariot. She had started her tearless, sobbing when she saw me, perhaps because I haven't visited for a fortnight. But she was soon back on form 'I'm frozen' she said as I wheeled her round Westcliff. 'Look at that maniac, why's he going at that speed?'; 'Oh, stay in the sunshine it's freezing. This is Hamlet Court Road, at last there's some shops.'
In one key-cutting, shoe-soling bar, we bought her a new pair of slippers, exactly the same as the ones she's complaining about, but blue not pink.
She held the cone sideways as she tried to curl her meaty tongue round the sweet white ice.
'Watch out Ma, you'll drop it on your coat.'
'Doesn't matter.'

Her characteristic whistle was put to air, mimicking firstly a police car siren, then an ambulance. She had her soft toy dogs on her lap which intrigued children and caused sniggers from some young mums, a lifetime away from their own infirmities.

I wheeled her along the seafront. People walked dogs, skimmed stones across the water, the incoherent yells of distant children indulging in faux panic at the tide's advance; a timeless seaside soundtrack. A flying fish kite gave her momentary delight. The converted public convenience owned by a French restaurateur which is called Toulouse she didn't laugh at, but conceded it was funny.

On and on we went. It got hot, she liked the big houses at Chalkwell and recognised some. 'We used to roller-skate along here, it was marvellous!' 'For sale, hmm how much?' at an estate agent's sign.

Towards the end she started fretting about my doing all the pushing and wanted me to sit in the chair while she pushed. But I continued up Victory Path past the tennis courts.

'I KNOW! GOD I'm never coming out again if I thought this was going to happen, I'd never of brought you. We're going the wrong way!' Briefly she was a young mum again.

Back inside Westcliff Lodge, Jackie said: 'Hello Nancy, did the doggies enjoy the walk?'

'Oh yes, where have I seen you before?'

'In here Nancy. It's time for tea.'

I left.

1st May

I arrived mid-morning today, Saturday. Ma was in the back room where the more hopeless cases are normally placed. She had a 1000-yard stare, her dogs on her lap. With my face in front of her she took a while to re-focus then the faux sobbing: 'Don't leave me.'

'I'm going to take you out if you'd like that.'

'Yes, I'd like that.'

'I'll get your coat.'

Aggressively – 'I've GOT a coat.'

I went to her room and got her coat. Out in the street she complained of the cold, pulled the collar over her face and ears. Down Victory Path the girls were playing tennis.

'Damn children all over the place.'

And: 'These women have got such fat bottoms!'

Further along at Chalkwell Beach, she said: 'God I know this place so well I don't need to see it.' Another complaint about the weather. Then she noticed the do's and don't's signs erected by the council.

'No dogs. Quite right, damn dogs, it's not their fault they just shouldn't care.' I wheeled her back to the car and drove her up to Belfairs Woods. Here we had a carvery lunch.

Her downturned mouth chewing turkey in concentration.

'What's that?' as she held a chunk of Yorkshire pudding on her fork.

'Yorkshire Pudding.'

'What's that?' As she held up a straggling piece of partly severed turkey on her knife.

'Turkey.'

She chewed away, the guttering on her top lip running up to her small nose folding and unfolding. Not as deeply etched as on so many elderly orifices. The not smoking I suppose. The lower lip supporting the liverish blue spot.

And a wide mouth hungrily masticating the slabs of turkey.

Then came the dreaded need to use the loo. I had hoped she would hold out long enough until I got her home again. But, no, this couldn't wait. I assisted her with her walking frame into the ladies' lavatory, which we both entered. Here I helped her off with her pads. She sat and defecated. I then wiped her.

'That's better,' she said with gusto. Having readjusted her pads got her skirt up we re-emerged into the restaurant. Nobody took a blind bit of notice. Nobody wanted to know. Nobody notices the old. Nobody wants to know what's coming.

'Oh, it must be so difficult when it's your own mother,' people say.

But no, not really. I still have the same conversation with her and she with me. Some framework is missing, but that's not important as we know each other and when she says she hasn't got a son, she's right, she hasn't anymore. I'm nearly sixty and can argue with her as an adult, no more deference from me. To her, a son is an obedient child.

Around the giant rose bushes, the beds of almost dead daffodils, the popping green oaks, I wheeled her. She smelled, touched and loved it.

26 June 1978

'E.M. Forster writes that the England, which Stephen Wonham was destined to inherit, is done for: "the growth of the population and the application of science have destroyed her between them. There was a freshness and

*out-of-door wildness in those days which the present
generation cannot imagine.''*
*'Two years ago when we went with Francis and Anna to
Nanjizel Beach in Cornwall we drove slowly down a
narrow, bumpy track between threadbare hedges,
brambles and bracken and when finally David and
Michael, their children, got out of the car where they had
been cooped up they stepped onto a floor of dry heath
stretching as far as the horizon. There was nothing else
there apart from a few sea birds. The two boys had never
seen anything like it and impulsively they both started
running as hard as they could...and were gone.'*

The wheelchair tyres ran over crisp curved rose petals,
then a bench to the memory of.
'Oh, Stanley Smith.' She read the plaque, 'He's dead.'
Then a little later: 'I can't stand that place. Downstairs all
the men and women sit there like this.' She hangs her
mouth open staring.
That's the damnable thing, she may have dementia, but
she's not demented. I've put her in a home with people
who are because: 'I can't be here when you fall over, Ma.'
Seems horribly lame.
Back at Westcliff Lodge I ask the carer why she's now
consigned to the back room. I know what's coming.
'I'm sorry to say this, but she keeps screaming.'
'And swearing?'
'Yes' she laughs, 'But Nancy is a very nice woman when
she's very nice! We've had complaints from some
residents. But it's her right to go in the front lounge if she
wants to.'
'No, she's OK in the conservatory,' I say.
'Don't worry, we understand Nancy,' she says.

I didn't tell her that when Ma asked where we were going once we'd got back in the car after lunch, I said 'Back to dribble palace.'
'Oh don't,' she'd said.
Once ensconced with her dogs again, I told her to look after them before leaving. 'Oh go and drop dead,' she said.

11th May

Mother in the middle room. Took a minute or two to recognise me, then the faux crying. 'Sound of Music' on the TV, Ma whistling to the songs. Cheese on toast supper arrives. She goes through the ritual of trying to get me to eat it. Calls me a 'brute' when I refuse. Likes the carpet 'It's marvellous.' Orders coffee. Doesn't drink it. 'I wanted tea!' I suggest she gives her Welsh Rarebit to Joan, who she says she's 'starving!'
Joan gratefully accepts. Carer sees Ma's plate is empty and gives her another helping. Ma then passes it to Joan who doesn't want anymore. So Ma, with a piece of Welsh Rarebit, in each hand starts 'conducting' the 'The Hills are Alive' waving her crusty batons. Old Cockney man eats a bowl of baked beans to my right, then with a hacking cough, returns them to the bowl. An old woman opposite sits staring at me silently. Her friendly son, Stanley from Eastwood, tells me she's been there 'two years this June,' in a depressing voice.
Ma is the fittest in the room. She could be there many years. It's depressing the thought of her going on and on. But, at least I'm not living with her anymore. She points to a man who has slumped down in his armchair and appears to have died. 'He's all right, but he needs lifting

up again. Come on.' She encourages and starts to rise from her chair to help.

'No, best let the professionals do it, the authorities do it,' says Joan.

The old man is eventually raised back up into the sitting position, bibbed and fed soup through a teaspoon.

'Stop pointing, Ma,' I say.

So she exaggerates her pointed arm and finger.

'She's so fat.' She says of a large Filipino carer, 'But you should see her brother, he's unspeakable!' She takes one mouthful of pudding, gives an approving groan.

'Is it nice?' I say.

'You have it.'

Fatal mistake, she will contradict all positives, next time I'll reserve commentary.

16ᵗʰ May

Ma in the 'lounge.' This is the large front room with the enormous TV against the chimney-breast wall. Joyce in her usual seat in the window, her inflated and oozing legs stretched out on a stool. Connie next to her as usual, un-smiling, but all seeing. Then, Bettine, who for once is not prowling but sitting. One unidentifiable man semi-comatose, and next to Ma, then Joan, who doesn't look as hungry as last time.

In the car and away to the trees and yellow rapeseed fields of Paglesham, where earlier in the day the cuckoos fluted. I had been anti-fouling my boat. Significantly when I said to Ma later 'I've been painting the boat you'll be delighted to hear.' She said 'Oh, I am dear'. For once even a subject which bores her to death, was comforting: something from that alien place, the past.

24 July 1984

'Stanley especially likes to see Dick as he is able to talk to him about his sailing days in the past for hours on end. Dick makes a very good listener and any other subject Stanley brings up he is immediately interrupted by his wife Joan who always apologises first then tells the story herself at great speed.
Stanley was still trying to tell Dick one of his sailing anecdotes and at last got his chance: "We were off the coast of Belgium and it was blowing half a gale and getting worse each minute and I said to old Fred, you know old Fred, don't you Dick? Lived in Westcliff all his life? His father had that little engineering business down the bottom of – oh, I can't think of the road now – somewhere near Southchurch Avenue – anyway I said to old Fred I think we ought to take in a couple of reefs and the next thing I knew he was down in the cabin flat on the bunk and that's the last I saw of him for the rest of the voyage. I just had to cope on my own, I was frozen and half-starved and I thought well this is all right. What a trip that was, I've never forgotten it after all the whole point of taking old Fred with me was so's he could crew for me some hopes of that I can tell you" (etc etc etc)'

'I'll never, ever, EVER be stepping foot in that DUMP again,' she says, as we look across towards the sea wall where cowslips are waving in the breeze.
'Oh don't bring me out here, we've been here before haven't we?'
'Yes.'

'Oh don't bring me out here again. It's beautiful. Do you know that bitch-faced cow grabbed me because I said something she didn't like. She twisted my arm, the brute.'

'What, one of the guests?'

'No, a girl like me.'

Yes, one of the guests, that was a relief. Ma showed me her blue-patched skin on her left arm. But it is the condition she has suffered from for a while. But then further up her arm two scabs as though the skin has been broken. I ran her back to my house. Cathy had a look and she thinks it's where she's scratched herself.

Ma lays back in one of her leather armchairs, which I now have and which she did not recognise and said: 'I wish I was dead.'

'Oh don't say that Nancy,' said Cathy.

'No I do, I'm so bored. And so damned depressed!'

We tried to cheer her and it worked. Cathy appeared with two of her Rupert books. The others have been 'stolen'.

Driving, while I tried to investigate the arm-twisting, she said to me, after I told her she must try and get on with people: 'Dicky, look, I know you. I know you like lots of people, and you want them to like you.'

She didn't add more, but she was accurate, at least that's how I was once. Once when she would have known me. She remembered that all right, how I once was.

In the rain I drove her back to Westcliff Lodge. She received a hail and a greeting from Katherine and Jackie, two of the carers, and was clearly pleased to see them, which was a relief.

I mentioned the fracas to them, and they told me that Ma had reported it that morning. They had called the senior carer who had confirmed the 'bruise' as Ma's condition, but conceded that Ma may well have been tussled by an 'inmate' and then suggested the condition was the result. I left as a strong smell of faeces wafted down the corridor.

28th May

Cathy visited Ma on Monday night. I was away on a job. Her visit was prompted by a call from the care home the day before – Sunday when we were in Leicestershire. This was a first. The home has not called us before, although I had fully expected it. Having spent the last year and more trying to curtail Ma's enthusiasm for what her late husband called 'bolshiness,' I dreaded her inability to recognise her own obnoxiousness when it mattered most i.e. when family, who are supposed to smooth over the bumps in the lino, were replaced by carers. Would the bumps come up somewhere else? But time is money and the home's investment in Ma is about caring for her well-being and therefore her longevity. An unassailable morality. Faultless. It leaves the relatives like hyenas with nothing to laugh at; will there be any money left? Well, it's hers anyway, we must resist counting chickens. Anyway, they called. Ma wanted to get the bus home and had no money. I expected she must have demanded she be put in touch with her mother or us, which means Cathy, the only mobile phone holder.

Ma was holding court in her own mind. In the middle room again and 'Oi, you' to the attractive and savvy manageress. Cathy's take on this is that Ma wants to be associated with beauty and brains – probably a sane enough choice but one she cannot match anymore. A 'deep seated jealousy,' which Cathy believes she holds, is welling up to the surface now that not even inhibitions, which she mostly ignored anyway, have almost completely faded.

After having pointed the superior finger and put them all down, she shouted: 'Because I'm a Best and we don't put up with that.'

Ma's latest credit card from the Halifax, which has my name on, and which means I can relieve her of 87 year's worth of savings, is marked thus:

Mr. R. B. Durham, POA for 11130 0022.

Ma's identity has been reduced to a sort code and an account number in someone else's name.

31st May

Mother screamed 'Dicky!' as soon as she saw me, the false sobbing followed by a hug and a rub and we settled down in front of Krypto The Superdog. Two men appear to be watching it, one woman is asleep. Another man appears dead. The film reminds Ma of Rosie her Beagle pet which was the family dog in the 1960s. She told me how she came home one day to find Rosie wearing a rictus snarl, which Ma mimicked. Ma knew something was wrong and she talked to the hound and stroked her and put her hand in the dog's mouth and pulled out a large bone, which had been stuck in her throat. 'There was nothing left on it,' she said.

I'd taken her some cuttings from the Banksia Rose, which Ma had proudly grown from a cutting in her garden.

7 May 1989

'We walked down to Blockley and outside Ye Olde Oak was a lovely bush covered in yellow foliage like buttercups

(last year I snipped a bit off it passing by, wrapped it I soaking newspaper and got it to strike. No-one knew its name.)

An elderly gentleman in overalls came round the front carrying a ladder, thought he might be a window cleaner, Clifford said no it's Sunday. He stopped and admired the bush and I asked him what it was. It was a Banksia Rose he said in pure Indian Army voice.

' "Sir Joseph Banks?" asked Clifford. "Indeed it was," replied the old gentleman, "He was responsible for bringing back many plants from all over the world." He added that his daughter had brought back two of these bushes from China but one was pinched overnight which made Clifford gasp over his choc-ice (I only pinched a tiny sprig)'

Later she called one of the carers 'Oi.' They took it in good humour and another replied 'She's not a boy.'

I said 'No, she said Oi.'

'I know,' smiled Daniel, the big African 'slave'. They certainly know how to handle Ma, but more importantly they know her demands are often just banter.

Later, as tea arrived and was delivered, to the other side of the room Ma said 'We're over here by the way.' Daniel laughed. This is classic Ma and I hope she can remain this way, inoffensive and good humoured. The room was overheated and I felt drowsy, and told Ma I was going to go home to sleep. She was fine about it and gave a much-dramatised kiss on the cheek, again the Ma of old.

13th June

Ma is sitting in an armchair head to one side, apparently dozing, with a large pink teddy bear on her lap. She's in the middle lounge with just the men again. Peter, a giant faced man 'staring into space' as Ma put it, with his mouth hanging open and full catheter bag sagging below his left trouser leg.

'He's not stupid, you know,' confided Ma, 'stop making that awful face,' she yells across the room. The room is covered by a dark green carpet scalloped with leaves and sober-shaped patterns which look like Fleur-de-Lys but which aren't. It's out-of-date and Ma loves it. 'Isn't this carpet gorgeous? I'd love to have it.'

Next to her sits a man, who, from his eyes, one can tell comprehends but who sadly can't be comprehended, he speaks in garbled sounds like a seal. Ted, who can communicate but can't talk and Ma who can talk but cannot communicate. Then there's Charles who appears semi-conscious with horribly blistered and mottled ankles poking out from food-encrusted trousers. He yells like mad when two carers lift him back into a sitting position so that the food they are feeding him will stay in.

The World Cup is on and it's Ghana versus Serbia. Big Daniel is agog. About 15 minutes before the end of the match, Ma wants to go to the loo. 'I'll take her Daniel, you watch the game,' I say, but Daniel insists on helping her in her walking frame round to the loo.

'It's a penalty shoot-out.' I say to Daniel, 'You go back I'll see to Ma.'

He does and I help her to the water closet which is seated on a raised platform, a throne of successful arrival. I notice someone has thrown a half-eaten banana down the pan. Ma fishes it out and I drop it in a large rubbish bin as Daniel returns 'We've scored,' and takes over.

'What a dreadful row,' Ma says upon her return commenting on the bedlam of supporters' horns roaring from the South African stadium.

'It's thousands of spectators blowing horns,' I say and Ma is bewitched.

'Really?' she says as she starts one of her long, high-pitched, declining whistles to join in.

'Thank you, Ma.' I say.

'Am I hideous?' she suddenly asks Peter, 'Am I hideous? Yes or no?'

Then she gives the man who understands but can't communicate, her sandwiches. Ted willingly receives them, he's already taken the biscuits which were delivered to Ma earlier. I offered him one and he took the whole plate.

Ma does talk to him but he garbles back. 'Oh, I'm not going to talk to you, I never understand what you're saying,' she says.

27th June

Ted is rubbing Ma's left cheek as I arrive. They are sitting in separate armchairs next to one another. The woman obsessed with knitting is winding wool into balls and placing them on her table. Bettine, the prowler, wanders in. Stands at the open door, it's 30c, and then sits down opposite Ma, her enemy, and tries to catch my eye. In order to see the TV, England have just lost 4-1 to Germany in the World Cup, I have to turn round and angle my head. Bettine angles *her* head to try and catch my eye. I ignore her. Confused though she is, there's enough residual Bettine for me to know she's a potential handful. Ted responds to his name and can now string a word or two

together. On the way out, I speak to two carers. 'Is my mother giving you any trouble?'
'No,' they reassure me, they said they were obliged to put Ma in with the men, which she prefers, and opposite Ted, but she wanted to be moved *next* to Ted.
'Ted knows Nancy fancies him and he's OK with that! When he's tired she feeds him.' I should hope he is OK with that, he's bald with broken shards of teeth and the garblings of a seal!
'No, we understand Nancy.'
'I mean she can be rude, or seem rude, but she's just being ironic,' I say.
'No, she's no problem.'
A new carer, tall dark-haired, from Moscow, speaks good English and found it amusing. I was kneeling down to talk to Ma, there was no chair, as though Ma is regal enough for this to be appropriate.
'Are you Dicky?' she asks.
'Yes.'
'Yes, your mother used to mention your name.'
Francis Smith, Ma's nephew and his partner Lynne, visited. Ma talked about his mother, Rhoda, her sister, and unusually acknowledged she was dead adding: 'Her sister's dying too.'

16 February 1943

'I took Francis upstairs and bathed him – he yelled when his face was done but soon cheered up when I soaped his head and the rest of him on my lap and plonked him in the bath. Such a soft, fat, wet slippery thing I've never held. Rhoda took photos of him with Frank's camera one looking at the rubber duck – he loves this – he is beautiful.

He is much more like Frank now bless his heart and his hair grows straight down in golden streaks above his ears not much on top.'

4th July

I wheeled her along Victory Path. She asked to stop to smell the wild roses. At Chalkwell Beach café, she engaged loudly with semi-naked children coming up from the beach for ice-cream. Revelling in their youth and chaos.
'I used to look like that,' she pointed to a young woman tanned and bracelet clad. The ankle straps a la Roman around another tanned girl's ankles snaking up from her sandals she commented on covetously.
Then a fat woman in a wheelchair caused her to worry about the carriage's payload.
'Betty died today.'
'Oh, how did you get the news?'
She started to say she'd read it somewhere before a brat demanding an ice-cream got her attention again.
'Betty had a dreadful life.'
'Why?'
'Because she married that man.'
Betty, was a cousin from Hampshire who died years ago.
'I love you,' she said holding my hand as she ate her cornet. 'I'd like to go on a cruise with you because everyone thinks you're so wonderful and would want to marry you, and I'd be able to tell them they couldn't.'
We had been on a 'sea cruise' together, back in 1952. Ma had taken me as a one-year-old baby to New Zealand to visit her retired parents-in-law. We returned on the frozen-lamb carrying freighter, Port Chalmers, by chance, once

the command of Ma's father-in-law, Captain Richard Durham.
My Mother had recalled this far off sea voyage while on a motoring holiday with Clifford after the ferry from Wales to Ireland had been delayed.

12 June 1990

It would surprise me if any ship ever sailed on time. I shall never forget waiting for the Port Chalmers to leave from Lyttleton. The ships's agent had booked me and little Dicky (aged 1) in an hotel but it was very scruffy and dirty so to his surprise I simply moved out and found another one more civilised and at least clean and there we stayed for over a week hoping each day to get a summons to go until I began to think I would never get home.
The hotel waitress was very surprised that Dicky ate meat! All New Zealand babies had vegetables only until they were five years (another of their crack-brained ideas as Dick's father used to say).
We sometimes took the bus to Christchurch, a much nicer place with green lawns and a river.
At last the long awaited message arrived to join the ship. We had a lovely cabin on the level of the deck. Dicky had his reins on all day and night. I used to tie him to the little shelf along the bunk with netting so he didn't fall out. Also sent for the electrician and asked him to disconnect the bell as Dicky would have a lovely time pressing this in and out.
There was no bar on the ship – we bought drinks from the purser and imbibed them in our cabins; he seemed to be inebriated most of the day, a sandy-haired man with

shaking hands who sometimes came out blinking into the sunshine.

Dicky soon had a swing fixed up for him and a playpen as well; one of the crew made him a porter's truck but it got thrown overboard in rough weather later on.

The passengers looked grey and old except for Audrey and Dorothy who persuaded me to go and ask the Captain if we might hold a dance, which was a huge success.

Dorothy had the disadvantage of travelling with her aunt who rather fussed over her but Audrey was making a first visit to England to teach. I used to take her and Dorothy down to Peter Thomas' cabin with a bottle of gin, the doctor came as well and whichever young officer was off watch.

The ship took only 11 passengers and one of the cabins was empty and used by the girls to iron all the officers' "whites".

Peter Thomas loathed the captain, they didn't get on at all well.

Captain Kidwell was a thick set man with glasses and was given to suddenly rising up from the table at mealtime and dashing upstairs on deck as though there was an emergency. He wanted to know everything.
 that was going on – about us, not the ship.

A large container made of planks and filled with seawater made a really heavenly swimming pool.

'Each day Dicky and I followed the "thermometer man", Dicky splashing in the scuppers at each little brass lid as he stopped and lifted out the tube to take the reading then off to the next one.'

I have a two-inch long, scar on the forefinger of my right hand which is shaped like a flap. Most of us remember how we attain scars but this one was a mystery until one day Ma told me I'd sustained it breaking a beer bottle which I had been rolling in the scuppers of the Port Chalmers. Years later when I asked her about it again she denied it!

When Ma's father-in-law, Richard Stephens Durham, retired, the Port Line, for whom he had worked as master and for whom, in a reserved occupation, he had carried frozen lamb during World War II from New Zealand to London, running the gauntlet of U-Boats and being decorated with an OBE, threw a celebratory dinner. It was held aboard the Port Nicholson in London's Royal Docks and was attended by my parents, myself, and my sister, Diana. Grandpa was not there so it was a bit odd, but back then, in the mid-1960s, I was more concerned with having long hair and wearing Chelsea boots, neither of which my father permitted me to do. Desperate to kick off the boring, lace-up school shoes I was obliged to wear, my hopes were raised when I noticed one of the men serving the food on the ship was wearing chisel-toed shoes, not as good as Chelsea Boots, but better than my toe-caps.

I pointed them out to Pa, thinking that because a crewman on a ship from Grandpa's old company was wearing them they'd meet with his approval: 'Typical of you to want to wear what a steward's wearing,' he said in disgust, crushing my hopes of sexual liaison once more.

Ma next told me of a woman at the home, who sits with her mouth wide open. 'I've got to look after her,' she said. I wonder if this is a deep-rooted sense of duty from her nursing days because Shenley Hospital, as well as treating 3,000 wounded servicemen also operated as a psychiatric institute. Ward 15 was dedicated to 'neurotic and mental officers.'

16 August 1943

'I had to accompany two neurotics to Ward 7 to see Major
Buckley, the neurologist. Pte Walters clutched my arm and
said: "Oh! I don't want to go in," and then begged me not
to leave. She is a typical neurotic, listless, sad empty face,
greasy lank hair, drooping shoulders and walks
awkwardly.
Major Buckley saw Pte Walters first. He is a tall, plain
man with glasses and a kind manner. Walters had to strip
into brassiere and pants which she wore almost ankle
length and he pummelled and pushed her, twisted her head
and neck and made her bend down and touch her toes. He
even had me out to twist my head over my shoulder as far
as it could go. He sat and wrote for ages and then had the
other one in. Pte Cousins; she was much younger and he
must have known she had on a pair of violet green satin
cami-knickers which she'd made herself for he only asked
her to take off her shoes and stockings. She was much
more graceful and did exactly as she was told. At the end
he questioned her on her health and she earnestly asked
him would she have to go back into the kitchen for it was
the heat and the damp that upset her, she was sure of that.
He looked up at me and I was smiling as it was pretty
obvious that the last thing she wanted to do was go back
into the kitchen. He assured her that heat and damp had
nothing to do with it. Returned to the ward and applied a
kaolin poultice, which I'd started to make hours ago.
The girl with fits was very carefully lifted into the
ambulance and taken to Chase Farm to have an operation
on her brain. Major Wynter accompanied her. The saline
drip went hanging from the roof.

Later civilian rations were discussed. We objected to having inedible bullet peas and that if we could only have some more sugar, things wouldn't quite so bad.'

1 September 1943

'This morning Richmond and I had to take charge of two ATS (Auxiliary Territorial Service) girls till they departed to Northampton Asylum. One of them, Mantle, was definitely neurotic and screamed blue murder when admitted last night. However she would at least swallow the dope given to make her sleep in the ambulance. PTE Warren, the other, was definitely not all there and would not touch the medicine glass saying: "No, I won't take it. It will make me sleep." Slowly but surely – Whitehill happened to be in the ward at the same time – and she spent at least half an hour, coaxing, wheedling, bullying and begging Warren to swallow this draught. She even had me interested enough to swear to Warren that it would not make her sleep and it would not make her sick, cross my heart. And I was thrilled when, still talking in her soft Manchester voice, Whitehill lifted the glass to Warren's lips and she drank it! The funny part was as Mantle flopped out as a result of this drug in a split second I had the screens round her bed so Warren shouldn't see. Fortunately Warren was in tears in Whitehill's arms, so I left them to it and returned to Mantle who was round by this time. She was an Irish girl with brilliant green eyes and heavy lashes, by no means unattractive, although she had ruined her hair with peroxide. How we got them into the ambulance I do not know and I wouldn't have been in S Boulton's place for the world! She had to go with them.'

Went to "Stars in Battledress". It was a very good concert.'

Back along Victory Path she reads a sign in the tennis courts where poor play is taking place between families and the pat, pat of balls underlines the heaving, hot summer weather: 'Trespassers will be prosecuted.'
Then at the home, a brief period of horror when I tell her I'm leaving, but this is soon over when Charles – his mouth orange from tomato soup and dew drops dangling from his nose, smiles and says Hello.
On reflection, it would seem her eagerness to talk and engage with children is because she's surrounded by folks who can't talk.
Like the solo sailor coming ashore after a long period at sea, she wants some social interaction. Why children? Because the adults around her are either hectoring, 'Come on Nancy eat your greens' or are no longer able to make sense. The real reason is that she still acts like a child, of the first juvenile term, and always has done. All her years of not wishing to understand finance, technology. All her instructions not to talk about war or violence, her ability to keep secrets, which is what her character of not being a gossip is really all about. Children like and make secrets, an aspect of keeping grown-ups at bay. Like Peter Pan, Ma genuinely empathizes with small children. Sadly, when they look at her they don't see a playmate. Yet, this too, she understands, as she knows the child only sees an enemy of their being…an adult.

11th July

With Richard we wheeled Ma back to the ice-cream parlour at Chalkwell Beach. She sat in the 28c heat, sun on her face watching a sparkling tide slowly ebbing. 'Just to see it is marvellous. There's no one swimming. Ah, yes it's going out, what a shame!' She had remembered last week's ice-cream, if slowly, although she is remembering less. Cathy went to visit for the first time in three weeks and she believes Ma sees her as an old school friend, because she starts getting bitchy about the other women: both 'inmates' and carers. It occurs to me that perhaps forgetting your life helps you leave it. There was a time some months back now, while still living under her roof, when Ma challenged my abrupt behaviour in dealing with her. The resentment of being saddled with her care, I was not handling in a particularly compassionate way and I did wish she would die. But it was because I found the confrontation of a decaying human being ugly; the corruption an inevitability I sought distraction from, the way of all flesh; a direction I wished to delay. But she thought it was about the money. Her estate and she, of course, was partly right. It was galling to think that her savings would drain away in care to sustain a wreck. Maybe I did not wish to hide my predatory thoughts. Maybe I felt that being 'nice' was too hypocritical. I denied it of course and as I think about it now, it seems to me that she still has or had, the ability to analyse and confront people with facts, yet while she is not scared of facing the truth, she goes into denial over reality.

1st August

Ma recognised me when I removed my sun hat.
'Dicky?'

'Yes.'

'Oh come here, I love you.'

Hugs and momentarily release of her pirated pink teddy bear. Then attention from Tim, one of the carers. Would I like a cup of tea? No, thanks then, again, from Thoma, oh well rude not to. Waitress service. Thoma was wearing blue, plastic gloves as she placed the tea on Ma's wheeled table. I gave Ma my biscuits.

'Don't leave your hat on the floor,' said Thoma, noting my casual use of its space. She did not add 'because you don't know what's been there, I do.' But she did not have to. Only toothless Joan is in the room semi-dozing. Later we were joined by staring Bettine and her tough-looking son who was holding a leaping spaniel on a chair which ate some of Joan's proffered biscuits. 'Not too many he's getting a gut,' said the son, who was wearing shorts showing off heavily tattooed legs. Well-built and friendly in an intense sort of 'get me-out-of -here' way. Then in came Lucy, the mutterer of endless prosaic domestic concerns.

Ma said 'See her,' pointing at Lucy, 'I wish she would drop dead.'

'Why would you want her to drop dead?'

'Because she's so stu u u pid. "Oh, it wasn't me. Oh, it's not my fault," she goes on and on.'

Next victim was Joan. Pointing again: 'You see that boy?'

'That's a girl.'

'Well done.' Ma rubbed my arm. Joan has cropped hair. All the while Rowan Atkinson has been partly ignored on the giant TV screen.

'There's one cow here I hate. She's a bitch.'

'Why?'

'Because she hits people, she grabs them by the hair.' Ma is not given to flights of fancy or lying, so this is worrying. But then as she aggressively asks for the windows first of all to be covered completely by curtains to keep the 'damn light out' and then smashed, I note just how vehement she can be with her commands and wonder about the claims. Looking at the dregs of her tea, she tips it out on the carpeted floor.

'Don't do that, Ma.'

'Oh, dry up.'

'No, that's not nice doing that.'

'Doing what?'

'Chucking your tea on the floor.'

'Where?' she yelled.

Of course the stain is completely invisible on the dark-patterned carpet.

'No, you shouldn't do that Ma. That's a carpet.'

'Same to you with knobs on.'

She pulled my hand to cover hers on the arm of her chair.

'Your hands are so lovely. Mine are horrible.' Hers are like speckled brown gloves on the end of her white arms in her sleeveless summer top.

I leave her saying I must go shopping for my dinner, which she is happy about. Shopping is the essential duty, the immovable given, the life force.

The postman delivers and Ma might have won £40,000. To find out, she needs to order an item guaranteeing her a free note-book with calculator which is worth £9.99. The other is a mail order book for 'wide fitting' summer sandals, worn by models in their 20s who would not be seen dead in them through choice. This 'concept' footwear is in peep-toe style. You have to have the most beautiful feet to wear peep-toe shoes. Hammer toes should not peep.

7ᵗʰ August

Still we are clearing away stuff from Ma's home. The worst junk is borderline junk – you can't chuck it but you are lumbered with storing it in case it's worth something. Then there are bits and pieces, which represent Pa, that I cannot bring myself to bin. Many are old cigar tins which he painted over and used to keep drill bits, screws and model yacht fittings in. Others are old wooden boxes nailed together to form compartments and in which are stored nuts, bolts and other rusting ferrous metals. But it's not the objects themselves that invite indulgent sentimentality but the fact that Pa's writing – in pencil – has been marked on them, or scratched on in the paint declaring: 'paint brushes' 'nails,' 'small bolts'. For some reason I have always put off eradicating his legend: what is literally and figuratively his handwriting.
On one old chest I discovered a cardboard removal ticket stapled on the back. The brown paper had the red legend upon it 'Julien, Falmouth' This sent a shiver of excitement through me as I was propelled back to childhood and the thrill of moving to Cornwall, John Julien, was the name of the removal company. The name was synonymous with the exotic promise of wild beaches, rolling countryside, high cliffs and impenetrable woods. The reality was warm rain, a country lane which ran in rivulets of warm rain mixed with pig shit washed by warm rain from the farmhouse sty next door; of a cold stone C of E school, a crocodile of children at lunchtime walking to a school dinner annexe, several streets away and long, wide battens used as canes

on the uniformed buttocks of talkative boys. Me, in particular.

The river of mail still pours in. The latest shows a scrawny-necked, old woman with the obligatory 'nice' hair holding a fan of £50 notes in her liver-spotted but red finger-nailed hands. 'Stacks of cash to give away' and 'free for you an exquisite gift worth £9.99' Why is it always £9.99? This will be bestowed upon my mother as long as she places an order for 'Fun Fur Mules' in Burgundy, black or navy and displayed by a woman's disembodied, wide-angled foot, with the obligatory cherry-red toenails poking out.

9th August

Ma is dozing, head to one side in the middle lounge. The TV is on with the strangely stretched face of Anne Robinson presenting her 'Weakest Link' show. No-one is paying it any attention. An old biddy is mumbling to herself in the corner. I sit next to Ma. After a while she stirs.

'Who's that?'
'Who?'
'Is that you?'
'Who?'
'Oh shut up.'
'It's Dicky.'
'Dicky?'
'Yes.'
'Oh darling, let me hold your hand. Why didn't you say it was you? How did you get in? Come on, give me a hug, both arms.'

She has a concept of jail, but no concept that it was my prosecution which produced the sentence.

Later after a continual stream of disconnected and incomplete statements, some of them half-conceived from the distraction of the TV, Ma said: 'Poor Dick. Poor devil. I wish I hadn't been so awful to him, but I was. But I didn't like him, well I did like him. But, he was too much for me.'

Later she added: 'All the girls liked him, but none of them wanted him.'

I found this very interesting and tried questioning Ma as to who she was referring to. But I will never know. Asked a question she gets affronted and confused. She had been talking about the man with whom she swam out to the barge with, mentioned earlier, so whether it was he the girls 'liked but didn't want' or Pa I'm not sure.

She also said she had to try and remember to be nice to everyone: 'I don't want to be nasty.' She also said she hadn't got any friends.

She then said: 'I'd like to take Catherine and you.'

'Where?'

'To Aunty May and Aunty Lucy for a cup of tea, they won't mind. But they could be dead as far as I know.'

'They are dead, Ma.'

'But I don't want them to be dead. I don't want them not to be here. I love them.'

Diana had rung up from the USA but a carer told me: 'Nancy was not in a good mood. She shouted at me when I told her to talk up.'

Bettine came in. I have decided it's better to communicate with her and I did so. She was friendly: 'Where do I know you from?'

'I'm in here regularly. I'm Nancy's son.'

She won't remember but it's worth a go.
Ted's been in hospital, he's out now but restricted to his
bed. I'm not sure if this is a permanent arrangement.

22 August

Ma was happily eating steak and kidney pie until I
arrived.
'This is ghastly, I'm not eating it.'
A stainless steel dish of fresh fruit salad and cream is
presented next, which she eats without comment.
On the giant TV screen is a programme about a gangly
man and his pre-mature wife who want to swap their home
in Windsor for a new life in north Devon.
It so happens Cathy, my son Richard and I have just
returned from north Devon on a mission to re-boot Ma's
memory.
She often talked, before falling ill, of her wonderful
childhood holidays spent at Aunt Winifred's hotel, the
New Inn in Muddiford. And of bathing on nearby
Woolacombe Beach.
We took photographs of the hotel inside and out and of a
stream out back and a pleasant wooded hill running up
beside it. The new proprietor presented us with
photocopies of the lounge and bar in the 1930s when Ma
would have been there. I stuck them in an exercise book
with captions and as Ma read the label: 'Aunty Winifred's
hotel in North Devon' on the cover she started her tearless
sobbing.
I talked her through the photographs.
'We went down there,' I said, 'on holiday.'
'Did we?'
I told her it was now haunted which made her laugh.

'Do you remember a stream out the back?'
A long pause.
'Yes,' she said in hushed amazement.
'Well here it is,' I turned the page to reveal Cathy standing under some trees by the brook.
'How beautiful.'
I recalled Ma telling me once how she used to go swimming with an elderly resident of the hotel who buried her clothing under the sand to stop her togs blowing away. Then I showed her pictures of Richard, aged 11, on Woolacombe Beach, with his surf -board.
'Is that me?'
In another retrospective diary entry, Ma recalls, how she and Rhoda, as bereaved children, were 'organised' by their Aunts May and Winifred, the sisters of Herbert, their dead father. They felt obliged to step in with advice, sleep-overs and even holiday breaks to give the girls' mother, Ethel, a break. As children they were driven several times in Aunt Win's baby Austin from Westcliff-on-Sea to her hotel:

31 August 1978

'The smell of wood smoke, the sound of running water and the sight of banks of foxgloves will always be associated for me, with the New Inn Hotel, Muddiford. At the back of the building rose steep woods with streams and little waterfalls and wild flowers; climbing up to these woods the floor became springy and covered with dry twigs so satisfying to walk on. We gathered the dry branches and lots of pine cones that were scattered around and took them to an old, old lady called Mrs Gammon.

*The hotel boasted a small pub with a stone floor and a
lovely damp smell of beer and in the front entrance I think
there were two petrol pumps.*

*Staying there on my own once I went bathing with one of
the guests, a Lady Ashley, I thought her very eccentric,
there was a strong wind blowing and she suggested we
buried our clothes in the sand to prevent them blowing
away. Needless to say when we retrieved them they were
very damp.'*

By now the couple looking to buy a house on a 'budget' of
£1.2 million have been shown over a place near Barnstaple
by a black TV presenter.

'I hate wogs.'

'Why?'

'Because I do. Don't be nasty to me.'

I then broach the tricky subject of her early morning wash.
A carer had told me Ma has become aggressive, swearing
and lashing out when they try and bathe her. The other
residents thought she was being murdered.

'Ma, in the morning…'

'Yes?'

'When they try to wash you. You must let them.'

'But I don't want to be washed.'

She is holding my hand with her left hand, her thumb
rubbing the back of mine.

'But you need to let them wash you.'

'No I don't.'

'But everyone needs to have a wash,' I say gently.

'Don't be nasty to me. I really love you. I want you here. I
want you all the time. But don't be nasty.'

She tells me she's not very happy and tries to explain why.

Then: 'I'm not making any sense.'

'Don't worry.'

'He's been crying his eyes out so don't look at him.'

Old Charles of the mouth agape sits opposite.

I open Ma's Devon-made clotted cream toffees and she cheers up while sucking on one.

I give one to Joan. I offer one to Charles who smiles but can't talk and I'm not sure I should hand one over in case he chokes. I move on. I offer one to knitting woman and she spits. I take that as a No.

Ma covets the photo book and the toffees, when I offer to put them in her room she picks them up and puts them on her lap.

Her dogs are nowhere to be seen, nor the pink teddy bear she's held hostage for some weeks. Just the plastic basket 'kennel', empty except for a crumpled email from daughter Diana and a tacky wallet with Ma's name glued on.

On the way out I speak to a senior carer, there are several new faces among them. She tells me she will 'monitor' Ma's aggression for two weeks, then call the NHS team and suggest tranquillisers if she does not improve.

I leave Ma hoping toffees will negate the sedation and return to sort her mail.

A free £12.99 'handy toiletry bag' is on offer if Ma contacts Healthy Living Direct to find out if she's won £65,000.

And Body's the 'eyecare and eyewear' consultants have written to say her eye examination is now overdue. It's like dressing up a human Guy Fawkes.

She had not wanted me to leave.

'I just want you all the time.'

'But, Ma, I can't be here all the time.'

'Yes, you can.'

'No I've my own family to see to.'
'Oh sorry,' she suddenly became dejected.
'You don't have to say sorry.'
'No, go on, off you go,' she says with stoic sulkiness.

27 August

Ted's back. He was sitting in the middle lounge next to Ma and what a difference in her since my last visit. She seems her old self again even taking courage against daunting Bettine. Bettine always stares directly at me and Ma which is unsettling and Ma shouts: 'Yes. What is it?' at her but it makes no difference to her fixated stare.
Ma decides we're leaving and stands up. Thoma dashes over with her walking frame and Ma, complaining about pain in her arms, asks me for directions.
 As I can only assume we're going to her room that's where we end up and have an almost animated chat about things which Ma can almost but not quite summon up.
'When we get the new house where can we put everything?'
Then I become aware she is carrying around with her a mental residue of all her belongings: furniture, books, pictures which I have spent the last year dispersing, in an assortment of charity shops, gifting away or dumping. The stuff worth keeping has been stored around my own home.
'Well, Ma, you know your will? Well I thought it was best to have a look at it and I've shipped that bookcase, the bound Shakespeare volumes, the praying chair, the mirror and other bits to Diana in America.'
'Oh have you dear? Oh thank God. I was going to ask you to do that, but I thought it would be too much.'

'And as for your diaries, your pictures and all your other stuff, I've got it packed away at my house.'
'Oh thank you dear.'
'No don't thank me it's all down to your…' I hesitated.
'Foresight,' she said.
'Yes and your consideration.'
It has clearly come as a great relief that all her belongings have been accounted for.
'I mean it's not marvellous stuff, but it's worth having,' she said.
Thoma knocked on the door to tell me Ma had taken a fall that day.
'I'm sorry we should have told you earlier.'
'Oh don't worry she's made of India rubber.'
We chat and Ma smiles at the fact we are having a conversation.
I take the opportunity to ask if there is any physical contact between Ma and Bettine. I am reassured there is not.
Apparently Bettine's dementia is rapidly getting worse not helped by a fall she had in the garden during which she hit her head.
Bettine is a prowler and has always been on walkabout. Tall, lean, and leggy she was probably a reasonable athlete in her day. She will stride through the home then turn at the gable end wall and walk back. She will then reappear.
'And when Nancy starts we just know it's Nancy,' said Thoma, who, with her Russian indifference to death, tells me several old residents who have been admitted to hospital have returned with the diagnosis that they will die soon, only to prove the doctors wrong while starting to regain some degree of health. 'Whatever state the human being is in, the end can never be predicted,' she tells me.

This is exacerbated by a cold war between the home and the hospital. In the home the residents come under microscopic examination from day-to-day, cheek-by-jowl, care. The carers actually live with their charges and know them, if not with professionally acknowledged medical expertise, then with behavioural muddle-through and constantly met demands. To that extent the residents live as few have ever lived: with servants. However, in the hurly-burly of hospital, they are on wheeled beds in uncertain territorial areas created with flimsy curtains. Such beck and call as there is comes after the processing of a thousand other patients. They live as they were once used to living: fighting for survival.

Old, ill people should be dead soon, should be dying, and will be treated in the light of this. Blood tests, urine tests are an unnecessary routine with a chronic condition, but it's a routine, which might throw up the terminal condition the overworked young doctors have a hunch about. Have a pre-conceived diagnosis about.

In the home the residents live under a watchful, but un-intrusive scrutiny into their daily life. In the hospital they live under intermittent rote visit to see how their death is coming along.

There is more mail to sort for Mrs N I Durham. This time an envelope with a clown face proclaims: 'Enter our £25,000 all the fun of the fair draw.' With 10 per cent off everything for a limited time only. And on the back I read that a 'lightweight handy step' which 'instantly folds for easy storage' and which was £7.99 is now £4.99. 'SAVE £3.00'. Or a 'solar shed light' down to £14.99. Or a 'foot rocker' which 'minimises heel,leg and back discomfort', down £3 from £12.99. Or the fully adjustable bed table now £9.99, that mysterious sum again. To purchase all these items you didn't realise you had been living without, 'All the Very Best' of Driffield Yorkshire tell Mrs N I Durham to 'place your order with our own UK call centre'. They've got her number: no nasty wogs to have to deal with.

Inside the envelope a shower of primary-coloured leaflets pour out offering other essential services: 'Beat the misery of arthritis,' and 'A guaranteed way to beat the rising cost of funerals.' I suppose having frittered your disposable income away, making savings on life, you can at least cut the cost of death.

I watched a giant sky-blue, ship sneaking up the river loaded with containers stacked as high as Kent. Among them will be another consignment of goods for 'All The Very Best' of Driffield and a thousand and one other bargain mail order locations. No wonder China's GDP is falling if its exports are based on such tat. Even western suckers wake up eventually.

5 September

I went along today at seven in the evening. Daniel let me in through the door without me having to press the 'bell' which sets off a continuous electronic howl until entry is achieved.

Daniel knocked on her door, room No. 9.

'Come in. Who is it?'

'Your son.'

'Oh COME IN.'

Ma is on the commode and slowly realising the impropriety of the situation starts a lot of sobbing because I'd arrived when she was so engaged. A lot of hugging to make up for this.

She tells me that some residents physically attack but she hits back.

'What would you do?'

'Ignore them.'

'What, you'd do nothing if they hit you?'

'Yes.'

She is perplexed momentarily, 'Well I wouldn't.'

'Good for you.'

'I'm so frightened. But I tell myself if I just wait I'll be all right, I'll get out. I'll get back. I want to show my mummy the bruises, the marks,' she points to the age spots on her hands.

'And I want to get back to England and I'll never, ever step foot in this damned place again.'

Tim brought us in some unordered tea and I start wondering if there's something in my mother's account. Are they are trying to suck up to me?

'How's your wife?' asks Ma.

'Very well. She wants to come and see you. She hasn't seen you for a few weeks. She's been very busy.'

'I wish you weren't married. I just love you so much.'

'You're my mother.'

'No I'm not.'

'You are.'

'How?'

I tuck her up in bed and sit on the pillow.

'How's Ted?'

'I don't know I haven't seen him since I last saw him,' Ma laughs at her own joke.

'This place is full of death.'

'What do you mean?'

'What do I MEAN?'

We sit in silence for a while. The room is peaceful, at the back of the large double-fronted old house. The bed is placed in the far corner opposite a WC and a hand basin compartmentalised behind a false wall to make the room 'en suite'. Ma is unable to use the facility and it instead houses her folded wheelchair.

At the foot of her bed is a white chest of drawers containing beautifully laundered, folded nighties, wool cardigans, and skirts: representing several Christmasses past and never worn. They are more to do with Cathy's desire to mark the day. For Ma not to be forgotten. A gift-wrapped conscience.

On the top is a TV.

At the door end of the room is a table. On it are her old Rupert books, and a pile of greetings cards. Over a radiator ledge stand framed photographs of her immediate family.

I stand up to leave.

'I hate it when you come because you always go. Good-bye dear.'

Downstairs I question Daniel about the violence he reassures me there isn't any. I specifically mention Bettine. He says she is 'very confused', knows not where she is, but is very placid and never lashes out.

I trust Daniel, who incidentally, has invited me to Ghana!

6 September

Following a visit by Ma to the 'Memory Clinic' at the Harland Centre in Southend, manager of the lodge, Stephanie Mirams has written a short report to the centre on any personality changes Ma has undergone.

'In my opinion, Nancy is a delightful lady with a wonderful character, however she has been known to reduce some of our visitors to tears with her comments. Generally, I would say Nancy displays anti-social behaviour to those around her. This is a pity as it means others do not enjoy her company and this can lead to exclusion, particular (sic) in a group activity, however, this does not seem to bother her in the slightest.

Nancy can be absolutely lovely towards staff, however, the moment they try to assist her with any daily living activity, particularly personal care, Nancy will lash out both verbally and physically. She will try to punch, kick and scratch staff and say we are trying to "murder" her as well as many hurtful remarks and name-calling. However this is quickly resolved when staff back off and a different carer intervenes to calm Nancy.

With regards to her appetite and sleeping pattern, we have no concerns. She eats and sleeps well and can be wonderful company when content.

My biggest concern for Nancy is her behaviour which does appear to be deteriorating as the months go on, so a review of her medication could be helpful to enable her to achieve greater fulfilment.'

A sinister liquid cosh, to render the patient senseless, or a sensible drug to induce well-being?

Out in the river the central channel was pushing in rapidly against the mud, but with a hundred tributaries to fill its onrush was side-tracked and momentarily slowed. In my mother's brain the intricate tributaries of cognition are slowly but surely disappearing beneath a sluggish tide of blank canvas.

10 September

The staff of Carr & Westley of Hadlow, Tonbridge in Kent are keen communicators and have sent through their Autumn brochure to Mrs N. I. Durham.

Their model wears skirts modestly down to her calves, which are reassuringly chunky but nevertheless shapely. Her large, well-worn hands sport French polished nails and are always posed in such a way as to display her wedding ring. Let us call the model, Audrey, she looks like an Audrey, a woman of 60-something who enjoys black and white movies of the 1940s. Audrey is happily married: you can tell by her smile. And Carr & Westley are delighted with Audrey as she smiles with her eyes and wears grey cardigans, plum and grey check skirts that drop to her ankle and floral print polyester dresses. 'Not too near the fire, Audrey.' Her feet are big and she does not know what to do with them: sling back high heels look like small barges which don't complement the coquettish tilt which Audrey affects in a bid to bring dynamism to standing still. Carr & Westley don't go in for trashy 'free' gifts that always come in at a penny below the final pound, or winning draws that require hours on the telephone. Their clothes are to be taken seriously: you can tell from the price. However there's an 'absolute guarantee' of money refunded or rather more alarmingly, goods exchanged, if returned unused within 21 days.

Ma's own wedding ring has gone missing. She's probably hidden it somewhere 'safe'.

14 September

I had dropped an email to Stephanie to explain I was a little concerned about Bettine, that Ma appeared a little frightened of her, and she replied:

'Dementia can be a cruel thing! The lady you mention is also suffering from it and it affects people in different ways but please be assured she is very caring and completely harmless. If anything, Nancy gives her a good run for her money, so to speak!

'I think it's important never to dismiss what Nancy says and it's important to listen carefully, so we "don't throw the baby away (sic) with the bath water"! To Nancy what she says is very real to her and usually stems from our attempts to assist her into the bath or shower, after she has had an accident. We cannot force people to accept care but we do try our hardest in these situations to get people to accept help, for their own dignity and comfort as well as other people's.

'Please do not apologise for Nancy's behaviour, it is not necessary, she is a lovely lady who will hopefully benefit from her next review with her CPN. We are professionals and we are trained to deal with these issues. I just hope it was not too distressing for you. Communal living can be tough for visitors, too.

'Anytime you have concerns, Dickie, do not hesitate to inform me and I shall investigate.

'On a slightly different note we are getting two kittens for the residents and whenever I mention them to Nancy and show her photos she gets incredibly excited which is lovely to see. Look out for Timmy and Peter (as named by the residents) coming soon!

Kind regards,

Stephanie.'

Which is a puzzle as Ma hates cats.

3 October

Ma is dressed in a well-laundered woolly cardigan over a
jumper, neither are from Carr & Westley, yet she seemed
contented and warm. Ted is sitting next to her, head to one
side, shirt unbuttoned at the neck. Lucy is babbling away
to herself about her mother, stolen spectacles and non-
payment of rates.
'I've not paid them, I know I 'avn't, Lucy. Someone's
taken my glasses, Lucy. I know they 'ave.'
Another decrepit woman with a face permanently cracked
open at the mouth, like a horror mask, keeps potting
imagined plants in the carpet and pulling the legs of her
trousers up and down.
They can't take your memories away. Paying rates, losing
spectacles, gardening, a lifetime of suburban bliss.
I asked Ma how Ted was.
She turned to Ted, 'Do you know Ted?'
'He is Ted,' I said.
'Oh are you? Ted, meet my son. Well say "Hello" then. Oh
you are hopeless.'
But, as we know, Ted's comprehension is not impaired by
being mute, while Ma's oral delivery is no longer linked to
intelligibility. Possibly a recipe for a perfect union.
I tell Ma about the kids, how Katie is thinking of studying
criminology.
'Cor, you clever thing.'

She is pleased the brent geese have arrived out on the mud-flats.
'The little darlings.'
And she tells me Daniel is the 'best person in here'.
Daniel, from Ghana.
She tells me a 'nice man' died on Saturday but I'm not sure if this is resident or residue.
She looks well. Good complexion, rheumy eyes still blue and focusing often.
Joan came in, sat on a chair and said: 'I want a wee. Am I on the right chair?'
'I don't think so,' I said.
She got up and wandered away.
Bettine wandered in and stood in front of the giant TV screen blocking out the Commonwealth Games broadcast from New Delhi. She tugged at the seat of her trousers and wandered away again. There is a kind of collective toileting time.
'Do I live here?' Lucy asked her visiting daughter.
'Yes, you do at the moment,' the daughter said archly.
'Do I?'
She combed her mother's hair then both Lucy's daughter and son-in-law got up from their chairs and left without saying goodbye.
Goodbyes get more difficult the closer they get to goodnight. Not for those about to die but for those left with longer to go. Will this be the last goodbye? Best not to utter it. It's a bit like meeting the terminally ill. What do you say in greeting?
Bettine wandered in again ignored the Commonwealth Games and looked instead out of the rain-streaked window. Water beaded down the pane.
'Hello,' I said.

'Hello. Where do I know you from?'
'I come here to see my mother.'
'Where's she live?'
'Here.'
'But where?'
'Upstairs. Room 9.'
'Oh. Are you going to see her?'
'Yes,' I said despite the fact Ma was sitting next to me.
There had been a handbag war. Ma had been given a shiny
brown leather handbag which Bettine had thought was
hers. Not sure what the outcome was but it's disappeared
now and forgotten about. The handbag. Your identity over
your arm. A life and death object. Must be a bit like a
cowboy and his saddle.
'How's your son?' I asked Bettine.
'Well.'
'How's his dog? It's a spaniel isn't it?'
'Yes. He's got pups as well. They're in a shed. Give me a
shout and I'll tell you where.'
Jackie came in and asked me: 'Who's Rhoda?'
'Ma's sister.'
'She asks for her every night when I put her to bed.'
Rhoda died in 1973.
As I walked out I said goodbye to Lucy.
'Bye, bye dear see you in the morning.'

17 October

Six old biddies were ranged in a variety of armchairs
around the giant, flat, TV screen that hangs on the north-
facing party wall. Captain Horatio Hornblower, alias
Gregory Peck did not have an appreciative audience.

Ma had her two 'doggies' freshly washed on the wheeled table in front of her and was hugging her garish pink teddy bear. Beside her was a new companion, Beryl, of relatively sound mind. In fact of demonstrably sound mind.

Lucy was rifling through her hand-bag pulling out balls of wool. Horror mouth was plucking at some sky-hooks.

Ma became jealous of my conversation with Beryl who does not know Ma well enough yet to pick up on her mood, although she stopped talking when Ma emitted a long, pronounced sigh.

Beryl said she had been there 'not quite a year.' The reason we hadn't seen her before is perhaps because the carers mix and match residents who they think may stimulate one another. It had taken a while to pair off Ma and Beryl and this was based more on accent than intellect, I feel. Beryl told me the carers do tend to rough-handle their charges at bath time.

'They scrubbed my face,' she ran a hand around her jaw, 'and they sort of shunt you over in the bath,' her voice was soft and well cultivated.

'But they've got a difficult job,' I said.

'It's terrible, absolutely dreadful, murderers,' said Ma.

'Has Stan gone?' said Lucy, the old Cockney.

Nobody spoke.

'I'm going to go home. Oh yes I am, Lucy,' she continued, 'has Stan gone home?'

Sooraya one of the carers said: 'Yes, he's gone.'

'I think I'll get the bus. Yes, Lucy, you should,' said Lucy.

No one talks to Lucy so she is not so much talking to herself as answering herself. As her statements are mostly rhetorical such responses are not taxing. The handbag is also there to help with the continuum of reality and Lucy's wool-ball carrier is searched again. It is something to fiddle with before action takes place. It is interlude made tangible. But, searched and snapped shut there are no more distractions. Now something must happen. Stan has gone. Lucy must go, too.

She stood up shakily from her faux leather reclining chair, the best one in the home, Lucy wants for nothing. Nothing material, anyway.

'Yes, I'll get the bus. I will Lucy. Has the bus gone? No Lucy,' she then tottered around to the back of her chair. 'Has Stan gone?'

'Oh shut up you stupid old cow,' said Ma viciously.

Then Lucy fell over landing on her right side with her head behind the chair of another resident who was dozing.

THE END in large red letters appeared on the TV screen and Gregory was replaced by a scatological sit-com from America.

I went over, lifted Lucy into an upright position and put a cushion behind her.

'Has Stan gone home?'

'Yes,' I said.

'I thought he had. He should be here, Lucy.'

I called the carers.

Tim came through. 'I don't want a fall on my watch,' he said.

'I don't think she's hurt,' I said.

Then Jackie turned up.

'Do you want me to get her up?' I asked.

'No we have to leave them in case something's wrong later.'

So Lucy sat slumped on the floor, her back against the wall, answering her enquiries as to Stan's whereabouts until two paramedics arrived shortly afterwards.

'Are you in any pain?' shouted the burly male of the duo.

'Is Stan here?'

'I don't know about Stan.'

'Has he gone home?'

'Who's Stan?' the medic asked Sooraya, 'has he been here today?'

'No, Friday Stan comes. He doesn't come on Sunday.'

'No, love Stan's not here.'

'Who?' said Lucy.

'Stan.'

'No Stan's gone home,' said Lucy.

At last she was engaged in conversation and she was able to provide an answer to someone else's enquiry!

While Lucy sat on the floor the woman whose chair she'd collapsed behind was sick. She projectile vomited over her lap, the chair and as she drew herself up to throw further, Sooraya dashed across the room with a wastepaper basket.

'How disgusting,' said Ma.

'Sorry, Nancy,' said the poor carer.

The ailing woman was quickly transferred to another room by wheelchair.

Now Ted, with catheter bag filled with orange liquid strapped to his leg is craned from his chair on a rig, steadied, and lowered into a wheelchair, is taken away.

'Say goodbye to Nancy,' said Jackie, for my benefit, turning Ted's wheelchair to face my mother.

Ted said nothing. Made no signal.

To break the silence, which all the residents are used to, I said: 'Goodnight, Ted.'

Beryl, said: 'This place is a jail. It upsets my children. You haven't got the freedom of movement you have at home.'

She can no longer walk.

Ma then piped up: 'I do love you. I just want you to be here all the time. I love you so much Clifford,' as she rubbed my hand.

'All I ever want is to see you and my mother.'

'Well you won't see her again,' I say, believing my cruelty is the kinder path.

Ma turned her enquiring eyes to me, 'Oh charming.'

'Well, Ma you are 87.'

'How do you know how old I am?'

'I just do.'

'Do you? How old am I then?'

'You're 87.'

A look of complete incomprehension passes over her face. 'You were born in 1923. For goodness sake I'm nearly 60 you gave birth to me in 1951.'

Ma tipped the last of her tea into her saucer and prepared to tip it from there onto the carpet.

'Don't do that,'I said, 'let me.'

I took the slop and tipped it into my cup.

'Oh you twit.'

Perhaps I'm witnessing a last shred of rebellion; to mess up the carpet, which, by the way, she covets.

I left the madhouse and drove down to the seafront. It was dusk and a very poor neap tide was imperceptibly creeping across the mudflats. Scimitars of silver, reflecting the dying sun, snaked through the black mud. A two-thirds waxed moon hung over the still river. A coarse-voiced girl let the silence know about her roller-skating skills as her two male friends rolled beside her. Her voice was deliberately plebeian, as she indulged in violation of the peace.

'At least it's a lovely evening,' she screeched. It was true there was nothing she could do about that.

I walked out to the end of a storm drain enveloping myself in the night and seeking silence. As the skaters rolled out of earshot, I could hear a faint cackle of winter geese on the mudflats surrounding me.

I could hear, too, the distant throb of engines and then spotted the speckled lights of a ship far out in the river moving east. It was high out of the water – light - on its way back to China. Its cargo of gift ephemera left in containers on the dockside.

22 October

'Hello, dear,' Ma said, then added: 'Beryl, this is my daddy,' introducing me to her new companion.

'No, I'm not. I'm your son.'

The professionals advise just going along with the misconceptions of those suffering dementia. But because Ma still has most of her vices, if not many of her virtues, I feel obliged to treat her 'normally.'

That is to say re-directing her misconceptions into real conceptions, not out of callousness, but of 'doing the right thing' or so it seems to me.

She still has a touch of irony in her babble, still is personal in her remarks about her fellow guests and will still flirt and put her best face forward when someone she likes enters her orbit.

In the room today is Betty who sits with her eyes clearly focussed on me. She knows what she is seeing. Her mouth is held open wide like one of those iguanas in the desert trying to cool down.

Then next to her sits Horror Mouth, poor Barbara, whose face looks like a medieval gargoyle, and whose mouth could drain Ely Cathedral after a downpour.

Lucy is lying stretched out on her faux leather recliner. Her skirt has ridden up showing bruised thighs, which are still flabby, almost youthful. One slipper has fallen off. Then there's Joan, whose bobbed hairstyle suits her and makes her look younger, but the illusion is shattered when she suddenly slumps forward into slumber.

Then in comes wandering Bettine. She's had her hair done, too. They all have regular visits from a travelling hairdresser. Somewhere between hair and handbag lies the ghost of identity.

Bettine went to assist with helping Betty out of her chair, but was scolded by Daniel who suddenly appeared.

'Don't do that she'll fall. I'll help her.'

'Why do you always say that?'

'She'll fall. She musn't get up on her own.'

Betty is then encouraged to sit up properly, meanwhile no one is watching Midsomer Murders on the big TV screen. Daniel starts to feed Barbara after dressing her with a bib. As her head is tilted back and her neck straightened, I am put in mind of the production of foie gras.

I've been asked if I'd like a cup of tea. I often say 'Yes' as a sign that I'm not offended by the festering folks, nor disgusted by the ineradicable pong that hangs throughout the rooms and corridor. It's a test of will: ignoring where the cup might have been and whose lips have puckered over it. It helps that the tea is always hot, well-brewed and the cups immaculately clean.

'Close your mouth, boy,' Ma suddenly shouts at Barbara, who sports cropped hair.

She does close it over the food being spooned into her mouth, but when dinner is over, her mouth will hang agape once more.

Francis Bacon had a thing about the mouth, how it could be both sexually gratifying but also let out some primal scream. In the Lodge the hanging mouth is neither it is just the vestibule to the gastro vascular cavity.

'That girl's got her mouth open, she can't help it,' says Ma of Betty, she also has a thing about mouths it would seem. But Ma's is based on her middle-class etiquette. You don't eat with your mouth open. You don't talk with your mouth full.

Betty, unlike poor Barbara, can still manage to smile with her eyes so Ma is able to understand her gape is involuntary, unlike Barbara's which is congenital, the carers tell me.

Irene, in charge of medication, came in.

'There's that awful fat woman...'

'Don't be rude.'

'If only you knew.'

Can there be something sinister in this?

Irene has been the one person to suggest putting Ma on tranquillisers because of aggression towards staff when being bathed.

'We are monitoring her,' she told me.

As Daniel fed Barbara we talked across the room about Africa.

'Have you been there?'

'No, not Africa proper. Only Egypt and Morocco,' I said.

'I'd love to go to sub-Saharan Africa. One day when I have more time.'

'You can come with me to Ghana when you have more time.'

A thinking Christian, Daniel does not blame the legacy of colonialism for Africa's lack of good government, he tells me.

'That was a long time ago,' he said.

And he is proud of Ghana, a country that has political stability, he adds.

Ma, taking issue with the fact I'm talking to someone else, starts talking over us to some imagined creature on the carpet.

'Oh really, dear? How fascinating. Yes, come on, come here, come on,' she waffles, waving at an invisible creature.

Daniel and I break off talking.

Ma's hand seeks out my own, then, tired of holding it she goes back to scratching the upholstered chair arm with her fingernails. Then she changes again and grabs the sleeve of my coat and eyeing me coquettishly says equally coquettishly: 'Do you think your father would mind if I called for you?'

'No, he wouldn't mind.'

'Really?'

'Yes, 'cos he's dead.'

'Oh really?' she was distressed.

'Oh really, I'm so sorry. I'm so sorry.'

Her supper arrived: bread and butter and a corn beef salad. She lunged at the slice of bread and dropped it on her lap.

'Bugger.'

'Oh good-bye dear, filthy muck,' she said as her plastic denture eventually gripped the morsel.

Back at home her mail is still arriving reliably.

'30 Day, RISK FREE trial includes FREE collection,' of a bendy reading lamp: 'Serious lights for serious readers.

FREE delivery SAVE £9.95. Designed for avid readers –
why suffer unnecessary eye strain and tiredness.'
Avid is a weak adjective, you'd have thought they'd have
gone for voracious, or compulsive or turned it around into
a noun like bookworm.
But perhaps selling to the elderly entails beige language.
'This patented technology is relied upon by professionals,
who must see well, like surgeons, scientists and watch-
makers.'
It goes on and on:
Tick: Breathtaking clarity
Tick: 30 Day RISK FREE TRIAL
Tick: Delivered to your door (as oppose to someone else's)
Tick: No assembly (flat-pack lamps?)
Russell Bryden, if ever a name sounded like two surnames
picked out of a phone directory, it's Russell Bryden.
However this Russell Bryden is from Dumfries &
Galloway, and he says of the bendy reading lamp: 'The
best thing since printing was invented.' I don't get the link,
but never mind.
With two months to go before Christmas the Damart
catalogue is empowering my mother:
'to skip the long queues during the busy Christmas season
and unwrap your new Christmas catalogue filled with a
wide selection of jolly-good (sic) gift ideas all at great
prices, ideal for the festive season, so relax and browse
through your catalogue designed to make this Christmas a
little bit easier…or shop online from the Christmas e-
catalogue!'
The exclamation marks, used throughout, denote festive
friendliness, and goodwill seasoning. The Three Wise Men
have been steaming up Sea Reach on giant container ships
for months. And cathedral-sized warehouses are toppling

with tat at cut –price cost: Christmas is not all about money after all.

Next, a heavy brochure from 'Hotter comfort concept Christmas 2010. Share comfort and joy this Christmas.' The brochure offers flat, plastic shoes with Velcro-straps in Teal, chocolate brown metallic and Sangria.

Sounds like the palette of Hieronymus Bosch.

A welcoming editorial is provided by managing director Stewart Houlgrave who has a rather nasty smile.

'Christmas is such a wonderful time of year and at Hotter, we've discovered the ideal solution for all that Christmas bustle – happy feet.'

Ma's feet are offered happiness in 'The soft-cushioned footbed and breathable leather lining of formal classic Schubert, ideal for festive parties.

'Feather light and flexible Sabrina, the perfect choice for busy shopping days.'

Clearing through old unfilled desk diaries, used as shopping lists; letters; postcards and scrap paper, in Ma's bureau, I found a note scrawled shakily in her hand, possibly the last thing she ever managed to write:

'Ho, (crossed out) How I wish I c could go back to that lovely land of murcis (crossed out) music laug a (crossed out) ghter.'

Now if only Stewart Houlgrave could provide that for Christmas.

23 October

A day later yet another catalogue arrives depicting a young woman holding a fan of £50 notes: 'URGENT. You could have already won our £40,000 prize.' Yes, it's them again:

'All The Very Best' of Wadsworth Road, Driffield in Yorkshire.

By claiming, my mother would also receive a 'glow-in-the-dark' clock with thermometer, although it is not stated whether the thermometer glows in the dark, too. And I cannot fathom how a clock complements a thermometer unless it's for timing hypothermia.

There is also a saving of £5 offered if my mother purchases two pairs of 'custom-fit, 24-hour comfort shoes. No laces, no zips, no buckles, no straps.' The female version is trademarked as a Mildred, the male version a George. There is a vein-lined hand holding aside a huge flap of either a Mildred or a George showing how the whole foot can be wrapped up like a fish supper in the 'comfort shoe.'

Then in case my mother is going bald there is a brochure asking: 'Scalp "show-through" ? Masse-Esse works on all hair types and colours for just £7.98.'

Inside the envelope this time are no less than seven brochures and a catalogue.

Next, 'The Best of British. Buy one adjustable bed get another FREE.'

A heavily made up woman in green satin pyjamas sits on a huge divan reading a magazine.

'If you have trouble getting out of your chair. Look No Further. Buy one Rise & Recliner Chair. Get another FREE.' Where is Ma going to put all this stuff? Such largess is being spread from Great British Mobility, based in a Somerset 'business park,' where, presumably, space is not an issue.

Next, 'How would you feel winning £25,000?' Age UK run a weekly lottery and are asking my mother to fill in a direct debit form for £104 a year to enter.

A Mr Graham Sykes of Yorkshire, says: 'It still hasn't sunk in. I am absolutely delighted, this will certainly prove to be a nice little nest egg for me and my family.'

Next, 'Millie Edwards. Inspired by the sight of a million flamingos after a holiday to Lake Nakuru, created a tropical paradise in the back garden of her three-bed semi in Staines. When Millie spoke to Yvonne, one of our friendly advisors, she wanted her love of flowers to be reflected in her Funeral Plan…with every guest at her service wearing a bright, pink gerbera,' promise Co-operative Wills & Planning, Manchester.

They don't tell us whether Millie Edwards is looking forward to her funeral or has already enjoyed it.

Next, Identity Direct from Southampton will insert your grandchild's name along with their 'Brothers, Sisters and Friends, all clearly woven into the story. Your name is printed on the title page. The children you love will never forget who gave them these colourful books,' which include Spider-Man, Toy Story and Winnie the Pooh. But hang on a minute these stories all ready have characters in them don't they?

Next, the catalogue itself. It has everything a human wreck could desire from a 'magnetic back brace, a battery-operated denture cleaner which uses "sonic vibration" to help remove stains, bacteria, tartar and food particles. Then there are foot alignment socks which 'help' (that caveat again) relieve bunions, hammer toes, plantar fasciitis (Google it), foot cramps and heel and ball pain, 89 per cent acrylic.'

Next 'lightweight incontinence pants with standing cuffs to prevent leakage, "perfect for slipping in your hand-bag"', men just have to wet themselves.

If Ma doesn't fancy that there's the Solar Cross Light, an affordable memorial which emits a warm, glowing light, no electricity, no running costs to "honour loved ones, remember cherished pets, or simply celebrate your faith." Then more random, almost desperate production runs, perhaps to use up acrylic off-cuts, include:

'Hinged earring screens; outside tap mufflers; hammer-in, stone-look garden edging; glow-in-the-dark rustic wrought-iron look garden fencing; portable bidets; solar garden-glow robins; toilet seat cushions; ergo-pen: "needs no gripping" ideal for arthritic hands; 13 inch standing resin meerkat "add a touch of humour to your garden, Marvin is sure to raise a few eyebrows from garden visitors and friends alike."'

My 87-year-old, widowed mother is also offered the chance to 'Spice Up,' her 'Love Life.'

'We have brought you a special collection of DVDs enabling you to learn how maturity can enhance and reinvigorate sexual relationships. Be aware, however, that this DVD collection includes extremely explicit scenes.

'So why not sit back, switch on and enjoy this fantastic collection?

Cheating Housewives 4, Nurse Betty, Real British Wives 2, Real Euro Couples 3, All You Can Eat, (God forbid), Hairy Down Below, Naughty Nanny, Riding Dirty 2.'

I watch another container ship sliding back down the estuary. Again it is high out of the water having discharged many thousands of tons of acrylic meerkats, garden-glow robins and Solar Cross Lights. It is returning to China with nothing more than the packaging.

A sweet revenge for the Opium trade.

All the imports flooding in for these mail order companies, much of which is discarded in house clearances, would once have been sorted and sold by Ma during her many years of charity shop work for Save the Children, Oxfam and Mencap.

She became a good friend of Red Cross nurse Mary Hawkins, who set up several Save the Children shops in Cornwall after a life caring for children in war-torn refugee camps.

31 May 1978

Dick and I collected a pile of junk and drove it straight to the Port Navas' Save the Children Shop. A week later Mary Hawkins offered to pay for the petrol and said she'd sold nearly all the stuff in one day, which was just as well as there was a carpet, some Venetian blinds, a rush mat and several boxes of kitchen ware and her little shop is about the size of a large bedroom.

Have had to mutilate Radio and TV Times for two weeks now by cutting out several pages of nonsense about the World Cup and players' life stories.

Bought a ribbon china antique plate with George V's face on it from a bric- a- brac stall in the market for £10 for Dick's birthday which he won't like but which I do.

26 October

The Daily Telegraph's lead story today carries the headline: 'Chemical cosh will be cut for dementia sufferers.'

The story reveals that the Department of Health and several care home groups have reached the conclusion that use of anti-psychotic drugs to subdue dementia sufferers is more likely to kill than cure them.

The report said 750,000 people are living with the condition in the UK and that the figure is expected to rise to 1 million within 15 years and top 1.7 million by 2051 as the population ages.

Only one in five receives any benefit from the 'chemical cosh.'

Ruth Sutherland, head of the Alzheimer's Society, said: 'Antipsychotics are a betrayal of people with dementia and their over prescription must be dramatically reduced. Up until now people have been trying to tackle this problem in isolation but it has been like doing a jigsaw puzzle in the dark. Dementia is a ticking time bomb that we must do everything in our power to defuse if we are to avoid a health and social meltdown. This mammoth task is not going to be achieved by one government department, one health body or one charity alone.'

Forty-five organisations have joined together to form the Dementia Action Alliance.

Ma has been lucky to escape being tranquillised as her aggressive behaviour almost got her 'coshed' by Irene Garcenila.

31 October

I thought maybe the catalogues were now arriving at Westcliff Lodge today. Ma was dressed in grass green nylon trousers and pink ankle socks with a ski-ing dog motif, and a royal blue cardigan with a large budgerigar on the back.

SKY TV was broadcasting talking heads in the US three days before the half term elections and for once a few of the residents appeared to be listening.

But after a while I realised it was just the sense you pick up on when a visitor to the home is paying a resident some attention. In this case it was a relative of Betty, a man in his 40s.

During a trailer for 'Fat Families,' to be broadcast soon, the TV screened a fat family running through a list of 'wrong' foods, ending the trailer with a loud belch.

'Class,' said Betty's visitor while she sat appropriately with her mouth agape. Lucy was asleep and Barbara was making barking noises and pecking her hand, like a bird's beak, at some invisible body above her head.

Ma's head would occasionally turn towards the screen but I think that was more to do with the commanding diction of their chief political journalist that she was attracted to. Beryl was talking rationally about how she didn't much like her sheltered accommodation.

'But this isn't sheltered accommodation this is a care home. Most of the people here have senile dementia,' I said.

'Oh, I didn't realise that,' she said.

Joan was asleep. Then she suddenly woke up and started picking her nose.

'I wish you'd leave your nose alone,' said Ma, 'stop poking about in it, horrible man.' Joan, with a bob, a flat chest, and in suit trousers looks like an androgynous student.

Then Barbara turned her bark into a sharp, staccato squawk.

'There's that mad girl. She's a pain in the neck if ever there was. She's got all her mouth cut out.'

Having told Ma she's living in a guest house, we now cannot complain if she observes 'guests' at face value and comments on their anti-social behaviour.

Beryl then added: 'I thought she was crying.'

'No,' said Ma.

'She looks like a creature..that one on the end of the bed,' added Beryl from some private nightmare. 'My family don't want me living with them anymore which is a shame, but Helen my daughter, has a full time job in the Civil Service. She does a lot of running around for me. I don't know where they are, they should be here by now.'

Last time I visited, Beryl told me her son was on his way over from Reading, but no-one showed up.

Ma started scratching her table making a noise like a trapped rodent.

Then Beryl suddenly stood up, 'Now I must go home. I've got to show my face. Go to my den. Don't let me hold you up if you're off somewhere.'

I stroked Ma's hair, 'Ahh, put him on my lap. I'd rather have him on my lap.'

I think she thought it was a bird stroking her.

One tiny carer came in and made a cupped wave at Ma who smiled and waved back.

Then the carer made the same gesture to Beryl who responded with a different kind of wave: her thumbs in her ears and open palmed hands shaking.

'That's what you do to children or babies,' said Beryl, who also has dementia, but who can still think and act independently. She fights at encroaching institutionalisation. She sides with Ma in a critique of other 'guests' and their peasant-like behaviour, a case of appeasing the stronger character.

More catalogues arrived today. 'Tick, tock goes the Westie Clock. A must for all Westie fans! This adorable wall clock in the shape of a Westie dog has a moving tail that wags from side to side as the clock ticks.'
And 'Protection from Identity Fraud. In the palm of your hand: easy shred scissors, five-bladed.'
Then there's a micro-waveable hot-water bottle filled with wheat instead of water, no 'risk spilling scalding hot water.'
Or 'Plug removal made easy. Limited dexterity or arthritis? This little item just wraps around the plug enabling easy grip. Pack of four £4.99.'
A 'hand-delivered' envelope promises a chance to win £65,000.
The ships move slowly but inexorably up Sea Reach gently manoeuvring the containers toward the giraffe-cranes.
Another 30,000 tons of tat for landfill or charity shop via mail order suckers.
Ma once spent her energies tabulating such junk. She was safe with order, she 'busied herself' with capricious distraction.

2 February 1977

'My dear Nancy,

I feel that somebody ought to write to you and say "thank-you" for all the months of work you have done for Oxfam. The Monday and Wednesday morning group will miss you tremendously but I shall miss you particularly in times of crisis. I have never forgotten the day last year when Treglowns suddenly dumped a whole legacy on us without warning. The entire shop floor was seething with bedding and household goods and underwear and every other kind of ware. It was chaotic! Suddenly you arrived, the essence of calm and efficiency and in an incredibly short time, everything was sorted, priced and organised. I suppose the rest of us did something but you were the presiding genius and I was filled with admiration for your speed and competence. I have never forgotten it.

With sincerest good wishes,

Gwen B'

31 August 1978

'When staying the night with the aunts, Rhoda and I were always allowed to play in the shop after closing hours; they sold knitwear and childrens' wear, and baby clothes: lots of bootees and mittens and there was Bear Brand hosiery and lots of items bearing a picture of a shepherdess and crook – or was it a nun? – St Hilda's was the brand name. The floor was covered in brown lino and so were the counters and the only form of heating was a paraffin stove rather evil smelling which gave out more fumes than warmth.
'Above the counters were archways displaying handkerchiefs and artificial flowers in gift boxes and fancy garters in pastel colours decorated with pearls and little mirrors, very frivolous, in see-through boxes. At the back were countless boxes of stockings and locknit underwear. We had a marvellous time "selling" things to each other across the counter and of course always left it exactly as we found it.'

6 November

The big screen is broadcasting Grand Designs, and as usual no one's watching.

Today the disinterest in television is shared by a male resident.

He's a beautiful yellow colour, almost the saffron of a Buddhist monk's robe. His eye sockets are vermilion which sets off his pallor further.

'Hello cock,' he says to his dream, 'fucker,' he adds.

'Down the pub,' he says, 'shithouse.' Is he back down the local?

Ma points at him: 'I don't think you know what you're talking about.'

Oh, but I think he does.

A new woman, big hair, in her 70s, wheels in a zimmer frame. Big smile on her face and left leg jumping like that of a spring lamb as she walks. She sits opposite me still beaming and stares directly at me. She crosses her legs, pulls up a denim trouser leg and puts a boot up on the zimmer frame bar. Her now bare ankle reveals a man's wristwatch strapped to it.

'I hate it,' says Ma.

'What?'

'Cream.'

She has been spooning a tub of pink yoghurt.

Suddenly Joan pipes up, 'Do you know why they're called teddy bears?' she waves at Ma's twin pink teddies.

'Yes, because of Teddy Roosevelt,' I say.

'Yes, after the Prime Minister,' she adds.

A carer enters the room and encourages Lucy to sing 'I do like that Doggy in the Window,' which she does with gusto.
'She's mad,' points Ma.
'Crackers,' agrees Beryl her acolyte.
Another, tall, woman enters the room and walks straight up to me threateningly, if a woman in her 80s can be threatening.
'Where's John?'
'I don't know.'
She stares.
Ma comes to my aid, 'I think you should tell us.'
The woman shouts in anger: 'I just want people to tell me where my husband is,' before being led away.
'She's mad as a hatter,' says Ma.
Beryl took my seat. Ma thought I was still sitting there and clasped Beryl's wrist.
I was not sure how Beryl, rational a lot of the time, would take this. She did not flinch. We were talking, she was in company and however bizarre the circumstances, the home cannot be accused of requiring conventional behaviour, even though many, like Lucy, hang on to it. A construct of distraction.
I sat on the side of Ma opposite Beryl.
'Where's Dick?' she asked looking at the floor.
'Here. Dicky, anyway,' I said.
'Oh darling.'
She now had two wrists to grab and rub with her thumb.
I noticed, as I listened to Beryl's past about cat-breeding, that she had cupped her other hand over Ma's. Human contact, however unconventional, is everything.
Bettine hovered in the doorway, sensing the ad hoc atmosphere of community.

'Oh, do come in,' said Ma.

Bettine backed off.

'Shame. I like her. She's a good-looking girl, that one.'

The chubby little girl on the sands of Woolacombe, can still covet a fine physique.

14 November

Joan, Lucy, the woman with the wristwatch on her ankle, the yellow man, Ma and Beryl, now wearing spectacles are sitting in front of the big screen on which large men are grabbing one another as part of the England- Australia rugby match at Twickenham.

Yellowman is animated and shouting. Fortunately the occasional 'fuckers' is so slurred and mal-delivered, it's easy to pretend he hasn't said it.

Joan started to tell me that her husband, George Murphy, was captain for England. But just then Yellow Man started shouting with disappointment.

'Prat,' he yelled. Unless he was supporting Australia, he must have been confused as England were winning.

'I'd like to be able to see my mum,' he suddenly shouted, 'some bloke 'it 'er and she 'it 'im back and knocked 'im aht,' the violence of the game clearly awakening fond memories.

'Plonker,' he yelled.

After two cheese and lettuce sandwiches, Ma, who had put up with Yellow Man's rantings long enough, suddenly bellowed: 'Shut your chops.'

'There, all right dear,' said Yellow Man respectfully, 'you're all right, girls and boys, men and women,' and looked lasciviously at Cathy, who was with me.

'You're all right,' he said again, his teeth suddenly shooting forward between his lips as he stretched them to attempt a smile.

The game finished giving us an excuse to leave.

'Well done England,' I said hoping to put Yellow Man's mind at rest.

'I suppose you're going to buy a bottle of champagne?' said Beryl.

'Aha champagne, would you like a glass for Christmas?' I said.

'Anytime,' said Beryl.

17 November

Westcliff Lodge organised a cheese and wine quiz night, 'You're alive,' exclaimed Ma as she saw me, 'I can't believe it,' I am her husband back from the dead. The fact that I had 're-married' and brought my wife along with me did not deter Ma's delight.

'I'm ugly as hell,' she added clearly not feeling at her best for her suddenly reappearing partner.

'Baby, baby…where did our love go?' Diana Ross and the Supremes got the evening started as Lee, the quiz-master in black tie warmed things up.

Ma's old slack-skinned legs pumped up and down in her tartan slippers as she sat in her chair. Cathy and I were in her 'team' for the quiz.

At the table opposite sat Ralph, a man with the complexion of finely refined flour, with his wife on one side and daughter on the other.

'Couldn't fit anymore in,' he said cheerfully, a naturally sweet nature shining through his eyes, which are almost unbearable to look at as they are self-revelatory, glistening and intelligent, like a harp seal's before the club.

Ma is trying to whistle along with Diana, but, frustrated in the role of spectator, she suddenly with perfect timing, asks in a clear voice:

'Do you ever stop talking?' as Lee momentarily stops his patronising patter.

Everyone - residents, visitors, and staff roared with laughter.

Ma encouraged, and now with the stage adds: 'Because I'm so beautiful.'

Now the audience laugh uncertainly as Ma's stand-up falters, 'Stop laughing,' she commands unnecessarily.

The show goes on, Lee's show, and Ma turns back to my resurrection. 'I can't believe it.'

Then, as if comforted by an unholy ghost, she's back to Lee.

'You mustn't ask these silly answers.'

And when that misfires she starts whistling furiously, her way of demonstrably ignoring the quiz questions.

'Which is a town in Australia? Is it a) Lesley leaps b) Jenny jumps c) Alice Springs or d) Susan slips?'

While the teams compile their answers, Diana starts singing 'Stop in the name of Love,' and tears spring to my eyes as I am transported back to the 1960s when Ma could whistle accurately to this song, part of a compilation on her giant tape-deck used to record Top of the Pops.

'Good boy,' Ma says to the little Jack Russell which has been adopted by the home.

'I can't keep living in this place,' Ma said looking alternately fiercely grim or laughing. Masks of another kind of theatre.

The quiz is over and Lee winds up. The manageress gives
him a box of chocolates and publicly thanks him.
'Good-bye, dear. Must you go? What a pity,' says Ma.
Cathy and I leave Ma who is now tired and is to be taken
up to bed.
Forty minutes later in a curry house, Cathy's mobile phone
goes off. Ma's fainted and been 'unconscious for five
minutes,' according to Irene.
Curry cancelled and I drive to Southend Hospital where
Ma is on a trolley tended by two ambulance-men.
She appears to be in good humour, pleased, but not
desperate to see me.
After 45 minutes she's wheeled in and transferred to a bed.
Blood test, blood pressure.
A nurse says: 'Can I look at your tummy?'
'Oh, do what you like,' says Ma resignedly.
Ma's feet leap as they're tickled, she yells as cold hands fit
electrodes to her bare skin, and then flinches as sticky
plasters are applied to hold the receivers in place on her
ankles, wrists and chest.
A child is crying continuously with volume.
'Oh, shut up. Take her somewhere else.'
We wait for hours surrounded by the paraphernalia of
health care: wheelchairs, bright lights, low false ceilings,
beds on wheels. A pecking order of professions but no-one
pulling rank. A chaos of hierarchy.
A red-headed sister joshes with a nurse: 'She's gingerist.
She doesn't obey me or the other redhead.'
'Oh this dreadful winter,' says Ma, 'you're very patient.'
'Yes, I'm patient and you ARE a patient.'
She dozes for a while then: 'Up comes Dick and he says:
"Have you had a nice ride in the country?" And I say, "No

I haven't got a car". And he said: "Well it should be called a walk". And I said: "Yes it should and I hate walking'"
At least her partner is now back in the third person.
She dozed some more then dredged up another dream: 'I'm frozen. Rhoda was never like that – frozen – I feel such a fool but I can't help it.'
It appears the home or the paramedics have over-reacted again. There's nothing additionally wrong with Ma and we're trying to get her to pee so they can test that as well. But she won't oblige. Finally the tall, striking black doctor Alba relents after my continued insistence that tests, tests and more tests are just box-ticking and she lets me take Ma back to the home. It's 01.30.

18 November

Today's Daily Mail reports on a care home which has created a room filled with objects from and decorated in the style of a lounge from the 1950s.
'The Alzheimer's room' is the unsubtle headline.
Apparently staff scoured junk shops to collect three flying china ducks, a classic Bakelite telephone, a Singer sewing machine, a Remington typewriter, a vacuum cleaner and a post-war pram, among other consumer goods of the 1950s, to recreate the good, old days.
Instead of being given drugs, dementia sufferers that are distressed, are taken forward to the past, sat in the room, and according to the home's manager: 'We go over their life history and within an hour they're completely calm and happy. It proves that you don't need to use anti-psychotics all the time.'
I thought the 1950s was a grey hangover from rationing, a post-war drudgery of austerity; a place where a snort of

cocaine would be most welcome, at least until Elvis turned up.

21 November

We parked outside the lodge and my son Richard, aged 11, sat in the car listening to a Radio 4 play.
'I don't want to go in there, Dad. It stinks and it's full of freaks. If Grandma was just on her own, I'd go and see her.'
Ma was happy enough among the 'freaks', a benign smile on her face, although she made no more sense than was expected. I gently rubbed her thumb to see if there was any pain from last year's fracture.
Ethel, one of the Filipino carers, made me a cup of tea. A strangely old- fashioned name for a young woman. I told her it was a pretty name, but she is too intelligent to respond to flattery.
An elaborately-painted woman dressed immaturely was introduced to me as Christine, Lucy's daughter. Lucy, I was disappointed to discover, is 95.
'She's strong apart from up here,' Christine tapped her head. She does not rate the home highly.
'You learn more about things as time goes on,' she said. Lucy's been an inmate for two years.
'It's the cleaning,' she pointed at the carpet, where Ma had chucked her tea, 'and things go missing.'
Ethel came in, rubbed my mother's hand and said:
'Nancy,' in a comforting manner. Then she turned to me and said: 'Ted died. Ted was Nancy's friend.'
Ma said: 'I don't like it.'
'Don't like what, Ma?'

'What?'
Christine told her mum she was leaving. 'I'm off now, Mum,' she said waking her up to impart the news.
'I'm off, Mum, because you're asleep.'
'What, dear?'
'I'm going now because you're asleep.'
'OK, dear.'
'I'll see you on Wednesday.'
'Who?'
'Wednesday I'll see you. Now, what happens on Wednesday?'
'Hair.'
'That's right you get your hair done.' The hairdresser, the reliable Messiah.
On the way out a large, black expensive-looking 4X4 van was parked on the driveway. And two burly men stood round the back doors muttering quietly.
'That's a private ambulance,' said Cathy, 'I wonder if someone's died?'
It was for Ted.

28 November

I heard a bleating sound and watched an elderly woman with bare legs and open-toed slippers as she was lifted from her armchair and deposited into a wheelchair. She was in pain. Her partner, a skinny, little man in a pin-stripe suit followed her out of the room his tie dangling from his zimmer frame and their departure revealed Ma who recognised me. She spoke in broken sentences, but even when you put them together they made little sense.

That was until she wanted to kiss me: 'With everyone watching.' There is status in exhibiting intimacy with youth, defined in the lodge as anyone not on wheels.

It is dark and overcast outside and the lounge is fully lit, but one thing which tells us it's still daytime is the broadcast on TV which is displaying English tourists in Austria trying to guess the names of a variety of dishes.

A close-up of a large cow suddenly loomed up full screen. Its bovine snout flexed and sniffed and sparked the only response from the room of non-watchers.

My mother yelled: 'You darling pet, don't worry.'

I read a letter from Diana, and show her the latest pictures of her family.

'Is this her poetry?' she asks.

Beryl, who always tells me her family are about to visit, but is alone every-time I visit, asks me what the high pitched whistle, which suddenly sounds, means.

'That's the noise the door buzzer makes. It does not go off until the door is answered.'

'Oh, it's probably my granddaughter coming to visit. Or maybe two.'

The sound ceases and I wait expectantly, but nobody turns up.

I show Beryl the pictures Diana has sent from America.

'Yes, I've got a daughter with long hair like that: Helen. She works for the Customs & Exercise (sic).'

3 December

Cathy and I arrive at the lodge at 17.30. Jackie answered the door and told us Ma was already in bed. We went upstairs and along the north side of the lodge down a corridor to Room 9 at the back of the home, which overlooks a courtyard containing an overgrown sycamore tree and horizontally stacked ladders and scaffold poles. Ma cares little for a 'view' but values silence highly. So the room, a peaceful sanctuary, couldn't have been more suitable had it been hand-picked . The heavy drapes are drawn and the room is comfortingly lit from a low table lamp and the glow of the TV. You enter through a door in the south-western corner of the room, which is spacious: seven paces long by five paces wide. In the far north-eastern corner is the bed.

 Ma is lying on her left side, eyes just open and looking at the TV.

When she heard my voice she was suddenly alert and overjoyed to see us.

We rubbed hands and Ma said: 'Well, you see, all the men were so dim.'

I asked her what she was having for breakfast.

'A bit of bread.'

'What no bacon and eggs?'

'No that's all you're having,' she shrieked with laughter, clearly thinking the question was made for my benefit. A carer turned up and pressed a red knob on the wall. I'd sparked off the visit by unwittingly treading on the pressure pad next to Ma's bed. A minefield of care.

4 December

I took a letter from Ma's old friend from VAD days, Gene Ruffhead (nee Whatling), to read to her:

'My Dear Nancy,
Another year nearly over. I'm afraid Eric has not been well he was in hospital from December to March. He went in as

an emergency and was a long time being diagnosed and therefore ages before any treatment. After many gastroscopies, endoscopies, scans, biopsies, X-rays, etc etc, an abdominal mass was found but not the dreaded big C so I'm glad to say he is at last improving.

Didn't we have a marvellous summer? I spent a lot of time in the garden doing nothing.

No bowls for Eric unfortunately but he is still President of Club so gets dressed up occasionally to present prizes etc! My brothers Bill and Peter are still taking part in the British Legion and RAFA anniversaries, but we are getting short of wartime friends. I don't hear from Jean Bennett anymore...'

'Jean,' Ma said.

'Yes, Ma. Jean and this is Gene, too, spelt G E N E.'

Ma just nodded and I continued reading.

'My two little great grandsons are very boisterous and unruly. I'd like to give them the odd smack or two,'

'Quiet right,' Ma, interrupted, I continued: 'but very much NOT ALLOWED! Claire is a modern mum and it's all quiet reasoning. Ha-Ha!

'Grandson Mark is just breaking up from his partner which is sad as they have such a lot of trouble ahead – dividing property etc. Everyone seems to have one member of family splitting up – suppose it's the modern trend.

'My writing is getting awful, are you computer friendly? We are not.

Needless to say our life is very boring, no shows, theatre or anything like that but we have had our moments in the past, so keep cheerful and smiling

'Have a lovely day on 25th.

Love as ever Gene.'

8 October 1943

'Yesterday I'd suggested that we should go ice skating as it would probably be our last half day together.

At 12 o'clock Gene and I rushed off and changed and Bennett joined us on the train. Gene led us through undergrounds, in trains, out of trains, here and there, up escalators, through tunnels and we finally got to Queen's Road, South Kensington...

Outside the entrance there were photos of ice carnivals and professional skaters in brilliant black and white. We crept in. It was under ground and once down the stairs the corridors were carpeted in a light fawn with steel bar ceilings. The air struck cold – there a few yards away was the rink, a dull white and in the centre graceful figures in short skirts and fluffy jumpers swooped and whirled around. In silence we entered the dressing room, several tall and graceful figures strode past us in white boots with the silver skate fixed on the sole. They balanced perfectly. We began to take our shoes off and wrench our feet into dark brown boots with dull skates underneath and began to take a poor view of our conspicuous uniforms and skirts below the knee. Then I refused to wobble along the carpet with my ankles trying to turn in and so I struck out firmly and found it was quite easy as long as you walked lightly. Fortunately no-one took very much notice of us and we went round the rink to the other side and here Bennett, nobly, was the first to walk down the steps and onto the slippery surface and we followed holding the side for grim death. After slipping about a bit I began to find that the movements were very much the same as those of roller *skating and began very slowly to slide one foot out and then the other. Gradually I let go of the side and crossed over to the other. Suddenly a gong sounded, the rink was cleared, and we watched professionals waltzing with each other, round and round, backs upright, perfect ease and grace in every movement. The music changed and they fox trotted together then tango'd and rumba'd. The Waltz of the Flowers was played so I hummed it with Bennett as we swooped round together with arms crossed and hands joined. We stayed as long as we could, our faces were glowing and I've never enjoyed myself so much in all my life.'*

One of Ma's slippers had fallen off. I re-housed her foot and left.

6 December

A new lifer arrived today. I found him with his head in his hands which in turn were resting upon his wheeled table laid with knife, fork, spoon and serviette like all the wheeled tables set before the arm-chaired feeders who in turn were spaced equidistantly around the walls of the dining room. The newcomer had a full head of curly white hair, which looked incongruous and I recall Ma's view that luxuriant hair looked odd on older men. Like Father Brown with Just William's mop.
As so often lately, Ma was slumped to one side in her armchair, eyes and mouth wide open.
I suddenly had a fit of guilt at having deposited her here in this waiting room of old, malfunctioning humans. I countered by telling myself that stuck in her own home

corralled in her bedroom was, whatever way you looked at
it, worse.

There was life here, however clapped-out, and movement
and sound, and some linguistic engagement albeit from
foreign-voiced carers who were unintelligible and who
applied unnecessary (in Ma's case) volume to their
cajoling. The silence of her own home reinforced only that
the human condition is 'alone-ness'.

Lunch was served: escalope of veal with roast potatoes and
greens in front of the giant TV screen which was showing
a satellite map of the UK under a cold blue shadow as the
weather reader warned of more snow.

Ma yelped at the touch of my cold hand.

'You poor thing,' she said then slumped back in her chair.

'I'm always frightened,' she said.

'Of what?'

'What?'

'Don't worry.'

Beryl said the TV was always tuned to a channel she did
not want to watch.

'Haven't you a TV in your room?' I asked.

'I've got an apartment at the Elms,' she said.

I felt an irrational resentment towards the newcomer. I'd
got to know all the others – what they could comprehend
or not. I knew whether the easiest form of communication
– patronisation – could be applied or not. But in front of
this newcomer I had to exercise caution.

'I haven't ordered any of these meals,' said Beryl, as one
of the carers, who I think is gay, brought me lunch, too.
The pong, that is always apparent and the luncheon offered
me from a man in translucent blue plastic gloves drives me
out into the thaw. The lodge's red brick walls and pantile-
hung gables are dripping with melt water of the biggest

snowfall in England since 1965. I mentally subtract 45 years from Ma's life and picture her aged 42, hen-pecking Pa and toasting crumpets in front of our coke-fuelled brazier fire as my clothes, wet from sledging, dry out, while we watch Dr Who.

24 December

Ma has been offered a guaranteed share of £10,000 from Healthy Living Direct, the chance to purchase a 'delightful Christmas four piece spoon set', or clockwork racing pigeons or a Hilda Ogden apron 'to celebrate 50 years of Coronation Street.'
Christmas has arrived just in time.

25 December

Just-sleeping Lucy, swearing Charlie and hang-mouth Barbara are in the middle lounge with Ma and Beryl while The Man Who Would Be King is screened.
Evidence of a hearty Christmas lunch is manifest in Charlie's lower dentures which are laid out on his table covered in semi-masticated food. Ma is wearing chipped pink nail varnish. In all her life I only ever knew her to wear clear varnish. Cathy and I gave her a peck and wished her a Merry Christmas. I returned in the evening with the children and we opened her cards and presents. She loved the china German house, which lights up, that I bought her in the Dortmund Christmas market.

'That was somewhere on the Arterial Road, wasn't it?' Ma said looking at the lit windows.

2011

2 January

Ivy, the woman with the wristwatch on her ankle, was visited this afternoon by her nephew and his wife – both in their sixties. The woman made loud, well-enunciated statements, in a I-will-get-through-to-you-in-a-positive-manner style. She would be one of those who 'brushed up their French' before a day's shopping in Calais.
'I've got a bit of arthritis, Ivy.'
Ivy who smiles continuously, said nothing.
'But you haven't got arthritis, Ivy, which is good, isn't it?'
'Yes.'
'That's a large TV. That's bigger than ours, Alby, isn't it?'
'Yes it's bigger than ours.'
'And have you been watching the cricket, Ivy?'
'No. It's like watching paint drying for me.'
'But you like watching football, don't you?'
'Yes.'
'Alby likes watching football, don't you Alby?'
'Yes. I enjoy West Ham. I like West Ham. I just like to see good football.'
Ivy did not respond, but Lucy, stimulated by the chatter, and angled into a day position of comfort from her adjustable faux leather armchair, provided her own visitor.
'I thought my mother would be up here. Yes, so did I.'
'Cor, that's hot in here. Yes that is.'
'We can't get out this way. No we can't.'
'So we'll leave these frames here. Yes, we will.'

'And can you get a cup of tea when you want one?' asked Ivy's inquisitor.

'Yes,' said Ivy.

'Well that's good isn't it?'

'Yes.'

'And were you nice and cosy here during the snow?'

'Well I didn't see any of it.'

'No, but it was nice and warm in here?'

'Yes.'

'Well that's good isn't it? And have you got your own room?'

'Yes.'

'Well that's good. You deserve that Aunty Ivy,' said the nephew.

'Gawd, that's hot in here. Yes that is,' said Lucy, 'Is that raining? Yes I think that is. He's got an overcoat on. Yes he has.'

Even Barbara made a few groaning noises and waved her incongruously well-shaped hands in the air.

Ma's hands, the pink nail varnish, now almost worn off, fingered at a late Christmas card. She buckled up the letter, from some long-lost cousin, which came with it, and held it like a truncheon.

'Aunt Nora shared a room,' said Alby.

'She's died,' said Ivy.

'Yes, she died. But before that she was sharing a room. But you're not, so that's good isn't it?'

'You look very good,' said Alby's wife, 'what's your secret?'

'Accept life. If you don't like it and can change it do. If you can't, just get on with it.'

'That's good. Very good.'

Ma was now looking across the room with a puzzled frown from all the chatter. First of all disapprovingly, then smiling, her face like a weather clock changing with the sun and clouds passing through her mind.

'I'm the best,' she said conspiratorially to me as we held hands with her thumb rubbing the back of mine.

'I'm a BEST,' she then shouted her maiden name.

'How old is your Simon? Your grandson.'

'I don't know,' said Ivy.

'He's go to be in his forties, time goes so fast.'

The room had never witnessed such great interaction. Even old lizard-mouthed Betty had her lips pressed together in concentration.

'You've got to go on the bus, haven't you? Yes I have. I'll go to bed. Yes so will I. We'll go from here in a minute. Yes we will,' Lucy was sitting up from her chair. 'My legs are wet. Yes so are mine. Right ready, steady go. Yes I'm going. Yes so am I.'

And Lucy with her alter-ego edged herself to the front of her chair and started to push against the arms.

'No stay there, Lucy,' said a passing carer.

'What? What's she say?'

'I said stay there Lucy, where are you going?'

'I'm going home.'

'No, home too far, Lucy, there are no bus.'

Old Joan woke up and I asked her if she was all right.

'All the better for seeing you,' she said through three teeth.

'My husband was a sailor.'

'Is he still alive?'

'Yes.'

'Where is he now? Still local?'

'Don't know.'

She did not know where her husband was but she still held him unconditionally in memory.

'All the nice girls like a sailor. All the nice girls like a tar,' she recited, 'so I must have been a nice girl,' then she nodded off.

Clifford telephoned yesterday and told Cathy he had suffered a nervous breakdown.

6 January

New Year chance of easy money from Healthy Living: a £25,000 prize draw entry if Ma buys a talking thermometer, a two-sided mirror or a reversible hood wrap.

8 January

Ma is slumped in her chair as Beryl is rubbing her left hand. I think it's more companionship in the abyss than anything Sapphic.

'They've all gone barmy,' was the only complete sentence I received until I was about to depart when Ma said: 'If you're not here when I want you there'll be trouble,' delivered with a jester's smile.

She seemed tired and said so.

Lucy was having her normal chat with herself and refused to take her 'meds' or eat her ham sandwiches and Swiss roll.

Bettine said: 'Move the door,' to Joan.

'What?'

'Close the door.'
'I don't need to close the door I've got nothing to hide.'
'Nor've I,' said Bettine.
'Oh my leg,' said Ma.
'Which one?' asked Beryl.
Ma did not answer.
Barbara gurgled as the last spoonful of carer-fed tomato soup went down.
Lucy muttered.
Bettine said: 'Leg?'
Joan went to sleep.
In came Ivy with the perma-smile.
Ma has only been toying with her food over the last few days until today when she ate her ham sandwiches plus one of Beryl's.
Bettine drummed her fingernails on the Formica topped wheel-table.
Beryl said: 'Someone's tapping on the window. Anyone can. You don't need a licence for that.'

14 January

Writing in The Independent, journalist Johann Hari reports on the horrific abuse his grandmother suffered in two care homes during the last decade of her life and how the Care Quality Commission's inspectors are to be cut back.
Under the headline Age Timebomb, Elderly Britain in numbers, the article cites some arresting statistics:
*10 million Britons aged over 65
*398,000 Britons in long-term care who are over 65
*474,000 total number of places in residential care homes
*1.4 million is the number of Britons aged over 85 and 87,900 is the number of centenarians expected by 2034.

He writes that bank bailouts will come from cutting many services and how he heard Bob Diamond, head of Barclays, on the radio 'bragging about how bankers should be rewarded,' while clearing through his grandmother's 'few possessions'.

He concludes: 'So in 2011, to reward the people who crashed the world economy, we are punishing the people who saved the world from the Nazis.'

23 April 1943

'Lieutenant John Vallier, who has only been commissioned six months, came over to play on the Mansion piano. He told me the reason for his broken nose and unconsciousness when brought in here. He fell over a cliff during manoeuvres at Fort William – a sergeant picked him up and turned him over – his face covered in mud and blood. "Gawd he's dead" said the sergeant at which Vallier opened his eyes and said: "Indeed I'm not"!

He is small and dark with white teeth and friendly, smiling eyes and surprisingly for one so clever and surrounded always by an admiring audience, not in the least conceited. I asked him to play Albeniz's Tango, and Falla's Ritual Fire Dance, and at Bennett's request he played the Blue Danube. He has no music sheets and hasn't practised for four years. Actually he is professional but won't tell what name he uses. Paderewski is his hero, his mother was one of his first pupils, years ago. Instead of declaring that "music has always been my one thought" etc, he told us he was simply made to practice when young and then it grew on him.

*He put everyone at ease by asking us to smoke if we
wished. He also played Toccata & Fugue, but the thing I
enjoyed most was Beethoven's Sonata in C. Rhoda used to
play this.
Then followed a composition of his own, a sonata, written
during the London and Plymouth blitzes. In three
movements. The first described, he said, the courage of the
British people, their unruffled demeanour whatever
happened. I didn't think it did anything of the sort but it
was a lovely movement; then followed a quick movement,
lively and very light and fast. He called it his Irish
movement. He saw three Irish children playing with
marbles in the streets during a blitz and noticed how their
mother was more concerned about fetching them to bed
than she was about bombs falling. The last movement was
slow and quiet, to represent the desolation of smashed
houses and ruined buildings after the raid.
I had to go for it was 10 past four and I was on teas and so
missed all his Chopin preludes.'*

Pinned in Ma's diary is a photograph of John Vallier in his
Army uniform. On the back he has written:

'To Nancy, a sweet girl who made life at Shenley very
happy.

Your friend,

John Vallier, August 1943.'

I then Google this man and under the category Keyboard
Giants discover he was a virtuoso classical pianist,
composer and child prodigy.

15 January

Eight old ladies in a room. They are today joined by a newcomer under a blanket who is staring nowhere, the eyes vacant because there's nothing externally more important to concentrate on anymore than her own-ness. Fish and chips are being served for lunch as I sit with Ma to my right and Joan to Ma's right. It means that my chat with Joan cuts straight across Ma.

Joan reveals that she was from West Ham. Her mother died of breast cancer when she was just four and so she was 'dragged up' by her aunt.

'My mother's sister. And her husband. Bastard,' the word brought us all up fast, 'He abused me. If he was here now I would,' she raised her knife greasy with cod batter, 'pull it out of his trousers and cut it off. It sounds crude but I would do it.'

She told me she had found out where his grave was and gone and spat on it.

'I can't stand cheese,' Ma suddenly said in the middle of Joan's confession, desperate to join in the conversation even if only armed with a non-sequitur.

Joan then repeated her story. Several times.

'I didn't have a happy childhood and I said if I get married and have children I'll love them to pieces. I'll give them the love I never had.'

She said her uncle had told her she'd go to prison if she said anything. 'I was terrified.'

She then continued with her fish and chips.

Joan has three daughters and told me they do visit although I've never seen them.

Ma, halfway through a beaker of liquidised food spilt some on her wheeled table. I mopped it up with a piece of tissue paper and left the 'morsel' of damp paper on the table. After 10 minutes she attempted to eat that as well.

23 January

Beryl is in an agitated mood. Hands shaking she accused the carers of being the 'Gestapo.'

'I'm very frightened here. They suppress you.'

'What physically?' I asked thinking the bathing issue had raised its head again.

'Yes, but mentally, too, eventually. I mean there's no-one else to turn to.'

I realised my interview technique lacked the probity of a detective's: I'd given her the answer in the question.

Ma picked up on the dissent. Three Filipino carers with unfortunately high-pitched voices and speaking with unnecessary volume in a bid to make their heavily accented English understood succeeded only in getting my mother to tell one of them to 'Piss off.' I'd never heard her use that phrase before.

She shrugged off the command with laughter: they all do, as the next utterance is just as likely to be friendly.

For example one carer couple who are married, Alex and Ethel, next bent down and sang a duet to Lucy: 'I do like that doggy in the Window.'

At which Lucy who had been dozing, woke up and waved at my mother who then said: 'Hello dear. What drivel,' to much laughter all round.

But no-one could appease Beryl, she accused the staff of lacing the orange cordial with tranquillisers and when one

Filipino, with a reedy voice started calling my mother, 'Nan, nan,' Beryl intervened: 'What's that? A goat?' Another carer tried zipping up Beryl's cardigan. Beryl unzipped it.

Ma had said when I arrived: 'I didn't think I was ever going to see you again.'

And as I left she told me to come back.

Beryl added: 'I shall end up committing murder. I was independent, I brought up four children, I had a house, now I've got nothing.'

As I left the room Alex told me that every night Ma is taken up to her room she says: 'Rhoda, are you there?'

30 January

The usual occupants, sat upright, arms placed on armrests, in their comfort thrones, backs to the wall, like the stone statues in the Valley of the Kings.

Something was missing in the 'middle room', there was no TV.

Suddenly on hearing my voice one of the Pharoahs spoke: 'Can you have a word with them? It hasn't been on for two days.' It was Joan.

'Perhaps they're saving on power costs,' I said.

'No. Power cuts don't affect the telly, do they?' she countered.

Ma's utterings are now entirely disconnected or at least appear so to anyone outside her mind.

'If I so much as,' she said, then, later: 'for Heaven's sake,' then, later still: 'Oh, good eat the lot. I'm not very.'

They seem to be the oral representation of assertion: the body's frail, the mind is broken, but the attitude is still there. The fight must be carried to the outside world. The liberty takers must be kept at bay.

Sometimes they register irrational anger: 'Stop banging that door, cheek.'

Ivy was sat next to Ma and offered me her seat.

'Is it your sister?' she asked.

Joan then caught my attention again as a carer, Ethel, entered the room. I passed on her request for the TV to be switched on.

The carer went to find the remote and Beryl told me how she'd been reprimanded for doing the same thing.

Ma, said: 'I haven't a clue.'

The TV crackled into life with a programme called Wife Swap and within a few minutes Joan was asleep, satisfied her needs had been met.

'Are you all right, Nan?' said Ethel.

'Yes, dear.'

Beryl said to Bettine: 'Your nan was my nan,' I think.

Ma, said: 'I knew it wouldn't last,' as she tried to extract a tissue from a cardboard box. I held the box so she could extricate one. 'Don't pinch all of it. Not that I like them,' then held the box to her nose and sniffed it.

'It's awful.'

Beryl then complained again to me about the way she perceives she is manhandled.

'I think they are just concerned you might fall over,' I said.

'Oh, I don't think so – that would be just another one gone,' she said chillingly, then reconsidered and added: 'On the other hand they don't want to get rid of their clients.'

'Who are they?' asked Ma.

'What?' said Beryl.

'I don't know. I don't know what it means,' said Ma,
'God, she's a funny woman. Where's your one, two, three,
four?'
Then challenging: 'Don't think I'm not coming up. We're
all going to die. This is where I went to the Girl Guides.'
Then reflectively: 'Damn and blast.'
All uttered from a mouth now with no upper denture. The
home had said the plate was hurting her mouth and that a
visit to the dentist should be organised. If anything was
going to seem like a potential homicide, then a man in a
white coat looming over a forced open mouth with tools
was going to fit the bill. In any case without the plate she
was eating again and even her appearance hadn't altered,
at least when her mouth was closed. Her high cheek bones,
and strong jawline held her face in place.
'Who does? Nancy, Rhoda?' something in Wife Swap had
sparked her off.
Then to me: 'Do what you like.'
Me: 'I will.'
Ma then pulls a face of mock disapproval, 'You are funny,
Dicky.'
'I know.'
'I love you. I wish you'd get married.'
'I am.'
'Blast.'
'I can't marry my mother can I?'
'And who's that?'
'You.'
'Oo-eer.'
Then she laughed a lot, but said: 'Life used to be funny but
not anymore.'

25 February 1943

'In King George V Hall, Variety Concert Entitled "The Gay Forties" Presented by The Burnt Oak Players.

'Well – the concert was the FUNNIEST thing I've ever seen IN ALL MY LIFE!!!!!!!! It was so AWFUL that it was simply a shriek. It began with a row of chorus girls in yellow sacks and black silk stockings, no wonder, said Harrison, they called themselves the Gay Forties for they were grey-haired and plump to say the least. They reappeared in black shawls and Spanish hats with flowers and sang a song about Marharita, when this had finished there was half an hour pause before a funny (?) turn came on. Three ancient men, one with a trumpet, and a little girl accompanying them at the piano, sang a song about dictators and every-time Hitler's name was mentioned the trumpeter blew a raspberry which was, of course, nothing to what the audience blew when they eventually went off. The audience roared all the way through but made up for their rudeness by applauding each item madly, they simply had to let off steam somehow. There was another half hour's pause and an item called "Over the garden wall" was announced. The curtains were pulled halfway to reveal a clothes line and two woman's voices emerged at each side, we couldn't see them, we couldn't hear them, not one word could be distinguished from another so whilst all this muttering was going on, the players being none the wiser, the audience took to its own resources, some sang, most talked, quite a few went out and Harrison gave me a Milky Way and showed me a news cutting of his wedding.
The curtains went up and 'Cinderella' was announced. The ugly sisters were ugly to the point of being hideous,

Cinderella was 50-odd and grey-haired, tall and skinny. Prince Charming was 40, parrot-nosed and mouse-voiced and rather short, Buttons was a hefty woman, bursting out of her clothes. If it had been just a tiny bit better than it was, it would have been boring, as it was, nothing could have been made more humorous. The men called out, whistled and hooted. I believe it even dawned in the players' heads that they were being laughed at. The funny (?) turn came on again this time to sing some funny Victorian songs. The men cat-called, booed, cheered and yelled, rang bicycle bells and tooted horns and then struck "I Yi Yippy" when they got sick of shouting. So the funny turn went and the poor little girl at the piano who hadn't played a single note followed them off looking very dazed. 'I think even we had had enough by then and we went before it finished.'

Ma spotted her soft toy dogs under the TV screen, 'That dear cat, I put it up there. I do wish someone would.'
On the way out I joked to one of the carers that maybe someone else could use Ma's denture.
'No, we have it in a pot, don't worry.'
My attempt at stand-up suitably deflated I departed.

6 February

Ma is in bed at 17.00 happily chortling at her portable TV which is showing Antiques Roadshow.
'I love you. I wish I could marry you. But I can't.'
'You can't marry your son, Ma.'
'I can. I can do what I like.'
Some white-haired expert floats into view on the TV.

'Do you remember that expert? Walter?'

'No, why? You haven't got any antiques.'

'Yes, I have I've got a bagful.'

'Let me have them.'

'No you're not having them. Anyway I don't know where they are so hard luck,' she said with much more chortling.

13 February

A pop group, Eyes Wide Shut, are on the TV. It's 10.30 and Ma is toying with cold morsels of sausage and a whole leathery fried egg, as she taps her fork on her plate to the band.

She suddenly grabbed the bowl of grapefruit segments and spilled the juice down her bib. I put it back on the wheeled table and guided her fork into a segment. With help from a teaspoon she managed to put it in her mouth. A carer told me this morning they did not attempt to feed her now because she would then refuse to eat at all.

'You've got a cold. Don't,' she suddenly said.

Lucy was still holding her one woman dialogue, albeit now more quietly and more as if by rote.

I told my mother Cathy sends her love.

She looked me in the eye: 'Thank-you.'

'She will come and see you soon.'

'No she won't. Is that true?'

'She will, she's just been busy with Richard,' I said, 'are you OK?'

'No', she said and laughed.

Ma's contrariness is part of her make-up. She doesn't actually mean to be negative, but senses patronisation a mile away and wards it off immediately. She knows

instinctively that to succumb to being patronised is final.
It's being mentally smothered.

'Oh well, I'm going now.'

'Good-bye, dear,' she says with courage. There's an
inevitable resignation. The good-bye has to happen. She
knows it and allows for it, like a soldier.

'I just want to see you.'

We embrace and air kiss. Ma in her usual exaggerated
manner.

Then 'Oo-eer,' at how soppy we're being, and then a belly
laugh, her eyes full of knowing laughter. I leave.

20 February

'Fish live in their own poo,' said a man on the giant TV,
which was screening a programme about defecating
whales. I looked around the room. Joan was crumpled in
sleep, Betty also, Lucy had stopped talking and was staring
at the floor, Barbara was lying on her back in her chair
looking as though she were contemplating the crucifixion
while being crucified herself.

'What a job, collecting whale snot,' said the TV presenter
as a marine biologist checked the exhaled air from a
beluga whale.

Beryl walked in and was told by a carer, pointing across
the room, to sit down.

'But that's a table,' she says like a smart-arsed schoolgirl,
looking at me, but no longer recognising me.

I feel sad. Beryl was the one person I could have a chat
with. A surreal chat for sure, but one which satisfied the
need for communication, however skewed.

I knew, too, that our patter stimulated Ma, who felt empowered by eavesdropping even if it was incomprehensible.

Ma is looking very well, good colour, bright eyes.

All the occupants of the room, including me, missed the link, but the next subject broadcast in the TV magazine programme is about building Bentley motor-cars in Crewe and footage of the vehicle's introduction in the 1920s.

'The Roaring Twenties,' I said, 'that's when you were born.'

'Why?'

After holding Ma's hand for a while she said: 'Shall I put them away, my hands? I don't want them mixed up.' Rapidly changing camera shots and loud rock music prevent any focus on the giant TV screen as young men and women are set a 'challenge' to photograph an 'iconic' image of South Africa apparently to extol the virtues of new technology.

'You must be awfully bored with me because I'm always tocking and bocking,' Ma said.

26 February

It's afternoon but already Ma's in bed watching TV having been freshly showered following a nappy failure.

'All I want in my life is to go back to England.' Thanks to the Filipino staff, Westcliff Lodge must seem like a small guest house in Manila, not that Ma knows where Manila is, but anyway it must seem 'foreign' to her. Different, a bit like Germany was just before the war.

'I do wish I'd never come.'

She looked at Cathy when I was talking or at me when Cathy was talking.

'I don't know if I did right or wrong,' she continued, 'I'm never satisfied with anything. You see there again I don't know what to say next.'

Her room is warm and peaceful, cosy.

The magnolia wallpaper must seem reassuring. The white wardrobe, white chest of drawers, table and three chairs. The Rupert calendar hanging by the en-suite loo. The bed in the corner. Stilled life. All is at rest.

But there was another colour once:

12 January 1989

'Phone call to say curtains ready to collect.

Bedroom carpet is rather a strange pink but unfortunately not in the least worn so no excuse to get rid of it and have lovely plain mushroom one with which anything would go. Was not in the least surprised to find the curtains were not the ones I had chosen. The assistant was horrified and rushed off to the manager's office and came back with the message suggesting we took them home to see if they were 'any good' if so he would of course reduce the price, if not they would immediately start cutting out the ones I had ordered.

Back at home the phone rang it was the poor assistant again saying that they would be reduced by £45 if I did decide to keep them. Said I would let him know tomorrow after seeing them in daylight.

13 January 1989

'Curtains proved very satisfactory and much nicer than the ones I'd chosen, very pretty with subdued pattern of pink foliage and the carpet appears to have faded into the background.'

Even the damnable clock has stopped at quarter to nine for the last few months, its battery dead.

Cathy thought Ma was tired, trying to converse more of a struggle than usual.

She put Swan Lake on her video recorder and Ma started to hum along, then whistle to it.

'I don't want you to go.'

'Is that a fire?'

'No it's the TV,' Cathy answered.

'A horse fell over, I think,' said Ma and laughed.

'It was a nice surprise,' said Ma, as we left, 'Are they all mad here?'

Ranting Charles has died.

8 March

Some new occupants have arrived and Ma is sitting next to Connie, a woman with eyelids like a camel, making it impossible to tell if she's awake or not. And on her right side sits a long-legged man called Ron with whom she was holding hands until he had a fit of coughing and she quickly withdrew.

She didn't recognise me although I was waving from two chairs' distance, but she halted momentarily when I said 'Ma?' The voice and voices she still does recognise.

I recall how the Ghanaian carer, Daniel, and Ma got on famously. I had been concerned that the received racism of her generation, would be a problem, but good breeding prevented her from actually registering any complaint and as soon as she heard his voice, she understood his intelligence and sensed his good nature and no longer noticed the colour of his skin. No-one notices what coat you're wearing when discussing the cold.

Ma has more mail. Her new bus pass has arrived, valid until 2016.

15 March

'She's upstairs. We had to give her a shower. She was a bit smelly,' announced Tim, the gay Filipino carer, who has dyed his black hair auburn, as I came through the door.

Ma, said: 'Is that Monty?' Monty Wood was the long-deceased husband of her cousin Marjorie. He was an authoritarian figure, a successful self-made businessman in the car tyre trade with a hard nose for a deal and a no-nonsense approach. He would be the sort of person you'd go to in a crisis.

'No,' I said.

'Well who?'

'Dicky.'

This sparked off a bout of tearless sobbing, the talk of devils and bitches and 'You don't know what I've been through.'

But whatever the means, the end was an old lady smelling sweetly of talcum powder, dressed in a clean nightie and sitting in a clean, warm bed.

I was still worried. Ma never lies, ever. But then so much of what she actually utters is confused, and hallucinatory. But then again there was Beryl's testimony. But, she, too, is a reactor short of a fuel rod...

The early evening twilight was playing on Ma's cheeks, and over her freshly-shampooed white hair combed back from her face.

I quietly explained that she required assistance when taking a shower.

'Oh, so they had to do it?'

'Yes.'

She then calmed down and was chatting away about how the tide had gone out and she couldn't therefore take a sea bathe, about how some 'ghastly hag' required elocution lessons: this phrase now beyond her she acted it out with the role of a posh-voiced teacher talking to a glottally-stopped pupil.

'I'm becoming speechless,' she said.

I spoke to the Filipino carer with the birth mark on her left cheek who told me they'd showered Ma twice as she had been 'playing' with her faeces. She has grown accustomed to being shackled into the hoist, which lifts her from static to wheeled chair and then again from wheel-chair to bath, and now quite enjoys the ride, although she still shouts. The carer told me how Daniel has now taken to drinking apple juice as it is thought it combats dementia.

I left and drove down to watch dusk fall over Chalkwell Beach. The high tide was just about to turn. Tiny wavelets licked against the shore like a cat at milk. The lights of Kent smeared down and over the flat sea as a wet, lowering sky of grey cloud compressed a pink smear of sundown over Canvey Island, which was peppered with orange lights. The lights of a train arrowed along the shoreline railway track. I turned and walked back up the beach, the rain-wet pebbles of which, glistened under the tall street lamps of the promenade. I wondered how much wear they'd taken since Ma's teenage feet negotiated them for her swims.

The benign River Thames was feared by one of the Filipino carers who saw in its vastness and proximity to low-lying coast, only the potential destruction that the tsunamis of her native land could wreak.

The silhouette of a container ship slipped up river.

21 March

Seven old ladies were lined up against the walls in their arm-chairs while young women paraded on the giant TV screen in a programme called Take Me Out. Young men arrived on a stage via a tubular-shaped lift and then voted for the woman who could become the 'love of his life' before being sent on a 'luxury holiday' to produce love or war.

Toothless Joan looked 20 years younger in the spring light, not because of Take Me Out, but because of a black kitten adopted by the home, which she spent an hour stroking on her lap.

Joan, poor, old abused Joan, was smiling. Bettine looked younger, too,

'Yeah all right, mate,' she said when I asked her how she was.

Beryl, sadly, is losing the plot. It would seem the finer the intellect the greater is the impact of institutionalisation upon it.

Lucy was being Lucy and talking to and responding to herself and also refusing to eat, her faux leather chair lowered to the level of a dentist's chair to, in the first instance, prevent her escaping to catch a bus, and later to allow a carer to run liquid food into her mouth via a baby bottle.

'No, you must swallow, Lucy.'

Ron, the only male, waved in a friendly way and gestured for me to come in when he saw me in the doorway, before tucking into his oxtail soup and corned beef sandwiches.

Ma, sitting next to him seems truncated as though her torso has shrunk and her legs are joined to her chest. Her blue eyes were clear and she conducted the dramatic tattoo from an automobile commercial by waving half a cheese sandwich as a baton. Every time she caught sight of it – the sandwich – was like a new experience.

Ivy was still smiling, this time smiling at the TV, her wristwatch purring contentedly, marking time, around her ankle.

Connie, from beneath her hooded eyes and lank fringe suddenly declared: 'I'm a bit mutton Jeff,' as she struggled to join the TV audience.

I reassured her by explaining the volume was low, which it was.

As I left I passed the ground floor bedroom of Betty. The door was open and she lay in bed her mouth still agape. We exchanged friendly waves.

Ma's post continues to arrive faithfully.

She's been offered the chance to purchase a crystal-studded Westie pendant, a Labrador puppy painting by numbers and a weather resistant, polyresin 'Mrs Bunny and Her Babies' for the garden, where 'you can almost see their little noses twitching as they peep through the foliage.'

It seems the mail order aficionados are determined to comfort their customers in their second childhood if not actually lead them to it.

Meanwhile the Affordable Choices Brochure offers videos on how to stay young and how to improve your memory, although from the footwear on offer it's clear that staying young does not necessarily include sexual intercourse: washable towelling slippers, cushionflex elasticated sandals, fuller fitting foam-padded 'day-shoes', wider comfort, lace-ups available only in grey, stunning 'punched detail' sandal in Burgundy and double-buckled, wedge-sole, peep-toe sandals in beige. Summer's on the way.

24 March

A domestic assistant at the lodge kindly took Ma to the doctor to collect the result of a blood test that determined she has high cholesterol levels and she is now taking medication for this. Hearing his male voice Ma said: 'Dicky is that you?' The poor fellow is now stuck with the name.

27 March

Connie must have been unattainable once. Tall and slim with a crop of now grey, but lustrous hair, she has heavy-lidded eyes and long, slender fingers. But now she leans forward, half asleep rattling her nails on her spectacle case, her face dissolving into a hanging sack of necks and chins. Ma was as bright as a button today. Newly-painted, garish, red nails. Her face like a child's: receptive with clear blue eyes. She laughed, and among her usual disjointed utterances even managed the odd sentence that actually made sense.

'Yes, they are aren't they,' she said when I commented on the redness of her nails.

When Barbara started gurgling and pushing out her right arm as if to slowly punch something, Ma copied the action. Lucy, said: 'I'm going to lie down. Yes so am I.'

Betty kept watching me, fishing for a smile. She has a lovely smile and one that obliges her to close her gaping mouth. There is nothing lascivious in her engagement she just wants to make contact.

Ivy, even dozing, had a smile on her face. She is so doggedly positive it has become second nature.

Lucy's not a smiler, although I doubt she's ever been. She's a 'I demand my rights' type or would have been once. A working class woman in a mock-leather chair, she was a woman who had always bettered herself, at least materially-speaking.

She would have been quick to find fault, only now her daughter does it for her instead.

I tried out some names on Ma.

Mollie Koch, an old Jewish friend.

'I never see her.'

Diana, her daughter.

'Oh she's barmy, she never does anything.'

Marjorie, her cousin.

'I had a good cry over Marjorie as she was so nice.'

Rhoda, her sister.

No response.

Bill, her brother-in-law.

'Poor Bill, he's dead.'

May and Lucy, the two old aunts she was very fond of. I
said they shared a bungalow near Belfairs Wood.
'No you've got that wrong.'
Herbert Best, her father. I told her what she'd once told me
that in summer he went for a swim in the sea before
catching a train to the City.
'Did he?' she said with astonishment.
Ethel Best, her mother. 'I think she knew them all,' I said.
'Oh, yes, of course she did.'
Aunty Bel, a deputy headmistress, from Ilford, her
mother's sister and her companion Aunt Anne.
No response.

28 March

Is love guilt? Is love only felt remotely? Why is love
difficult to express? Why is loved craved for? In the end is
love just memory? A rose-tinted sentimentality after the
rough-edged reality has been smoothed off by times'
sands?

23 April

It's Easter Sunday and the temperature in Ma's room is 29
degrees centigrade.
'Can't we get rid of the smell in Grandma's room?' asks
Richard as we leave some cuttings of her favourite Banksia
rose in a vase. But the Westcliff Lodge 'pong', while
benign compared with most multiple-occupancy homes, is
all -pervasive.

Cathy, Richard and I wheeled Ma along the seafront to Chalkwell for an ice-cream. She was pleased to get outside until we rolled her along Victory Path, the wooded footpath which runs along a section of the Southend-Fenchurch Street railway track, between the embankment and several tennis courts, where she alternately said the light was 'dreadful' or 'marvellous' as we flitted in and out of the shade.

Upon our return to the home Joan was quite aggressive: 'You've got a nice, little, cushy number here,' she told me, 'but I'm going to get out and I'm going to report you. I'm going to get you into trouble. It's all very well you saying "Oh dear". You're not taking a blind bit of notice of me.' Lucy's daughter broke off some of her mother's Easter chocolate egg, before changing her mind and packing it away.

'It's too hot to leave it here. I don't think she knows who we are anymore,' she said before going into a long diatribe about the traffic congestion and a discussion with herself about which would be the best route home. Genetic revenge.

Ma was genuinely sad when we got up to go.

'All right, dear,' she said with resignation. It's easier to leave the room when her eyes aren't on you. That said, her eyes now, appear hollow. You search them for something known, for something being registered, for them to be observing. But it's not there. The vacuity can only be dispelled after a period of interaction. Once I've gone she locks out.

30 April

Triangular red, white and blue plastic flags are still draped over the large double-gable of Westcliff Lodge, yet to be removed to mark yesterday's wedding of Prince William and Kate Middleton.

Inside, the curtains are drawn in the middle room where Ma is sat alone against the west wall, neatly stacked in with a row of empty armchairs all with their lap tables drawn neatly in. Opposite are sat, like a panel of interrogators, smiling Ivy, three-toothed Joan and sardonic Beryl. Against the south wall in her normal position, is Lucy.

Joan berates me for suggesting they were given champagne yesterday: 'Fizzy wine,' she said, this was confirmed by Irene who told me Ma had two glasses. 'We gave them flags to wave and there was a cake with William and Kate on it,' she said.

Today the wedding is over and the giant TV drones instead with monotonous football results.

25 April 1943

About three o'clock I went to the hall and could hear the piano being played; through the sitting room to the music room and there was Vallier, and on the couch was an Austrian girl with fuzzy hair dressed in those awful "blues" the ATS patients have to wear. She was from Ward 18. I leant on the piano. Could he play the Emperor Concerto? He could and played the 1st movement, also Rachmaninov's 2nd, and Schumann's 2nd. He was upset over the announcement in England of Paderewski's death. It was cold and indifferent as was Rachmaninov's. Had it been England's champion footballer there would have been long, regretful speeches in the news.

Ma picks up her three-sandwich supper in one go and allows a carer to prize them from her to feed her one at a time.

'I love you, Dicky.'

'I love you, too.'

She gives me a beaming smile.

Later as she grips my right hand: 'I'm very fond of you, Dicky,' perhaps dispensing patronage is the last of her power.

At least it means she can form phrases still and at appropriate times. But apart from that I could get no sense from her at all and so instead spoke with Beryl, Joan and Ivy.

Joan said she was 'frightened' because she can't remember anything: why she's here, who brought her here, her age.

'I can only remember my name, Joan Murray.'

I told her I knew her and had spoken to her many times. At this she was surprised.

Ma kept slumping over on her right side but never closed her eyes and was quick to become alert again for no apparent reason.

'I'm off, Ma. Cheerio.'

'Yes, OK, dear,' she said rattily as I'd forced an acknowledged good-bye.

7 May

Lucy's daughter hands her mother a biscuit from hands with intricately painted nails. They have a pink base with a Japanese-style filigree pattern over the top. They are a work of great kitsch and must have taken hours for someone else to do. They contrast markedly with her mother's toe-nails: long, thick, scalloped and ridged yellow blades which stick up at crazy angles from her sandals.

Lucy sucks on the biscuit as her daughter recounts her day in high-pitched sentences which she converts, irritatingly, into rhetoric with the addition of 'Yeah?' at the end of each.

I dread Ma listening in and am not surprised when she starts parroting the daughter's speech pattern.

The daughter throws Ma a suspicious look, but the situation is saved by Beryl who starts to shake, leans over and emits a brown gush of vomit all over the long-suffering, not-quite, Paisley carpet.

Lucy instinctively draws up her bare, red-scabbed shins and her daughter starts to tell me instead about her son who has just gone to the loo. 'He's brain-damaged and was born with a hole in his heart, but he's 41 now and handles it well,' she said, 'he's coming back. I won't talk about it, he doesn't like me talking about it.'

Suddenly I feel Lucy's daughter has every right to indulge herself in ridiculous nail-painting.

As her son settles down beside her she continues: 'I am here today because my son lives next door and on a Saturday I can knock off two visits in one.'

'That's Rhoda's clock,' Ma says suddenly looking at the large clock on the wall.

Cathy and I leave.

'I'll see you soon.'

'When?'

'Later.'

8 May

I plucked a whisker from Ma's chin, 'Be careful, Clifford, that hurt.'

I tried to scrape a dropping of soup from her blouse with a spoon, she became agitated and aggressive, 'No don't Clifford, I'll murder you,' and pulled her blouse away.

I had bought a new trilby hat which fell off my chair arm and Lucy picked it up. A moment of communication?

'Go on, Lucy, try it on.'

She did and we all applauded.

'That's new, Lucy,' she said, 'Yes, I know that is. You can wear that tonight and take Connie out,' she added.

I retrieved it and put it on.

Lucy now noticed it was on the correct way round, although how she knew she had it on back to front is anybody's guess.

She tried it on again, this time pulling it down low over her permed, white hair.

'Lucy, the gangster's moll,' I said, but no-one was interested second time round.

Beryl started singing, 'Sailors on the ocean go bob, bob, bob,' and waved her hand, 'I don't know the rest. Does anyone know the rest?'

No-one did, 'I remember it as a little girl.'

She then started singing the Grand Old Duke of York. 'I'm just trying to cheer you up. Or maybe I'll make you cry.'

I shook them all by the hand and waved before leaving.

'You nearly lost that,' said Ivy, smiling as usual, and referring to my hat.

10 May

Outside the room, close to the window, the police are shouting. We can hear every word and lie silently in the dark, holding our breath, not quite sure whether this is because we want to hear what's going on, or in case of being discovered. They are making arrests. 'Come on Quasimodo,' one officer shouts. Our room is dark and then the light is in the room. A voluptuous, pink figure, naked and perspiring is in the bed. On my bed. I beat her off with the sole of a sandal. As I hit her wet skin I think, 'Christ that must hurt.' It is my mother and I wake up. It's 00.41, a new day marked with an unfathomable dream.

'Easy-to-lay, no-spill edging. Pebbles make a very attractive feature in a garden, but can be a nuisance as they move and can look untidy,' Mother's latest mail shot announces. 'Effortlessly crack eggs with one motion, without getting any bits of shell on your food,' with an 'egg cracker and separator.' Also 'an attractive, bendy, lightweight "normal looking" shoe with a hidden secret; a super stretch upper made from Elastane.'

These shoes, a wonder of ergonomics, which don't look as though they could bend, are for those who suffer from 'awkward or swollen feet, bunions or corns,' or those whose 'feet change shape during the day.' The bendy boots will 'conform to the contours of your feet yet when you remove them they will immediately return to their original shape.' Such distortions can be shod in beige and black.

From Stanford-le-Hope to Harwich powerful dredgers are carving a trench in the sea-bed, hoovering up sole nurseries, and ancient wreck artefacts to accommodate the giant container ships from China bringing in the Elastane shoes; loaded to their marks with England's terra firma to be.

12 May

Subject: PRIVATE AND CONFIDENTIAL – Matters of concern, the email began.

'Hi Dickie

I hope you and Cathy are well.

It pains me to say that I have received an allegation of abuse about a carer at Westcliff Lodge concerning the care of Nancy. A colleague has informed me the carer deliberately stood on Nancy's foot. The carer in question has been suspended and I have called the Police to investigate. Disciplinary proceedings are underway with a view to dismissal.

Needless to say I am mortified that anyone in my employ would be capable of such actions and to someone as lovely and vulnerable as Nancy. Please except (sic) my heart felt apologies for any pain or suffering Nancy experienced, on Nancy's behalf. She is a wonderful person and I would never knowingly allow anyone to ill treat her in any way. I believe the Police intend to arrest the carer concerned and prosecute her.

If you would like to talk to me in more detail, please ring me at any time.

Kind regards,

Stephanie Mirams,
Manager.'

So there it was in black and white, testimony that not all claims the staff act like the 'Gestapo' are hallucinatory. I could imagine the situation: a carer trying to feed Ma, at a pace or with a method not to her liking and Ma's aggressive reaction and the carer's loss of patience.
When I went to see her that day she thought I'd been to visit her mother.
'How's mummy?'
'Fine.'
'Good.'
'I suppose you want to dash off as usual.'
I mentioned the email I'd received and told Ma the police were dealing with the affair.
'I didn't know what to say to the carers,' I added, 'but are they being nice?'
'No,' she said.
I lifted the bedclothes to look at her feet, no sign of injury. No need yet for Elastane shoes.
'Don't worry,' she said.
'I do worry, Ma, if something's wrong.'
'Where's the doggies?' I found a soft toy and gave it to her to cuddle, 'Hello diddams, are you all right? "Yis'" she answered on the toy's behalf, then added: 'how daft!' and laughed at herself.
'He's like Buster,' referring to her childhood dog, I said. I have given up trying to install reality. It seems kinder just to go along with delusion.

'Yes, he is.'

She put the toy down and looked far away.

'I must get wet again,' she said.

'What in summer rain?'

'Yes.'

Cathy and I then drove to Shenley Park in Hertfordshire where Ma worked as a VAD nurse.

I was, again, 'being' her memory, trying to empathise with events in her past life in order to try and bring them back to her.

Shenley Park is now a place where the public roam looking at the garden and drinking tea. It's hidden in narrow lanes with overhanging trees, disembodied now from the rest of Hertfordshire, by the M25 which whooses by, and corralled instead by the same highway into a leafy part of north London.

A Scandinavian-style tea room with bare timbers was full of young families, eating sandwiches, drinking juices and chatting.

5 August 1943

'Tomorrow there is to be an inventory before Sister Luxton finally goes. Captain Dady, chief of the Pack Stores, comes around accompanied by Corporal Lloyd who is well known for his meanness and the two of them will try to confiscate anything and everything they can lay their hands on.'

6 August 1943

'Everyone towards 11 am began to rush round hiding things. Two brooms were locked in the coal hole because

they were our own and we did not want them put down on Lloyd's list. Tipple had three jellies and some odd cutlery in her pockets, soap was hidden in the library cupboard. Some tins of tea and sugar, which we had saved, I put at the bottom of the salvage barrel and piled high on top with newspapers. We save it so that the patients will never go short and yet if Dady and Lloyd found it they would send it all back to the stores. Tansley and RSM Chidlow were made to sit on 12 sheets between them out on the surgical balcony and five bath towels were placed alternately between the wooden bread trays until Hall rushed frantically in and snatched them out saying: "They'll count those, they'll count them," meaning the trays. Prosho had laboured long and hard at the Pack Stores and has obtained for us at least 50 more draw sheets than we should have although they are all in constant use. I can't think where we stowed all these, however we were determined he should not have them. The procession arrived, short, blunt-mannered Captain Dady full of his own importance, bad-tempered Corporal Lloyd with his wretched list, looking daggers at the VADs and Sister Boileau white-haired and worn-out and worried. They were accompanied by Sister Day, flapping and talking and trying to hold onto every article and prevent its going on the list and Sister Luxton with her gaoler's bundle of keys, smiling slyly and answering Dady back, sometimes grabbing an odd mug or milk jug before he could get it and snapping out: "Hands off! Private property." We followed in the background giggling and laughing, occasionally darting off to hide something we'd forgotten. Eventually they arrived in the kitchen and Sister Boileau looked ready to drop, she even asked us for some coffee

which we gave her on a plate saying: "We haven't any
saucers, sister."
Captain Dady did his best to get into the loft where Sister
Luxton had hidden a few more valuables and as he
ascended the ladder she cried: "Here! You haven't
checked this down here," and down he came each time.'

The walled garden was an oasis of silence. The white
Porters Mansion where Ma was billeted, now comprised
several, privately-owned town houses, with self-
consciously trimmed yew bushes in set pieces beneath
giant Scots pines and very old oaks. An arcadia on a hill
above London which we wandered through as though in a
dream until our reverie was broken by a fast-moving car as
a B road cuts through the flora without warning.
When I made my report of the visit to Ma and showed her
a computerised version of the photographs of her old
accommodation block, it drew a complete blank.
The synapses wiring together my Mother's mind recalled a
rope and plank bridge I'd once seen spanning the Kabul
Gorge in spring. The rush of air from the thundering melt
waters coming down from the mountains and passing
beneath it was making the bridge sway and peppering the
planks with spray.
Its precarious attachment to each side of the gorge seemed
under constant threat of parting.

20 May

Ma is 88 today and described her birthday perfume as
'disgusting,' although she loved her £4 Primark bracelet,

except: 'Can you make it longer?' She meant shorter as it dropped off her wrist. I pulled it over her cardigan sleeve which may help.

I was aware of a newcomer to the lodge which turned out to be my mother's second cousin Bryan Wood. He'd had a stroke some nine years beforehand and his wife, Sylvie had been living with a half person for all those years.

I introduced them, but it was impossible to tell if either recognised the other. Bryan, once a cultured, witty and urbane man has not lost his charm or good manners and greets everybody warmly, but can only say: 'Nice, very nice.'

Ma stared and laughed. Apparently she woke up singing this morning.

28 May

Unusually Ma was in the front lounge today, which is reserved for those who have a smidgeon of comprehension left. An even larger wall-mounted TV screen was broadcasting very loud and aggressive children's cartoons which were being ignored by the residents.

Ivy was there, too, and became fascinated by my portable computer.

'Oh, so that's what they call a lap-top is it? How do you get that information on there? In a little slim thing like that? We're becoming too clever for our own good,' she said.

Bryan was there, too, making his characteristic friendly gestures, smiles and noises of approval.

The gesture he is most comfortable with is a sort of knowing, 'perish-the-thought' shake of the head, followed by, inevitably, a smile.

'New dress, Ma?'

'No.'

She had ordered the dress at a sale earlier in the week, organised by the home.

'Nice cardigan, blue with those sparkly beads. You look like the Queen Mother.'

'I don't think so. I'm cold.'

I pulled her cardigan back down over her chest.

'You're a nice man aren't you?'

'Yes.'

She was holding her own hands, I noticed. No-one left to hold them for her or just cold?

She asked about the tide. I'd been down on the beach at Chalkwell earlier. A strong south-west wind was causing small waves to break and rubber-clad wind-surfers to enjoy the ride. A lone thorn bush was twisting in the wind its pink flowers already turning brown. Out in the sun-speckled river a huge container ship with stacked monoliths of boxes was backlit against the sun. In silhouette it looked like Manhattan sliding towards Thames Gateway.

I think one reason Ma and others are allowed into the 'front room' is the demise of this territory's 'Godfather', Joyce, who held court in the great bay windows, who was not demented and who took strong exception to interruptions from half-wits.

She's joined the 'disappeared.'

There's never any sense of death at Westcliff Lodge, it's a microcosm of life on the 'outside,' as the lodgers, one by one, just aren't there anymore.

On the way home I stopped at the nearest filling station, a dreary 'one-stop' cornucopia of pre-packaged meals tempting you to abandon any effort at culinary innovation, and pistoned in a tankful of fuel. At the pay station I bought a lottery ticket. Such establishments are ideal markets for selling lottery tickets. Like the labour-less food, the pre-cut bouquets of flowers, the effortless current affairs catch-up available from tabloid newspapers, a lottery stub was the potential ticket to end all struggle.

'Hope you're lucky, sir,' said the lanky youth with a strangely narrow, medieval face.

'Thank-you,' I said.

'And don't forget who sold you the winning ticket,' his bad teeth grinned cheesily.

'I'll come back and rescue you if I win,' I said.

He leaned forward, bent over the counter, and shook my hand.

'And remember, that's on camera,' he added jerking a thumb at the CCTV mounted over his domain.

1 June

I thanked Stephanie and the proprietor of Westcliff Lodge, Jenny Green, for their immediate and candid reporting of my mother's abuse and noted that it came at the same time as the Panorama TV programme about Bristol's Winterbourne View care home which resulted in four arrests and the suspension of 13 staff.

2 June

Jenny Green emailed to say:

'RE: Alleged abuse against Nancy. I will leave it to
Stephanie to update you on matters referring to the Police
and Ms Katherine Escoto, as events are 'in progress' as I
understand it and until resolved, we remain unsure about
any information we may provide. Regarding the
disciplinary procedures, I can report that they are not yet
concluded as Ms Escoto has one more day to appeal
against her dismissal from Westcliff Lodge, two weeks
ago, for gross misconduct arising as a result of abusive
behaviour against several residents at Westcliff Lodge.
That is her statutory entitlement arising from employment
legislation.
Having worked at the 'coal face' of elderly care in private
homes, NHS psychiatric hospitals and within the
community since the age of sixteen, I have observed
enormous change in this sector.
I think the real problem lies with the lack of status for care
work generally, coupled with the rising veneration of
youth in our society. There are parallels with the status of
motherhood and parenting.'

8 June

Something different for Ma in the post: The Civil Service
Retirement Fellowship Newsletter announcing that this
will be its last publication because the local branch has
'just enough money to meet the cost of printing and
distribution.' As a 'surviving dependant' – father, who was
a Customs & Excise officer, died in 1984 – Ma had been
the recipient of this little gem for 27 years.

The last issue's cover had a spaniel puppy waving a paw, with the headline Goodbye and the lead story was entitled, 'Rainbow Bridge':

'Anyone who has had to say goodbye to a pet dog will know just how painful it can be. Well, just recently a number of us who attended dog training classes had to say goodbye to the lady who regularly – no matter how ill she was – turned up in all weathers to help us make our dogs good citizens.

'Sadly she caught the "dreaded" and within a year we lost her. Pam left a legacy of well -trained dogs – and handlers – who are all extremely grateful for what she did for our pets, and we all felt privileged to have known her.

'An example of how much she was loved was that between 30 and 40 dogs lined the route to the crematorium – and not one animal barked or misbehaved.'

Then followed publication of Pam's story Rainbow Bridge, where hound and master meet up in the 'hereafter.'

Jenny sent me another email: 'Dementia is such a cruel disease, it's quite bewildering how for people afflicted with the condition, a huge piece of their lives just seem to drop away from their minds. However, such people remain receptive to atmosphere. For relatives the whole process can be quite heartbreaking to witness. I prefer to view the condition of dementia as an altered state of mind rather than a "loss". In addition, and fortunately, in my experience most people with the condition experience significant levels of contentment which is comforting for relatives and carers alike.'

I took Ma to hospital for a chest X-Ray because of her chronic cough. Fear seems to bring on lucidity: 'Don't drive so fast, Dicky,' she said, travelling through the third dimension at a pace with which, even degraded senses, find hard to compute, is clearly a worry, I realise, and slow down even though I'm doing no more than the 30 limit. After the X-Ray I drove her through her home town, Leigh-on-Sea, and she looked with great interest at the passing buildings along the main shopping street, Leigh Broadway.

'Do you recognise them?'

'Yes I do,' she said emphatically.

Then we turned down Leigh Hill, where she had lived for two different periods of her life.

'Do you recognise it?'

'Yes,' not quite so certain, this time. Shopping leaves a bigger imprint than residing.

'There's your old house.'

'Yes. Oh, I wish I could have some.'

We drove into the Old Town and she remarked upon the mudflats, the tide was out. Then we drove along to the scruffy golf-driving range where we sat in the car and she semi-dozed while I offered her a buttered scone and she sipped a little tea as a fresh south-west wind rustled the leaves of a line of poplars and, far away, a cuckoo sounded. Ma sat contentedly with the summer sun shining through the windscreen. Jenny Green is right: she can comprehend 'atmosphere.'

Have received a bill for £39.98 for a dress Ma 'picked' from a clothes sale.

12 June

A newcomer has arrived at the lodge. A distraught woman, with bad teeth and luxuriantly curled hair, called Gladys, she cried: 'Can I go now?' to me as I entered through the front door.

I ignored her.

'Can I come home with you?' she entreated a carer.

'Are you going home?' No response.

'Can I come?' Still no response.

'Are you going home now?' Again nobody says anything.

'Can I come?'

'I'm not going home I'm just moving about in here,' the carer snapped. Carers at the lodge, in my experience, don't snap. But Gladys never stops her entreaties and no amount of appeasement or reassurance will make her stop. She goes on and on and on. Tension builds. I feel my own nerves being wracked in hoping that no-one will be unkind to her.

'I want to go wee-wee,' she tried again.

'Stick your bottom out of the window,' said Beryl callously.

Self-pity or any sign of weakness gets short shrift from the residents. It's a reminder of their own predicament.

You have to get tough to survive in a commune.

A Jewish woman has driven down from London to visit her 63-year-old sister, Sue, who has an unusual form of Alzheimer's Disease. She understands all that is said but can no longer read or write or express what she means even though she talks coherently and appears cognitively perfectly normal.

20 June

Ma was sitting with a semi-cold cup of tea and a bowl of skinned porridge in front of her, just one chair away from her beloved second cousin, Bryan. They were totally unaware of each other: on separate planets with fading gravitational pull.

Ma's chest growled with a heavy infection as she coughed. She's on a course of antibiotics for a virus making the rounds. She took a while to believe I was there and brightened when the penny eventually dropped.

She jumped whenever I touched her anywhere but her hand, which sported the incongruous nail varnish, this time pink, over her perfectly convex nails about which she used to mockingly boast.

'I love you,' she said.

'And I love you,' I replied.

She nodded her head from side to side gently as though checking out a still-doable function.

It's like watching a nuclear power station being decommissioned: the bodywork still stands, but slowly the lights are going out.

'Please help me.'

She faces it alone. Perhaps that is what she is now aware of.

I had to leave for a job in Dover. I belted along the M2 at 80 mph, Verdi's La Traviata blaring and licking the salt water running down my face.

27 June

There has been a complex development in the Cold War. Ma suddenly started refusing to take fluids so a doctor was called and he ordered her intake, or lack of it, to be measured and if it remained low then she was to be taken to hospital and re-hydrated via an intravenous drip. If she refused to take the drip only I, as her Power of Attorney, could countermand my mother.

The carers, meanwhile, kept trying to persuade Ma to drink. A hospital visit is a 'failed' in their book.

But Ma had continued to refuse fluids all week while I was away on business and Cathy had been backwards and forwards to see my mother and deal with the tug-of-war. I arrived at the lodge today, armed with my POA (Power of Attorney) documents, in preparation for her move to hospital.

I met Jenny in the lobby and after a long discussion about NHS politics, she finally said, baldly: 'I don't want her to die in hospital.'

'Thank goodness, someone is prepared to talk straight,' I said. I felt Ma would be very agitated by the noise and chaos of a hospital. And Jenny believes nature should take its course as all a drip would do would be to delay the inevitable.

She countered claims by the GP that Ma was losing weight by producing her medical record, which proves she is the same weight now as when she was admitted. She has, in fact, put on a little weight since being at the lodge. She then lost a little but has since stabilised.

Jenny said that is there is an 'acute' need for hospitalisation then that is when to act, but that no ambulance should be called over a little dehydration.

We then went in to see Ma.

She was drinking a little tea, a little chocolate milk from her baby bottle and she ate a slice of toast and marmalade. She looked bright-eyed although the skin – over her face – has aged a touch.

Jenny announced the home was to receive a pet dog.

'Ma likes dogs.'

'Do you like dogs, Nancy?'

Ma did not answer.

'Remember old Buster?'

She lit up immediately.

'Do you remember Buster?' she said.

'Yes,' I lied.

'Dear old Buster.'

I chatted to Ma about where I'd been over the past week. Devon. And I mentioned the places she once knew as a young nurse. Torquay, Exmouth.

'Exmouth,' she repeated.

I rubbed her hand and a thumbnail moved gently back and forth rubbing mine.

'I love you,' she said, and then 'Do you love me?'

'Yes, very much.'

'What?'

'I said I love you very much.'

'Oh that's all right then,' she said with a big smile.

I told her I was off to Croatia on a job.

'What would you like me to bring you? Some toffee?'

'Oh, no.'

'Some chocolate?'

No answer.

Then remembering how Cathy always sourced cheap bracelets, which seemed to go down well, 'A bracelet?'

'Oh yes,' she beamed and I left her looking forward to her new clasp.

Ivy was reading the Daily Mail.

'Been doing some gardening?' she asked.

'No I've been doing some sailing.'

'Oh well not everyone can do gardening. I used to like gardening, til I came in here. Now I've lost my get up and go. More like get up and gone…'

Jenny let me out and told me how one resident, who died in the lodge, was 100 years old.

'I'll never forget it,' she said, 'there was a summer storm raging and rain pouring down and the door burst open and this woman with a horrible face, screamed: "Where's the rings?" I'd not once seen the resident's family in the three years she was with us. I didn't even know who they were.' I suppose the last material thing a woman loses are her infernal wedding rings, and before the cold sets in, the offspring prepare to scrap the corpse. The betrothed themselves, are parted long before death.

2 July

Disembodied sentences today. 'I wanted to go and see Marjorie, but that was dreadful,' of her long deceased cousin – the mother of Bryan, now sharing the lodge with my mother.
'Life can be infuriating at times.' We can all drink to that.
'There was this man. A very nice man. In fact I liked him very much. Then I found out he was this crazy man.' It's only a guess, but there was an Italian army officer, Francesco Motti, who Ma met somehow, somewhere, who had the same narrow face and dark looks of my own father and whose photograph Ma still had among her bric -a -brac of mementoes. Strangely I found the photo under some of Clifford's folded clothes in the chest of drawers he used. Was it a picture which touched a raw nerve? Possibly. But it was a two-way jealousy: Cathy found a photograph of Clifford's deceased wife, Sheila, in her wartime WRENS uniform hidden under some cardigans of Ma's!
I told her how Cathy and I had been to an evening of opera singing held in a local barn. It had been excellent.
No response.

Then I mentioned the family holiday we'd arranged for North Wales, and jokingly said how we were going to see 'the Wellish, isn't it.'

She got that and laughed.

Ron heaved himself up into his zimmer frame, walked across the room and sat opposite us. Ma watched. As he settled I noticed he had a black eye. 'Conversation,' stopped.

Ron got up again and wandered unsteadily away, seeking another conversation to eavesdrop.

I gave Ma her Croatian bracelet then I tried to feed her some chocolate milkshake.

'Get away from me.'

Later, at home, Irene called to say that she had managed to get Ma to drink ice-cream 'smoothies' mixed with fruit. Success. Irene had also spent time patiently sitting with Ma trying to determine why she was refusing food and drink.

'I don't want to be fed,' Ma had eventually said.

9 July

I found Ma propped up in bed watching a talking sponge and a talking goldfish bowl on TV.

'Oh look, it's snow,' she said as the cartoon characters walked across a white plain.

'Rhoda, such gorgeous features,' she said of her sister's prominent cheek bones, and then 'Ghastly, terrible. It's mummy and… I can't remember.'

Ma's diaries stop sometime at the end of 1943. I don't know exactly when as the last nine pages have been cut out leaving a half inch of entries at the spine. A tantalising scroll of my Mother forever gone. She does not pick up her pen again until 1978.

One reason for the silence is that her Mother did not make a full recovery after her hysterectomy and died from cancer of the uterus in July 1945 aged 57. Why does everyone have to die?

Down for breakfast and I find tea, toast and marmalade, porridge all laid out and will every mouthful towards my mother's mouth. I don't talk as that will distract her act of lifting a spoon or cup.

Suddenly I feel a hand on my knee. A mummified thumb, with red nail varnish, is scratching at my leg. I brush off a morsel of porridge from my knee and hold her hand.

She is distressed when I announce I'm leaving.

'OK. Goodbye, dear,' she says as I depart and I rub the anti-septic squeezy stuff into my hands, available on the way in to prevent the spread of germs to the residents, on the way out to wash away a sticky residue of marmalade.

On the mail front mother has been offered from Healthy Living Direct: 'Comfort Grips Cutlery with soft, rubber grip handles. Adult Full Size Meal Protector, a wipe-clean bib. Swiss Age blemish cream,' which has age-spotted hands turned to non-age-spotted hands in before and after photographs.

Walking stick shock absorbers: 'Reduce shock to your arms and back when walking.'

And an 'Automatic can opener.'

28 July

A carer from Westcliff Lodge called to say: 'Nancy is asking for Dicky,' I haven't visited for two weeks and she's noticed!

31 July

Ma now looks like a little girl. She's got smaller. Her
bright face smiling. Her blue eyes focusing although
uncertain as to who the figure is in front of her.
An old, little girl. Perhaps that's where the phrase 'old girl'
comes from.
Going back to childhood seems an acceptable way of
winding down.
'Are you going to marry me?' she asked me as a little girl
might ask.
'Can you choose your own?'
'Yes,' I did not mind confirming the latter question.
'But I didn't think you had one?'
'I haven't,' I said.
She was talking incessantly, smiling and chuckling.
Happy, content. Slightly shrunken.
Ron was curled up on the sofa opposite.
'Oh look at that little boy,' Ma said of the 85-year-old.

27 August

The 'sun lounge' suits Ma. She is bright, chatty, laughing
in there. She's on her own in there. She mind's not being
alone. She'd rather that than sit like one of a line of
dementia exhibits in chairs, around the walls.
There's more space here and more light and no wall-hung
TV. Instead a music station, which is always tuned to some
mediocre radio station playing out-of-date popular songs
too loud and which I always turn down.
Ma was chattering nonsensically: at least the sentences
made sense as stand -aloners but not consecutively.

'Is she trying to sing?' asked Margaret the Polish carer.
'Could be.'
'We had karaoke the other day but she did not want to sing.'
'Yes, she's spontaneous, aren't you, Ma?'
'She is a free spirit,' said Margaret.

3 September

Ma has lost none of her fear of pain. She has a finely honed sense of impending physical intrusion. Margaret had found me a nail file with which I did no more than gently lever out the dark, crumbly matter from beneath her mauve-painted fingernails onto a baby wipe. It's not that I enjoy taking part in my mother's personal hygiene – in fact a visiting hygienist charges Ma £30 a shot for such work – it's just I have an irresistible urge to de-grot people. It's something even a layman can do. Dirty fingernails are so obviously easy to counter. It's the same with blackheads: I can't resist squirting them. I find it difficult not to focus on them when talking to a sufferer. Those little black moles ready to pop out and be done away with. The kids and my wife no longer let me perform this satisfying service. So now I can indulge my dubious passion on Ma.
A carer brought tea and biscuits. Two NICE biscuits and a chocolate Bourbon. Ma played with the latter for a good while until she snapped it in half. Then with a newly-dredged fingernail started scratching at the chocolate centre and put it to her lips. The two NICE biscuits she clapped together like cymbals.
She chatted with her characteristic disconnected words and sentences. Clearly trying to say something, but it is the something which always eludes her, or which, at least

never surfaces linguistically. She can trot out 'joining up' words but cannot express what they are joining to. She can erect the pylons, but is unable to hang the cables. It's most strange. As I've said before it's grammar that's tough when learning a language and nouns which are easy. It appears when the human computer is dying the reverse is the case.

'I want to go back to where I know what to say,' was the startling exception to this condition, and made perfect, if surreal sense. I doubted it was just random luck: pulling three cherries up on a betting machine.

Rain came in on a falling glass, but it was still warm. I drove away passing a grey-haired man in a tan smock, navy blue sailing hat and welly boots. An Estuary sailor. A weekend yachttie braving the muddily safe waters of the Thames, wet from the rain and rising wind, imagining the greater depths and serious tempests his playground is on the fringes of. Getting a taste of the epic before tethering his plastic boat to a chain buried in mud and watching the shallow tide retreat to the ogre of the ocean before walking home for tea and a book about shipwrecks.

I sat in the car doing much the same: listening to Mahler's First Symphony being performed at the Proms and imagining thunder and lightning.

31 October

A letter has arrived for Ma at Westcliff Lodge from Essex Magistrates' Enforcement Office.

'The court has ordered compensation to be paid by Miss Katherine ESCOTO. The amount is shown below.

'On 21/03/2011 at Southend on Sea in the county of Essex assaulted Nancy DURHAM by beating her. Contrary to section 39 of the Criminal Justice Act 1988.
'Compensation order made £100.00.'
My mother will be paid 'in instalments or a lump sum.'
Miss Escoto was deported.

11 December

Ma is reclining in a faux leather chair which is vaguely familiar. Then I recognise it's Lucy's.
She died three weeks ago. She was 96.
Ma said to me: 'What are we going to do about Dicky?' as we sat holding hands.
'I don't know,' I said.
'Only I don't want him to leave.'
She has been reluctant to see me go of late. Two weeks back I went to see her two days running.
'Come every day,' she exclaimed as I walked in on Day Two.

24 December

There is an expectant atmosphere in the middle room as a full complement of residents sit around in their chairs, feeling suddenly wanted. At this time of year even those who do not get a visit from one year's end to the next can expect their annual hug.
Then Joan is brought in clasping two greetings cards.
'I don't know who they are,' she says, 'I don't know anything. All I know is my name is Joan Murray.'
'I know you,' I said.
'How do you know me?' she says assertively.

'I know you from visiting the home.'

It's out now. I refer to the lodge as the home, as there no longer seems any point in diplomatically describing it as a guest house for Ma's benefit.

'But I don't know what I'm doing here. I don't know any of these people,' Joan nods at the residents staring benignly at the carpet.

'I don't know who brought me here.'

I screw my eyes up to read who the cards are from.

'Perhaps Len and Sam,' I say.

'No, it's not Len it's Ken,' she says, a moment of daylight breaking through, but the chance to build on a fact is suddenly stripped away, 'I don't know who they are.'

Then I notice one card says Happy Birthday.

'Oh, it's a birthday card,' I said.

'How old am I then?'

'I'm afraid I can't help you, there.'

'Only I'm frightened, I can't remember anything.'

'Well you've nothing to be frightened of in here.'

'No, I don't mean that. I mean I don't know why I'm here.'

'I'll have a word with the carers to see if someone can tell you who brought you here.'

'Well if that could be organised, if somebody could tell me who I am.

'I need to know who I belong to.'

It's a chilling statement of dependence. We come in alone, but are loved, cherished, and pampered out of any sense of solitude. We'll get the chance to discover what that's like when we go out.

Ma suddenly announced: 'I love you,' to me before slumping over again.

On the way out I checked with Irene to see if Joan's cards had been hand-delivered. She confirmed Joan had received a visit today, a rare event.
'Do they live far away?'
She shook her head.

2012

14 January

Ma was taken to Southend General Hospital last night, her crackling cough and hacking chest necessitating investigation. She was curled up under a blanket in a metal-framed bed with barrier-like sides under stark light. She coughed and dozed, still managing to laugh at some deep-seated memory, still comforted by my voice and still able to hold my hand.
Proprietor Jenny Green said her condition was not a 'life-ending situation' but that a hospital visit did now make sense to try and re-hydrate Ma as she has not been eating or drinking or taking her antibiotics for the chest infection, for three days.
Yet the consultant at the hospital told Cathy before I arrived that she should 'prepare yourself for future decisions.' For example, he continued, if Ma's heart stops while she is with 'them' they would not resuscitate her and that dementia sufferers pulled out intravenous drips because 'it distresses them'. So I wondered why she was there at all.
She had an X-Ray today and I got half a cup of tea down her plus she consumed a pot of trifle for breakfast, then later another half a cup of tea plus two pots of jelly and half a digestive biscuit.

Her right eye is slightly lower than her left, her mouth has been hanging open and she still has a vicious hacking cough, which seems to exhaust her and makes her lop-sided eyes water. The fine wrinkles on her brow are more marked now, the thumb of her left hand crooked.
Someone in the ward makes a loud sneezing noise.
'Hello darling,' she says with a beaming smile, then her eyes become vacant and pensive on something within, then they re-focus on the external world and she looks with alarm. She occasionally rocks her head from side to side and now and again reaches into the third dimension with her right hand to touch me, or my scarf.
Occasionally there are a few words, a disjointed phrase or sentence.
'I don't know what they're doing,' was one.
Occasionally her head tilts back and her eyes close, once while still holding the corner of a digestive biscuit, with her violet silver nail polished hands.
In a bed opposite a woman with dementia is sitting up and receiving a memory test from her doctor.
'Who's sitting on the throne at the moment? Who's the monarch?'
'Oh, I know it, I know that.'
'I know, it's probably just on the tip of your tongue,' says the doctor, 'Can you count backwards from 20?'
'Ninety.'
'How old are you?'
'It's a secret.'
'What year did the First World War start?'
'The First World War?'
'Yes.'
'Oh I know that.'
'Where are you?'

'In bed.'

'Where is the bed?'

Outside the window I look at empty, memory-to benches situated under naked cherry trees. Bird lime covers the wooden slatted seats and cigarette butts lie in squashed squalor around their legs. Brass plates are engraved with the names of lost souls.

Hanging on the back of my Mother's wheelchair are her drugs and some notes from the lodge: 'DO NOT ATTEMPT CARDIOPULMONARY RESUSCITATION.' The document adds: 'CPR is unlikely to be successful' (ie medically futile) because of, the hospital doctor this time has added, 'frailty dementia.'

The form continues: 'Record of discussion of decision (tick one or more boxes and provide further information)' Box 'No' has been ticked and the words 'compassion and daughter-in-law' added.

So there it all hangs on the back of the subject's wheelchair, as she awaits an ambulance to take her back to the lodge. Her future demise decided by her nearest and dearest, their adjudication available to read first hand, like a 'penny for the guy' sign. I thought of the executed 'enemies of the state' who had their status written in crude letters on cards hanging around their necks in 1930s Germany.

A lot of banter is on hand in the Acute Medical Unit. The busy, front line staff of porters and nurses josh each other in an affected jolly manner, oblivious in their youth, to the ebb of their charges.

One of them, an African, does not join in. Does not affect jollity. He is more dignified. Suddenly he approaches my Ma's bed and apologises as he close the curtains around us.

I peep through the curtains and watch half a dozen well-dressed men and women, red-eyed and hugging one another as they walk quickly through the ward.

Then a corpse is rushed through behind them on a wheeled bed.

One of the jolly porters says loudly: 'No, clear the room, they don't want any of it,' about the dead woman's last wardrobe.

18 January

Ma is back on form. She's eating intermittently and is very volubly aggressive, telling Beryl to stop staring at her and hoping out loud that she, Beryl, develops Ma's cough. Beryl can be a cool bitch and keeps on staring and innocently asking: 'Is that cough permanent?' Mad Gladys is angrily, loudly and repeatedly asking me if I'm a doctor.

Ma: 'Will you do that for me?'

Me: 'Do what Ma?'

Ma, with gusto: 'Nothing, just be here.'

I make my excuses and leave, already late for work, but a carer asks me to return to assist her giving Ma antibiotics. I do so.

'Come on, Ma, take your medicine.'

'You're not HERE,' she shouts angrily. When I say goodbye, however disappointed she maybe to hear it, she is irritated when it appears meaningless.

'Come on, Ma, for me,' and she takes her 'meds' at last. An order has been put in for rice puddings, which she seems to enjoy.

21 January

'Help, help,' I could hear Gladys as I entered the lodge, 'help, help, I want to go to bed.'

Her lovely curly white hair bobbed in front of me then she turned and her presented her protruding yellow teeth caked in plaque: 'Help, help, I want to go home.'

She walked into the middle room. There against the walls sat eight figures like Lincoln memorials in their chairs, Ronald, Bettine, Joan, Betty, Barbara, Beryl, Ivy, and Ma. Gladys stood in the centre of the room.

'Help, help.'

No-one took any notice and Gladys sat down and with her head in her hands continued: 'Help, help.' A carer sat beside her and gently asked her not to shout.

'Not me,' Gladys shouted, 'It's not me.'

She then fell silent briefly then started up on a new tack: 'Help, help, I wanna go toilet.'

Then she shouted: 'Hell, hell,' unlikely deliberately, but unwittingly describing her inner turmoil.

Then back to 'Help, help.'

At which point both Beryl and Ma bitchily mimicked: 'Help, help.'

Which only encouraged Gladys, who missed the sarcasm - perhaps others needed help? - 'Help, help,' she said.

Ivy's smile at last vanished, vanished for the first time in my experience, and she said curtly: 'SHUT UP.'

Lunch arrived to curb Gladys' tongue.

I changed Ma's cardigan and top as they were soaked with juice. She seemed contented enough. Happy to get a hug and animated by some tap-dancing film on the TV.

She managed to eat a morsel of chicken and a few peas. 'Nancy's eating. Well done, Nancy,' said a carer.

And Jackie, the tall African, usually the night nurse, said, genuinely pleased: 'Nancy always bounces back.'
The little Filipinos are sweet-natured and always want to show off their work, hopping round Ma like birds: hugging and trying to kiss her on the cheek, but this invariably backfires as when I'm present Ma wants no substitute!

26 January

I am miming to Michael Buble, who is singing 'That's life' on the radio. Ma is alone in the back room. I prance around the room in front of her holding a banana as a microphone. Richard, my 13-year-old son sits beside her. Ma suddenly turns to him and says: 'He can't help it, he thinks it's funny.'
Is this anecdotal evidence that stimulation of a spontaneous variety, as opposed to that by rote, can still send electricity across the synapses? Ma has not phrased a sentence as complex as that for months, years. What's more it was pure Ma!
She was eating a ham and tomato sandwich on her own and perfectly happy in her isolation. Irene told me the TV in the middle room was distracting her from eating.
She's always been perfectly contented on her own and the back room is peaceful. She can hear the rain on the conservatory roof, which underlines the primal need of shelter.

7 February

A thrilling aspect this morning as the estuary is throwing up light from a heavy snow, which covers the far away fields of Kent and the marsh and even the mudflats on the Essex shore. The worms beneath await the tide to rescue them from their icy carapace.

The car is snowed in and I do not go to Westcliff Lodge, instead it comes to me. Ethel, the carer who is married to Alex, another carer, calls up to say 'Nan is missing you, Dicky-pie.'

I am thrown by this peculiar intimacy, until I realise Ethel thinks it's what I've been christened. One of Ma's pet names has been taken as read. So Ethel puts the phone to Ma's ear, 'It's Dicky-pie, Nan.'

A horrible caterwauling sound came through then I hear Ma's voice mimicking the high-pitched carer: 'That's what you do.' Then she stops mimicking, 'You devil, go away you beast, get off me.'

I do not know if she recognised my voice.

26 February

Ethel told me today that Ma stopped punching her and Irene a long time ago when personal care had to be administered. Ma even said to me, of Ethel, 'Get that same nurse.'

Ethel said: 'Now she sits up in bed and says "Come on, I want my tea" waving a finger.'

'Well, you girls look after her well,' I said.

'That's because we love her,' said Ethel who said Ma also reads her name badge and calls her 'Mummy.'

Her mother's name.

Ma is also now acknowledging Bryan and told Irene he was her cousin.

5 March

I've just got home from Southend General. Ma had a 'collapse' at the home. She had five different blood tests, was under an oxygen mask, fitted with an intravenous drip, and had been given an X-Ray.

All of which produced this diagnosis from the young, tall, consultant, the gilt of whose youth was wearing thin presumably from overwork: 'It's not pneumonia.' The applied science had not backed up his prognosis.

Perhaps he's overworked from unblocking beds. Once he's managed to harden up a hunch that you are dying, you queue up somewhere else. To the left termination, to the right we'll work on you.

He had one last throw of the God dice: 'Did she smoke?' he said dismissively, not even bothering to use a more diplomatic tense.

'No, not really.'

I felt pathetic. Please just be nice, I thought. I wanted to appease him. Just a kind word. I wanted him to like my Mother. Maybe just a kindly smile? I felt embarrassed that she had eluded a category for this clever young professional. Stupid woman. I felt like a peasant. All right maybe just a patronising smile?

He looked at a clipboard. Then he was gone. It's not pneumonia, it's not pleurisy, stands to reason she should be dying, but she ain't. It's out of his hands.

'Did she smoke?'

It was like saying, 'Was she young?'

Then I felt angry with myself for my puppy-like hope for just a tad of care. He could have done with a piece of reality Essex: 'Yes, you lanky, privileged piece of shit, who's education I've paid for with my fucking taxes. Fuck fucking off!'

We retreated with, or at least my Mother did, our useless dignity, to the lodge with a list of antibiotics and tea, and warmth, and hopeless, science-lite affection.

31 March

I took Katie along today. Ma was sitting confronted by a trolley-load of soft toys her expression going from a frown to a smile.
'I think she's confused. That's what babies do,' said Katie.
'You naughty boy,' Ma said. I think it was directed to the pink teddy bear.
A squeaking trolley brought the tea. It's the sound of the institution. At home those wheels would have been oiled.

26 May

The lodge is on the fringe of the slightly less well-heeled part of Westcliff-on-Sea to the east and on the periphery of much wealthier Chalkwell to the west. A magic tunnel-like, footpath leads you through from one to the other with the commuter railway embankment on one side and tennis courts on the other.
City brokers flashed past in sleek white trains behind giant poplars, as I wheeled Ma out from the fusty, museum of human dinosaurs into 28 degree heat.
'Oh,' she said as the sun hit her sallow cheeks, 'lovely.'
We stopped at one tennis court and listened to the lime green balls popping off racquets.
'You used to play tennis,' I said.
'Aren't they a scream?' she replied.
The Arcadian alleyway is bisected by mansion-lined Chalkwell Avenue where each grand forecourt supports

several shiny, brand new, automobiles splayed out as though at a motor show.

Louis, an old Jewish acquaintance of mine with his wife and child in a retro-pram with tassels on the hood, came rolling towards us. Both wagons stopped rolling as we met head on. I explained to Ma how she once pushed me in one of those.

'Bye, bye,' she said as we parted. Manners maketh otherwise ignored relics.

In Chalkwell Park we watched the white-clad cricketers batting at dust in the netted practice pens, but she did not respond when I reminded her how brother-in-law Bill once played the game.

'Oh look at that little,' she said as a four-year-old boy wandered past in sun-hat and dummy.

We rolled into the rose garden, passing benches where widows had adorned garish plaques to their husband, on the backrests before being added themselves.

We sat with our backs resting against some funeral director's sentiments and Ma became fixated on a pecking but suspicious blackbird. I managed to get her, with help from a serviette, to eat an ice-cream until her reverie over the bird was broken by the sound of a plane, a Spitfire, it being the time of the much-loathed, by Ma, Southend Air Show, which she tried to accompany by making a trumpet noise as it dived.

Diving planes no longer mean bombs to her. But during a visit to Torquay she recalled the time they did, when she was working as a Red Cross nurse at the local hospital before transferring to Shenley:

7 October 1987

Rained all day.
Dartmouth and across on the ferry to Kingswear and on to
Torquay.
By the side of the Hotel Regina is a passageway and it was
here in 1942 that we ran and flung ourselves down on the
ground when a German plane with a large black cross,
machine-gunned that area after dropping bombs near the
town.

We came home along Imperial Avenue where she did not
recognise the grand house of her seminal Christmasses-
past, courtesy of rich Uncle Stanley.
We passed several children walking with their families.
'Hello darling,' Ma said. Children, all children, she relates
to. They are of her world. Adults keep letting her down.
They keep dying.
As we approached Westcliff Lodge she said 'Good.'
For her it is now home.

5 June

Does the Queen have dementia? After all, according to the
Alzheimer's Society, one in six people over the age of 80
suffers from Alzheimer's or vascular dementia or a mix of
the two. Do queens get dementia? Well they are more
likely to than kings as it's more common in women.
Today is the last day of Queen Elizabeth II's 60th
Anniversary Diamond Jubilee. On the large TV screen she
was shown being driven from St Paul's Cathedral to the
Mansion House and then onto the Guildhall for a 'small
lunch engagement' of around 250 people.

It's very difficult to tell if she is a sufferer. The close-ups only show an elderly lady waving modestly. But then when I wave at the residents of Westcliff Lodge they wave back. And if you are being waved at by thousands of people as you pass by, even if you are not sure why, you'd have to be pretty far gone not to respond in kind.

Take the Queen's Christmas Day message -the only time we get to hear from her- if her long-term memory is OK and a valet is mouthing the words, off camera, she might just manage it. When I prompt Ma she can sometimes, with practice, string the odd sentence together.

What about when the Queen goes walkabout? She only waves at children and says 'Hello', much the same as my Mother does as she is wheeled past in her chariot.

If the Queen's long-term memory is OK she may recall a middle-aged woman with an expectant face standing at the kerbside of Kimberley Park Road, in Falmouth Cornwall on 6 August 1977. The Queen was there with her husband to celebrate her Silver Jubilee and my Mother was there with her camera to celebrate it as well.

The Queen's hair was brown and she was wearing a buttoned-up red and white check coat and a cream bowler hat, the details of which I record like all good newspapermen should. I know these details because my Mother was standing that close on the pavement and papped the Queen through the window of her chauffeur-driven car.

I don't know why her coat was buttoned up – through the other side of the car windows you can see people in shirtsleeves – perhaps it's an early sign.

My mother has written on the back of the photograph: 'HM outside 42 Kimberley Pk. Rd.' The number of the house recorded as though this was a personal visit.

The Queen's face is a pudgy white colour with a circle of red lipstick in the centre like a target. The circle is a smile. A genuine smile, and although it's unlikely that 35 years ago the Queen was suffering from even the early stages, she is...waving.

It's as difficult now to know as it was then...

There was a time at Shenley Military Hospital when Ma did not want to get too close to royalty:

21 June 1943

'We have the Queen's niece here now – the Hon: Ann Bowes-Lyon. Very concerned in case Madam should think of putting her in with us – however Madam didn't.
She is rather tall and graceful – a sweet face, but not pretty at all. Very neat and pink and white and so far as I can see not in the least bit snobbish. She has been a VAD for three years. Her name is next to mine on pay-slips, Pte Bowes-Lyon!'

11 October 1943

'Bowes-Lyon has got over her awful sickness and now glides around in a red zip dressing gown and red suede slippers fascinatingly embroidered. These she bought in Austria. She is tall and slim and terribly vague. She has a soft, sweet expression and a very soft voice. I should think she is a bit Irish. She can be very cutting at times and very firm with the girls. Read later on in the admission book that she is 34 and her next-of-kin is her father, the Hon: Patrick Bowes-Lyon.'

Westcliff Lodge organised a Jubilee barbecue and suitably for the 'Blitz spirit' a cold wind from the south brought rain.

Cathy and I have had to go through Ma's annual assessment for the home. A large file is kept on her diet, behaviour and condition, to keep abreast of things. This is done mainly by keeping a note of her weight rather as a farmer does a pig or cow, as, like livestock, my mother can't talk either.

She is putting on weight again although the chest infection has returned.

Bryan Wood's wife Sylvie told me about an article in an old person's magazine, Saga, in which it is reported that some dementia sufferers can get their care funded by the NHS.

'The homes don't mention it, as public-funded care is not as great an amount as private, but hurry they are changing the rules soon,' she said.

So I printed off a 44-page set of guidelines from the Age Concern website and armed also with the Saga magazine will now set off to hike across another life-crushing prairie of finite time in battling with bureaucracy.

10 June

Ethel is having difficulty getting Ma, now very alert, to drink. Beside her are baby bottles with tea, chocolate milk, water and juice. All full.

'Come on, Nan, drink some.'

Ma tilted her head away from the teet.

'Nan, open your mouth.'

'Come on, Ma, have a nice cup of tea,' I joined.

Eventually a mouthful was deposited but not swallowed. Ma kept it in her buccal cavity like a reviled mouthwash, lips compressed, cheeks blown.
Ten minutes passed.
'Swallow, Nan,' said Ethel.
'Nan, swallow,' said Ethel's husband Alex.
'Come on, Ma.'
'Give me a kiss, Nan,' Ethel tried another tack.
I left them working on the blocked gargoyle and went home.

11 June

The cough wracks her, exhausts her, but still she swings her old lion's face towards us as Ethel, Alex and I try to persuade her to swallow a thimble-full of orange-coloured, antibiotic.
It seems improbable she can 'bounce back' from this latest chest infection and I sense, uncharacteristically, for me, disappointment.
Now I want her to live long enough to be 'assessed' for funding.
Come on Ma, stay alive, the state might pay for your hellish existence.

2 July

It's assessment day and I meet Lynn Freeman, NHS Community Matron for Continuing Healthcare in the dining room where we sit alone. A pleasant, Scottish woman of middle years, with a heavy cold she tells me I can appeal if the decision does not go in Ma's favour. I tell her that if it does not I will. And we then go through to meet the assessee in the conservatory.

Ma is slumped in her automatic reclining chair – apparently the purchase of same, plus the purchase of a 'profiling bed', an automatically adjustable couch - all 'helps' the case for funding.

I do not make any greeting. No point in stimulating Ma with any voice recognition. Nor do I perform my middle distance poise trying to get her to focus. We should keep it objective, after all.

'Hello, are you Nancy Durham?' asks the matron.

Ma does not respond verbally or visually. Keep up the good work, Ma, I think.

'Yes, this is my mother,' I say.

'Nancy, are you OK?'

Nothing.

'Nancy, I'm here to assess you, is that OK with you?'

Nothing.

We retreat, with Irene, to a garden shed 'admin block' in the back garden of the lodge to work through a list of categories to see whether Ma is eligible for funding. It is a tick-box system of grading, the more ticks the patient invites the more points she scores towards a magic number for eligibility. They include cognition, 'Nancy has no ability to assess risk or keep herself from harm or neglect, she is reliant on others for all care, her cousin lives within the same home, Nancy was not aware of any of this.' Lots of ticks.

Mobility, 'Nancy is completely non-weight bearing, she is unable to cooperate with repositioning, she is hoisted for all transfers, she has a poor sitting position in her riser recliner, she is positioned in bed and chair with cushions.' Tick-box heaven.

Continence, 'Doubly incontinent, occasional urine infections.' Tick, tick, tick.

Behaviour, ' Nancy is resistive to care, she can be aggressive and she will lash out at times of personal care and agitation, she is physically frail and risk of harm to others, although minimal, is present, she will decline food at times and spits medications out also. Staff manage by leaving Nancy to calm down and go back later, she will usually accept care at this time.' Go for it Ma.

Psychological and Emotional, 'Nancy takes an antidepressant, staff feel that reassurances help at times but due to cognitive impairment difficult to assess fully.' Jury still out.

Communication, 'Not able to communicate needs at any time, in any way, staff anticipate all needs due to familiarity with Nancy.' Keep up the good work, Ma.

Nutrition, 'Nancy often refuses meals, she is fed by others and this is a laborious task at times, staff have to return to feed Nancy often to ensure an adequate intake of food and fluids, she has lost weight.' You are doing fine, Ma.

Skin, 'Nancy has a pressure relieving cushion and mattress. District nurses have seen Nancy recently has had a red sacrum, they have prescribed barrier cutimed cream. She requires two hourly turns at night and frequent checks during the day.' Coming along nicely, Ma.

Breathing, 'Nancy develops regular chest infections, she has no diagnosed respiratory illness but does have problems with her swallowing. At these times she goes off her food and becomes particularly unwell.' I rest my case.

Drug therapies and symptoms, 'Medications administered, is both non-compliant and non-concordant.' Moderate, could improve.

Other significant care needs, 'None reported at this assessment.' Must do better.

Summary of needs and recommendation:

'Nancy evidences complex and intense care needs with a level of unpredictability with behaviour and a primary health need and is eligible for CHC funding at this time.' Oh, you beauty.

Dementia isn't considered a disease like cholera, yellow fever, or bubonic plague. It's just something you get for living too long. It's your own bloody fault for getting old. Just because you've looked after yourself and never gone running to the doctor or the hospital to get fixed you can't expect the National Health Service to step in at the last minute and waste its time caring for the moribund. However, contrary to this, if, without the care from others, the condition of the person concerned worsens it then becomes a health issue and now she's ill enough to be unhealthy I discover that Ma might be eligible for continuing health care in the past. This is called 'retrospective continuing health care.' It's like looking backwards on a moving bus.

The NHS doesn't do 'care' care, it services people's health, which is health care. However if it cared for patients at the CARE stage they might never become a health issue!

27 July

Ma is slumped in her chair, her head to one side as 'I do like that doggy in the window' trills from the CD player, along with a medley of popular tunes. A carer is trying to get fluids inside her by dipping Rich Tea biscuits in tea and dropping the soggy result into her mouth.

Gladys 'Help' asks if I'm a builder and how much work I'm getting. The son and daughter of Ron come in to visit and nervously don't acknowledge me. It's as though they are embarrassed to be there. I later consider my own grey beard, and grey hair and realise they think I'm one of the residents. Back in the car I put the Stranglers on and break the speed limit to reassure myself that I'm not a care home resident.

Ma has been granted continuing health care from 24 July 2012 and I now have to apply for this to be retrospective and try to reclaim the £74,000 of her money which has gone to Westcliff Lodge, already.

Ma still asks for Rhoda when she is taken to her room in the evening. She is 'turned' at least twice in the night by carers. As they come in to move her she often calls out 'I'm dry' to save them another job.

11 August

I rolled Ma out into a hot, sunny day but she remained slumped over for most of the journey along Chalkwell seafront. I wheeled her to the site of the long-demolished Westcliff Jetty, where the shiny flint foundations gave her a good footing into deep water for sea-bathing.

It meant nothing to her.

29 July 1978

'Swim at Port Holland. Dick said he'd left it "too late to go in this year"

but whilst floating out on water saw minute figure gingerly walking down to water's edge and finally striking out. Said afterwards he doesn't really enjoy it but feels he should make the effort!
After a swim I always feel about 18-years-old – this lasts for half an hour and then back to normal.'

I also rolled her up Chalkwell Station ramp-style bridge where once she rolled me in a pushchair in a summer rainstorm.
We stopped to watch a little tennis along Victory Path.
'Shall we go home for a cup of tea?'
'No.'
'Do you want to watch tennis?'
'Shut up.'
Eventually as we neared the lodge she looked at it and said: 'Turn round.'
And yet I am not sure if she knows where she is.

13 August

Sing-a-long songs are being aired on the CD player: Bridge over Troubled Water, As time goes by, and Chattanooga Choo Choo at which Ma's slippered feet start pumping. But the disc was scratched, 'Chat Chat Chat Chat ter ter ter ter ter noo noo noo noo noo,' it confused Ma who stopped beating with her feet. It was a kind of electronic Alzheimer's.
'Stop patting me,' she said as I, feeling the need to communicate in some way, tapped her wrist with my hand. The carer feeding Bettine in the next armchair, spun round, surprised at the coherent sentence, 'What did she say?'

As I left I said: 'See you soon,' to which Bettine replied : 'Plenty of room here.'

10 October

Been in and out over the weeks, not much to report as Ma says little if anything these days. Her last phrase was 'Hollyoaks' which she read out slowly from the TV screen like a child finding her first words. Does it go further? Does she follow the plot? Enjoy the storyboard? Recognise the conflict? The jeopardy? And the resulting cliffhanger for the next edition?
Does it matter?

29 October

Ma is sitting comatose. I move my head trying to get her to focus her circled retinas on my face while gently shaking her knees. Eventually the mouth closes, her eyes do focus and she has the expression, briefly, of Nancy Durham. I go to check her room and say 'I'm just going to check your room,' she says 'Oh dear' then subsides into silence once more. She spends more time in this state than in a focused state these days although Ethel will come over and screech 'Nan,' as though her being comatose is unusual.
'Nan is sleeping today,' she says to me. But it is hard to believe that she suddenly becomes talkative when I'm not there to observe it.

10 November

Ma is looking bright-eyed and in good health. She ate two biscuits while being confronted with, I use the phrase deliberately rather than 'watching' Roger Federer play against Juan Martin Del Potro in the ATM Finals. With her mouth open ready to receive a morsel she lifted her right hand up to it, the biscuit, in her left hand remained stationary.

28 June 1989

'The Australians have mercifully won the cricket so there won't be any annoying interruptions of the tennis, but unfortunately it poured with rain at Wimbledon so some of yesterday's matches were shown instead. Finally we got Lendle playing against a qualifier, which was very dull. Then two women which was even worse; Harry Carpenter kept taking us round the outside courts instead of the centre court where Connors was playing as he was saving that up for "Match of the Day" tonight."

23 December

I arrived to find Ma, like a little monkey swaying across the lounge hanging from a domestic mobile crane, her arms and legs dangling from a harness, as she was wheeled over to her reclining chair before being lowered into it. She has just been 'toileted.'
The reclining chair and the profiling bed we purchased second hand and in good condition for £400 the pair. A new profiling bed costs £2,000 alone. We comfort ourselves with the cliché that 'it's what she would have wanted.'
Not unreasonably. Ma would have been horrified to think her savings were ebbing away on such items.

2013

12 January

I popped in at teatime. Ma propped up in her profiling bed, eyes closed and listening to Fred Astaire and Ginger Rogers performing 'Just the way you look tonight' on her portable TV.
Her later diaries seem like a race to note down the runaway train of life: birthdays come and go; people die; rounds of Bridge continue; TV Wimbledon flares briefly and is gone; the sun comes out; the skies cloud over; charity shop donations are received, listed, sorted, priced and sold.
The editing is less drastic; few if any pages are cut out and little is scrawled over. That's because what is recorded now is nothing more than a prosaic diversion from what must come. The wood is much closer now, the long and winding road towards it much shorter.

14 February

Cathy called me at the office, the home have been on – they have her mobile phone as she works locally, while I commute to London.
Would I call Irene and then Dr Nagel. Irene wants to send Ma to hospital for an IVF infusion to whack the, by now, severe chest infection. Dr Nagel disagrees. First I call Irene who explains that she believes Ma needs antibiotics delivered directly rather than orally as the infection has again laid her low. I agree with her that a hospital visit is in order.

I then get through to Dr Nagel after an hour or so.
'She's gone downhill quite rapidly. She has a lung infection and a bit of a temperature. She's drowsy and dry in the mouth.'
It becomes apparent that it is my decision, as I have Power of Attorney, to make the call.
But Dr Nagel does not think the visit worthwhile: 'It's better just to see what nature does. If she recovers all well and good, if not it's nature's way of dealing with things.'
She tells me she had a mother the same age and that this would have been how she would have proceeded with her. 'Mrs Durham is not distressed. The only thing that causes her distress is being moved.'
I then change my mind and agree with her. I do not want to go against Irene's decision, but on balance I think this time the GP – of which there are several in the practice – is right. Also I know that Irene's decision is an emotive one, I'm very grateful for her concern, but it is a non-professional decision. It is a 'caring' decision.
'I'll call Irene and explain,' I say to Dr Nagel.
'No, don't worry, I'll call Irene, it's my job,' she says.
I sense a whiff of battle. I do not want Irene to feel she's lost.
We both call Irene.
I appease Irene and explain that perhaps, this time, the GP is right. I thank her for all her concern and apologise for countermanding her.
I've always appeased the staff. I don't want them taking out their frustration on Ma when I'm not around.

16 February

Ma is restricted to her room. She has just coughed up the apple juice Alex has fed her. And her coughing is wracking her whole body. She is red in the face and the coughing is exhausting her. It is hard to watch.

'It's Dicky,' I said in her right ear, 'I'm here. I'm always here.'

'Yes,' she said and smiled.

The next day I called the GP again. This time I got through to Dr Nagel, there are five GPs at Ma's surgery.

I explained I was worried about the coughing and wondered if there was any kind of treatment to help ease it.

'Codeine syrup, but it will make her more drowsy. Coughing is a way of fighting the infection,' she said.

I told her I heard pneumonia mentioned again.

'Pneumonia is just another word for chest infection,' she said.

She asked if I would like a doctor to visit Ma again. I said I would appreciate it.

Then I called the home to let them know and discover Ma has 'bounced back' again! She's downstairs, eating and drinking and 'chatting'. The oral-fed antibiotics appeared to have worked after all, plus the coughing?

We receive news that Clifford died a few days ago of heart failure.

When I asked where Joan was, a carer said: 'She died on Thursday,' in front of the others. No-one seemed to notice.

Ethel said: 'Dicky, you know them all.'

As I continue to read through Ma's diaries they seem to have become an existential tract; with the numbers of the days struck off with a flourish. I make a diary entry therefore I am.

22 May 1985

'To Southend. Bought grey skirt. Lift home with Anna. Grey cardigan. Cleared side of house. Put beans in. <u>Gas Board.</u>'

2 July 1985

'Walked to Deal and back. Long swim opposite the house. Diana rang up. Cauliflower cheese and bottle of wine. Drink at Dover Yacht Club and called in to see Lee. Le Conte beat Lendle.'

Sometimes the days are not struck off and instead the entries are timed:

1 October 1985

'2.45. No bridge. Met C in Broadway – he phoned later – and we went for a swim off old Leigh beach. He drove back and I went down for another. Met Vera Mayo. Golden and sunny.'

2 October 1985

'3.13. Compost bin arrived. Jenny helped me assemble it behind the shed. She is going to lower all her vegetable peelings over fence in bucket. Swim.'

21 April

Ma uttered three phrases on the trot this afternoon, while seated in the conservatory. 'You are nice,' 'I do love you,' and 'I don't care.' I went up to her room to check on her wardrobe and found it shrouded in darkness, the curtains drawn. As I entered a figure leapt up from Ma's bed. Ethel. Taking an afternoon nap. She was hugely apologetic, but I reassured her that it was fine by me and pleased to have confirmed the sanctuary-like quality I'd always noticed for Room No. 9 and the fact the bed is always kept scrupulously clean!

18 May

It's the nearest Saturday to Ma's 90th birthday two days hence and we held a party for her at Westcliff Lodge. She was seated on a centrally-arranged blue, faux leather chair adjusted so that her feet were dangling. She was like a queen in dotage but still at court. She'd been dressed in a light white cotton dress embroidered with blue flowers and was holding a helium-filled balloon with 90 in pink. Ethel and Alex were casually dressed: it was their day off, but they had come in anyway to help arrange the food on tables along the sides of the room. Ma was animated, her eyes sparkling.
Cathy had arranged a Power Point presentation of Ma's life in photographs which were on the large TV screen and which Ma appeared to look at.
Guests included Rhoda's son Francis, from her first marriage, and her two daughters, Helen and Janet and her son Robin, from her second, to Uncle Bill. Majorie's son John Wood and of course his brother Bryan were there and husbands, sons and daughters of the various tribes. My

sister, Diana, over from the USA, was there, too and as far as anyone could guess, Ma enjoyed it especially early on. As the afternoon wore on she seemed to wear with it and was unable to take in all the sudden stimuli and surfeit of attention. And next day, according to Irene was 'knackered.'

Jenny Green was also there, up from Devon especially. 'I'm not missing Nancy's 90th.' And in conversation I mentioned that Clifford had been giving Ma paracetamol daily, to which she said: 'Was he trying to bump her off?'

6 June 1993

'The date of Dick's 75th birthday.'

My father. He died in 1984 aged 65.

23 September

Ethel and Alex have returned to the Philippines, their visas having expired. They had formed a bond with Ma and Ethel had given evidence in court against the abusive carer, a fellow countrywoman. She told me that when she told Ma she was leaving for good Ma wept.

I gave her £200 as a thank-you for what appeared to be her exceptional attention to my Mother.

29 June 1993

'Walked round to return photo to Francis; sun came out – clouded over later.'

21 October

NHS Continuing Care officer, Nikki Wood, visited Ma today for her annual check up to make sure she is ill enough to warrant continued funding.
She asked Ma if she knew who I was.
Ma just smiled.
'Are you feeling well?'
'Yes.'
'Are you in any pain?'
'Yes.'
Ma just smiled and repeated the only word she could muster for the sake of good manners.
We then repaired to the garden shed to go through the box-ticking again. This time with Janine, deputy manager, as Irene was off sick.
Mobility. No change. There is none.
Behaviour. Reduced from high risk to low risk as Nikki has deduced Ma is only verbally aggressive, not physically so.
Continence. No change. Ma is doubly incontinent.
Cognition. Is Ma subject to depression because of her situation? Or is she fighting off food and medication because of cognitive deterioration? Nikki decides it is the latter.
But despite some hitches enough boxes are ticked and the funding is to continue for another year.

30 June 1993

'A little warmer, foot better as am increasing walking. Loads of newspapers to waste bin near Clifford's flat.

8 December

Christmas party at the lodge. Ma watched a troupe of panto singers perform Jack and the Beanstalk and made unintelligible noises, but pulled characteristic faces mostly of disapproval.

31 June 1993

'Bridge here; Gloria and Jane bid up to five clubs, I had eight of diamonds to the A.K. void in clubs and AKQ spades. So I bid five diamonds; Sandy's hand went down and she had the queen I lost the two losing hearts and that was all.'

15 December

They say cats are born blind and Ma reminds me of a newborn puss these days. Her well-defined face has the broad cheekbones of a cat. It has shrunk into a tightly-closed mouth like that of a feline and her eyes are invariably shut tight. Then one will open as one imagines a kitten's does as it first beholds the world. Her hands are also bunched into little claw-like fists. Of course she doesn't need them anymore as she is fed, watered, dressed, toileted and transported. I pushed my finger into her right fist and her fingers closed over it but it was not possible to tell if this was anything other than a reflex action.

3 July 1993

'Cold, strong winds. C. painted his bedroom windows.'

25 December

The family gathered round and Ma uttered a single phrase: 'What's the point?' Whether this is a fragment of yesteryear or a contemporary statement remains open to question.

21 July 1990

'Sat out in garden. The new circular clothes drier makes ideal sun canopy; tea in garden; all was peaceful as neighbours away.
'No rain; garden kept watered all day otherwise hydrangea blossoms crinkle like paper, the grass is suffering, the beans and spinach doing well. The sun burns down all day without a break.'

2014

27 January

One of my Christmas presents was a subscription to Saga magazine from Cathy. And, of course, the New Year being the time to market holidays - the next thing to 'look forward to' - there is a special offer to its readers a 'Road of Remembrance' trip to Flanders which costs £699 for seven nights and 'includes12 meals: seven breakfasts and five dinners.' The mealtimes itemised because as far as any ageing demographic is concerned the trough is as good a calendar as any.

18 May

My weekly visits are short and sweet, now. It's just a habit, a 'watching brief' as she is invariably dozing. Ma had a birthday cake with her name engraved in iced sugar. She was slumped to one side, her legs much thinner, her face skeletal in profile. But she still smiles for youth. A beam for Katie. She said nothing. Although one carer told me: 'She couldn't stop talking yesterday.' And another told me Ma says: 'Thank-you dear,' as she is given a cuddle when being put to bed at night.

Wandering Dot, with her default worried expression wandered in, said 'Oh, dear,' very quietly and wandered out again. Tall John, the fireman who I used to meet at Leigh station when I was on an early shift, and who, much to my surprise is now resident here, also wandered in shoeless.

He greeted us all in his usual, well-mannered and friendly way and then left. Dot wandered back in and said: 'Oh, dear', before wandering out again rubbing her painfully thin shoulders.

A newcomer to the conservatory is a slender woman with a large wig which slips forward over her eyebrows occasionally.

The one Anglo-Saxon carer there at present is sharper in dealing with her at 'toileting time' than the Filipinos would be.

She commands her to stand up.

'I'll fall.'

'No, stand up, we've got you.'

'I'll fall.'

'No you WON'T,' later one of the Filipinos returned and asked her if she was happy.

'Be happy. Are you happy? You must always be happy.'

To which the woman replied: 'Not as happy as when I was young.'

2 November

Eden, a new carer from Manila has arrived and is feeding Ma as Carol, a new resident, asked for ice-cream.
'After lunch, Carol.'
'Why can't I have it now?' says Carol, a powerfully well-built woman who is always perfectly charming and polite to me, but who can be aggressive to the much smaller carers.
'After lunch, Carol,' Eden continues both trying to placate Carol and feed my Mother at the same time, 'You like ice-cream?'
'I love ice-cream.'
'After lunch, Carol.'
'I live here. My mother lives here and you're for it.'
'You can have ice-cream after lunch.'
'Well stick it up your arsehole. You are so ignorant. You ignorant bitch.'
I sat next to Carol and gently explained Eden would have to feed everyone lunch before she brought the dessert. The ice-cream.
'I wanted something else but I've forgotten what it was.'
'How's Peter?' I asked. Her husband had been a regular visitor, but the visits invariably left him in tears.
'Who?'
'Peter, your husband.'
'How do you know him?'
'I've met him in here.'
'You're better off without,' she whispered conspiratorially.

23 November

Iris who sports a wig, I say sports advisedly as wearing a wig, in the sense that it is an alternative to hair, would be inaccurate, in Iris's case it's more like headwear; walks in crookedly, a bandage of fibreglass matting around her left leg and sits in a chair. She is hungry, but it's not a meal time.

'Get me dinner...oh.'

'Get me dinner...oh.'

'Get me dinner...oh.'

'Get me up...oh.'

'I'll fall.'

'Get me up.'

'I'll fall.'

'Get me up for dinner...oh.'

The 'oh' is a sign-off of resignation, perhaps that no-one is responding, but it lasts no more than a few seconds before she's forgotten no-one has responded and starts the aggressive demand once more.

'Get me dinner.'

Ma made an incomprehensible noise when I said I was going. Difficult to tell if she wanted me to stay.

'Get me up...oh.'

2015

2 February

The home called today to say Ma has 'deteriorated.' She has been in bed for several days and I have visited regularly. The only response I've had to my visits was a one-off wail, I could not tell if it was of humour or despair.

23 July 1990

'Jenny back from caravan came round to collect Charlie, her budgie which we look after when they go away. Very furious and said she now had a dustbin lid on her roof. Asked her to clarify and apparently her next door neighbour has put up a satellite dish, practically all over on her side. Jenny furious. Ron Cox furious.'

4 February

I was called to the lodge today to meet Jenny and Irene who are changing Ma's care plan. She is now officially under 'palliative care.'
She was lying in the foetal position in her bed the TV on showing 'Around the World in 80 Days.' Her eyes were open – just. She was looking very drawn, her jawline marked.
I chattered about nothing.
I asked her to give me a smile.
She did, a faint, barely perceptible, lop-sided grin.

24 July 1990

'Muddle over bridge. Jane wanted us to go up to Tattersall Gardens, went next door to tell Frank who was annoyed as he'd got bridge table out and garage locked.'

11 February

Although confined to her bed Ma has rallied again. She has eaten a bowl of porridge and a yoghurt and was 'singing' at 11 am to Matt Monroe despite still being wracked by a chesty cough.

12 February

Invariably when I say I'm leaving produces the only response from Ma during a visit. 'I'm going shopping now, so I'll see you later,' the way I avoid actually saying the word goodbye in case, in retrospect, it becomes a poignant statement.
Today I said: 'Well I'm off for breakfast now, see you later.'
She opened her eyes and said, very faintly, 'I'm happy to see you.'
Taken aback as this was the first phrase for many months, I said: 'I'm happy to see you.'
We exchanged smiles and she closed her eyes again. Ma is a 'morning' person.
Earlier during the visit a single tear fell from her right eye, but I sensed this was a mechanical rather than an emotional reaction.

10 April

The BBC are reporting that being overweight can cut the risk of dementia according to an investigation by The Lancet.
Since being made redundant last November I tend to take the bus. My old man's pass giving me free travel and if The Lancet story is accurate bus drivers have nothing to

fear from dementia. I've noticed that bus drivers, at least the First Direct bus drivers are obese. The one who drove me today was a typical example, not so much fat as round. Young and perfectly round and because of his youth he seemed comfortable with his sphereness.

His First Direct issue boots were round. His uniform Velcro'd up over his round, youthful body made him appear even rounder. He was round from the front elevation, round from the back elevation, round in profile and round, probably, in plan. He seemed roundly benign, roundness not being the physique of a man of action after all. He sat in his bus driver's cubicle a round peg in a square hole.

As the bus stopped at a 'stage' he switched the engine off and set up an anxiety among the passengers. We sat wondering if the bus would ever mobilise again as fine rain melted down the windows, in silence, occasionally flicked aside by a single, fast swoop of the windscreen wiper.

The round driver opened his little stable door with the tubes of change stacked like machine-gun bullets on the inside and activated the folding front doors of the bus which hissed as a colleague – also round – squelched aboard in his First Direct boots.

Suddenly I realised what was so incongruous about them: young men wearing ties. And as spheres the ties give them a radius, as globes longitude, as balls, symmetry.

12 April

I suppose it's only natural to step up one's visits to a close relative following advice from their carers they are soon to be gone. And I have or rather I did. Upon the realisation that demise is either moving at a snail's pace or has, in fact ceased in its trajectory, I suppose it's only natural to step-down one's visits. And I have.

Next I suppose it's only natural to question why one makes them at all.

So you're not dying then? So what am I doing here? And yet if I'm visiting because my Mother is dying the logic of that is I should be comforted by finding a corpse.

Does a visit benefit my Mother? Almost impossible to gauge. A fleeting moment of recognition may be welcoming, but is just as likely to be upsetting for her: there he was gone.

Does a visit benefit me? Much more likely the case. I have 'been to visit my Mother.' I have been a dutiful son.

So it's back to the weekly visits to 'be there for her.'

6 May

I had a long dream last night about Ma in her home. Several plates of uneaten beef in slices are scattered about the floor. All the other guests are lying down on beds but in common areas. But Ma, who I'm chasing, is upright and moving through corridors which are getting narrower until I can't squeeze through and she disappears as though through a caving pot hole.

7 May

It's the day of the 2015 General Election and, having been to my polling booth early, I'm on the bus to Westcliff Lodge and sitting behind a Bangladeshi man who's dressed in a suit and wearing the yellow and mauve tie of UKIP. He was on his mobile phone to his local HQ reporting how he had just visited one polling booth and was off to another.

I could not help but think of the role of the kapos in Nazi concentration camps.

Back in February, Rob Tinlin, the electoral registration officer for Southend-on-Sea Borough Council wrote to Ma threatening her with an £80 fine if she did not register to vote. They know her name, her address but now registering to vote is done online and she must do this via a 'computer, tablet or smartphone' or by filling in a form if she has none of the aforementioned.

'To find out more about the changes or the circumstances in which we will impose a fine go to www.gov.uk/yourvotematters,' his letter ended cheerily. Fuck off, Rob.

20 May

The phone rings. It's 06.20. Ma is 'coughing up blood' a carer says, but Cathy, who answers the phone, finds it difficult to understand the poorly enunciated English.

I arrive an hour later. It is a false alarm. Ma is not coughing up blood, but blood has been found in her stools and she has been coughing a lot.

A duty doctor was called out.

'We all love her here,' said Janine the deputy manager, 'yesterday she was downstairs responding to Beryl and laughing: "Har, Har, Har" as she does.'

I found Ma dozing peacefully, curtains drawn against the bright sunlight, and a night lamp still burning. I left her birthday cards and presents unopened on the table. She is 92 today.

27 February 1995

*'Decided that pink hydrangea must be moved out of sun –
pruned it well down and removed the Victorian iron
support.'*

26 May

Following the advice of Westcliff Lodge management I
went to make enquiries today about funeral arrangements.
I arrived at a local funeral directors to discover the door on
a security lock and felt self-conscious standing in the
bright sunshine on the bustling High Street and dreading
being seen by a neighbour. There would be only one
reason I would be standing there. Already one gauche
neighbour known as 'Mad Miriam' who is obese and
wobbles up and down the Hill on one walking stick
screeched across the road: 'Is your Mother still alive?'
Stifling my anger at her thoughtlessness I shouted back:
'Yes. She's doing well. We're moving her back in soon.'
Go and spread that around you old bag, I thought. But she
won't, as good gossip falls on deaf ears.
Eventually I'm given entry to the dark side and meet Alice
a stocky woman with blunt teeth and a grey parting
showing through her dyed copper hair. She explains the
'procedure.' An interim death certificate is issued by the
GP and a full one by the registrar at the local town hall, the
'Civic Centre' in Southend's case. At that stage a 'disposal
notice' is also issued.
'That's the one we need,' she said.
There are set costs. The fee for the crematorium is £1,465
and the boxing and transportation of the corpse to the
furnace is £850.

'If you would like your loved one preserved for their dignity we offer an embalming service,' she said. £89. The provision of hearse, pall-bearers and attendants £550. Extras include 'mourning stationary', 'catering' and a 'full range of quality memorials, please see our brochure and separate price list.'

Where are 'All the Very Best' of Driffield, Yorkshire when you need them?

Additional charges include 'Bringing the deceased person into our care outside of normal office hours,' £122.

Alice, rather a butch lass, wearing a black trouser suit, said ministers could be provided from Catholic priests to Humanists.

'You can have a service where God, the Lord, cannot be mentioned: no hymns, basically an atheist service. Or you can have an independent service with a Humanist, but which includes a favourite hymn and people can pray…it's much more flexible.'

I felt as liberated as Henry VIII must have done having invented the Great Compromise.

On the subject of coffins, I was shown a list:

'The Coffin and Casket Selection,' which started with the Glen Coffin at £350 going up to the Autumn Oak Coffin at £2,586, although the latter, Alice said, 'Are more geared to burial.'

If you're going to shell out over two grand you'd want it to last a bit longer, I guess.

The 'Urn Selection' includes a Wessex at £88, rising to an Ocean at £206.

Alice gave me a thick dossier headlined: 'Helping you every step of the way with advice, support and care.'

Cathy and I visited Ma later in the day as she was being changed and she was making a sort of parody of a lament as though turning personal violation into a joke.

By 2000 my mother's handwriting in her diaries is distinctly shaky. Emily has two 'm's; b's at the beginning of sentences are just circles and the letters have increased in size as though by enlarging them she can maintain communication.

20 March 2000

'Birthday of Herbert Best.'

Her father who died in 1928 aged 50.

28 May

Ma is now regularly taken 'downstairs' to the conservatory, once more where I found her this morning 'singing' to 'What's New Pussycat,' and later 'Tower of Strength.'

Dot is still on walk-about, muttering 'Oh dear,' and frowning each time she re-enters the room, which for her is a novel experience for every reappearance.

Ivy is dozing. Then angry Carol is helped in by carer David, who has just completed a sponsored walk of the Pennine Way to raise money for the lodge.

'He's a bad man, he's hurt me,' says Carol.

'No, Carol, he's nice,' I say.

'NO HE'S NOT,' she scolds.

Ma starts chanting to 'I just don't know what to do with myself' as David manages to switch Carol from her wheelchair into a static chair.

'There, she'll chill out, now,' he says to me, but instead she kicks over her feeding table.

David sets it upright again and puts down on it toast and jam, porridge and tinned fruit to which Carol said: 'Thank-you' before falling hungrily upon it. David then says to me: 'Nancy's no trouble but she closes her mouth when we try to feed her.'

Beryl II, sitting next to Ma, is gentle and smiling. Pretty much always her state. Incongruously a black & white photo of her cutting her wedding cake with husband Keith is hanging, not in her room, as you might expect, but on a wall of the conservatory where all can see it.

She smiles at me as we listen to 'The Man who Shot Liberty Valance'

And I ask her when the photograph was taken.

'Not that long ago. I can't be sure,' she says.

29 May

The latest issue of The Spectator magazine carries the following sentence: 'Each nightingale has a personal repertoire of 250 phrases made from 600 individual sound units.'

If that's enough to enable a bird to sing then that's argument enough to vote against any Assisted Dying Bill. We should let old folks trill away.

4 June

Ma is making caterwauling sounds continuously. She ate her porridge but refused a drink at 0900. I know this because an 'Input/Output Position Chart' is left on a clipboard on her table and is filled in daily by carers. This form is to 'prevent malnutrition and dehydration by encouraging fluid output and offering nourishing snacks in between meals to increase calorie intake. To daily monitor urinary output and bowel movement and promote good circulation through passive movements and relieving pressure on existing sores.'

Boxes are ticked and abbreviations noted: TBON (toileted and bowels opened normal); PC (Pad wet and changed); WBOL (pad wet and bowels opened, loose/watery stool). And so on.

Like the grey and orange nylon harness used to crane Ma from bed to wheelchair and from wheelchair to static chair or loo seat which now hangs on the door of her en suite lavatory in full view of the room, the chart of her bowel movements needs no longer to be 'put away.'

In the same vein I took a pee I her hand-basin: the loo itself was buried under more paraphernalia of care including a mobile commode.

Her portable TV has broken. It was showing Swan Lake, which was stuck on 'scene selection' playing the same music over and over again. She might have been listening to it for days for all I knew.

I asked if she'd like the music turned off.

She shook her head.

But I bought her a new CD player and packed the useless TV under her table. She doesn't 'watch' anymore, just listens.

25 March 2000

'Katy and Emily round with presents and each had a go on the stair-lift.'

7 June

Ma is dozing in the sun, bib on. I have to go away on business. I lean over, whisper in her ear: 'I'll see you in a week,' and plant a gentle kiss on her ear.
She gives a very faint, but unmistakeable smile.

21 June

Will this be Ma's last longest day? Her face appears as a death-mask, but one which comes back to life. A haggard skull, open-mouthed in her cot.
She lives in an upholstered trough holding her mouth agape like a baby thrush in the nest.
Down in the summer-heated conservatory I watched Carol, arms like hanging porridge, collapsing her baggy mouth over toast.
No turn should be left un-stoned I think as I watch a talent-free talent contest on the giant TV which is once again ignored by breakfasting Carol and everyone else.

17 July

The skeleton beneath is trying to climb out. Porridge is clearly enough to sustain life but only at the bread line. My mother's jaw-line is extruding, her cheekbones, too, and the bone over her eye sockets has left her eyeballs in deep pools. The skull is showing its hand. The tissue has to give way.

Her once luxuriant hair is now grey, thin and stiff like combed hay.

I noted this on my smart phone in a sotto-voce voice-over. To my horror my Mother appeared to be listening, so I asked her in a louder voice if she wanted some music, hoping to mask my indiscretion.

She appeared to say: 'No.'

'Very good,' I said and walked to the door.

'Yes,' she said and I walked back to ask her if she had a choice, but now she turned to caterwauling.

I bent to kiss her again, the act of departure, and her face suddenly took on its tiger aspect, eyes flaring and comprehending.

'Bye, bye,' she said angrily.

I think, I hoped, this was only because as my face touched her head she jerked towards me and my beard pricked her.

12 August 2001

'Planned to have a meal at Waitrose. Waitrose crowded each bought goose feather pillow and went home.'

30 June

Today I received a letter from Jennifer Edge, 'team administrator continuing healthcare retrospective review'

'Dear Mr Durham

RE: The late Mrs Nancy Durham DOB: 20.05.1923 NHS Continuing Healthcare Retrospective Review'

She is asking for copies of Ma's private health care records which 'could be used within your claim' to get the money refunded which she has already spent for residing at Westcliff Lodge.

I sent her what she requested and politely pointed out that my Mother's obituary has yet to be written.

2 September

Ethel has been in touch with Cathy via email. She is back in the Philippines and her father is facing medical problems. Could we lend her £300? A quick discussion and I feel it's the least we can do, especially as Ma will be paying.

We confirm we will send the cash and ask what is the best way of getting it to her.

Via Western Union, she says and raises the loan to £400.

I walk to Western Union's office and wire the cash, wondering if I'm being 'touched' but reasoning that it's money morally squandered if so.

21 September

One in three babies born today will develop Alzheimer's, reported the Today programme.

An expert said that being 'doddery' masked the onset of dementia to which the veteran reporter, John Humphreys, asked hopefully: 'We're simply living longer…aren't we?'

The talking head from Alzheimer's Research UK said it was time to 'bring dementia out of the shadows, end the "stigma" surrounding the disease and make it an heroic subject like "the Big C"', unwittingly using the euphemism for cancer which has helped preserve its own stigma.

23 September

Just one phrase: 'Thank-you', the wheat from the oral chaff, in response to: 'Would you like some music?'

18 August 2001

'Dicky now 50!'

That's me.

25 September

Glaswegian Janet McKay, an 88-year-old dementia sufferer left her home, got on a bus and went walkabout in an industrial estate before dying eight days later. No-one noticed. No-one looked. Only a CCTV camera was there when she died.
Police have said they are sorry for not following up her disappearance with more zeal. 'We apologise to the family for any distress caused at this difficult time.' But only the press are blaming them. Mrs McKay has become a 'story' because in a busy world she is the second or third example of people dying outdoors in Scotland before the police have found them.

20 August 2001

'Video set went off for repair.'

9 October

'Thank-you. Thank-you,' eyes shut. In response to: 'I've put some nice classical music on for you.'
The CD player was set to Classic FM – too many adverts, which would once have driven Ma mad – I retuned it to BBC Radio 3 and left a note for the carers asking them if they could please do the same.
At the door I looked back. Ma was lying with her bed-clothes swooped round in a great swirling S fanning out into a giant fin-shape. Her white hair splayed on the pillow, her cadaverous face falling into a black hole of mouth, she looked like an aged mermaid.

2003 November

'Was just coming down in stair-lift when a small figure at the bottom said: "I will tell you when to stop, Grandma" and did so. "Oh, thank-you, dear, just in case I might go through the wall."
Richard followed me into kitchen, "I know you like giving everybody lots of lovely food, Grandma," he said eyeing up the apple tart on the bench, cut him a slice.
Cathy gave me a lovely school photograph of Richard and they departed'

The words of Ma's last entry were undated, trying to break out into block letters and without full stops.

Down in the lobby an elderly man wearing a black jockey hat with the name Jim Prince printed on it is trying the door handle.

He engages me in friendly but garbled conversation. It is more a selection of known noises representing the prosaic: I can't actually make out the words but I know the sounds: 'He's all right,' 'Coo, I should say,' 'Flipping heck,' 'I told him so.' They are noises one makes all one's life. They are a parody of communication, more about reaction than instigation. They are the OKs of agreement, the all right thens of compromise, the eeyores of an unthinking life.

I notice he has his slippers on the wrong feet and point this out to a carer in non-critical way, saying it clearly doesn't matter onto which foot a slipper resides.

But she is concerned that it shows a lack of attention and immediately sets about getting Jim to remove them and re-arrange them on the correct foot. The end result is that they still look 'kippered'. He has worn them so often incorrectly they've become ambidextrous.

27 October

Ma died today at 16.00. And after all that I wasn't there. We were driving along the Scottish coastline of the Solway Firth having just stopped to look across the wide sands of Southerness. The cloud was lowering, the wind rising, the light dying.

Cathy had a text on her phone: 'Call Westcliff Lodge urgently.'

She turned and looked at me with alarm on her face, and read out the text, 'Should I call?' she asked as I was at the wheel.

'Yes, do.'

'Nancy's gone,' Janine, the deputy manager told her.

She had been coughing sufficiently badly for the GP to be called and when he arrived he advised to keep Ma 'under observation.' This had happened many times before and there was no reason to think it wouldn't happen many times again. But in the afternoon the observations showed this time it was different.

When we returned from Scotland I went to speak with Janine. She took me into the empty dining room and closed the door. Death now safely compartmentalised she told me of my mother's last minutes of her 92 years.

She reported that the GP had said the fluid/mucus coming from my mother's mouth was not just the result of infection, but secretion. He advised keeping my mother upright and comfortable. Later at 14.30 Janine checked and Ma was sweating her 'phlegm was coming out.' Janine has seen enough old folks departing to know the signs and frantically tried to contact me. But we had not told the home we were going away, my mobile phone was in the boot of the car and out of battery anyway. She called Jenny who advised her to keep trying. She did so and eventually raised Cathy.

'I think she's trying to go,' Janine said using the present tense as she recalled the day, 'her phlegm out then she close her mouth. I think she's trying to go. I say: "If you want to go, go." I don't want her to suffer. I pray. I say: "You can go if you want to. I couldn't get hold of Dicky Pie. I tried but I couldn't" She was so quiet.'

Many struggle, Janine said, but Ma went quietly like she'd decided.

At the side of the road in Scotland I thought about the blue hydrangeas speckled through the wooded coast and recalled how Ma loved them. Or did I think that? Was I imagining I thought that? Over the mobile phone I thanked

Janine for being there and asked what the procedure was. She said she would organise the undertaker, the Co-op, they use.

Appropriate, I thought, Ma had used the Co-op all her life. In fact my earliest memory was of holding her hand and entering the grocery part of the store just before a bitterly cold 1950's Christmas. Bare floorboards, men in white coats, a maroon-painted bacon slicer, tins of biscuits with pheasants in the snow painted on the lids…

By early evening we arrived in Hamilton to stay with Cathy's Aunt Netty and Uncle Billy. Uncle Billy shoved a large glass of red wine in my hand. They were my family now.

A call came through from 'Dave' at the Co-op.

'Are you Nancy Durham's son?'

'Yes.'

'May I offer my condolences?'

'Thank-you.'

'We have taken her into our care,' he said.

As long as she was out in front, ahead of me, there was a sense of going forward, and, however tedious, of a continuum, of a line, which drew me ahead. Now she had stopped I felt as though I was moving away on the other side of her, that the line was spooling out behind me. Each hour after 4pm on the 27th of October drew me further away from her. Every day the line snaking back to her death got longer and the distance from her increased. But like some surreal astronaut, whose airline carries him through the universe, like all sons I was linked by an umbilical cord of belonging which can never be cut.

And yet I had a palpable sense of loss. Perhaps the time beyond is what's called bereavement.

Dave explained the death needed to be registered before a 'funeral plan' could be organised.
And after all that I hadn't been there.

28 October

Trying to meet the demands of the state that I must register my mother's death from a remote location has its difficulties, but everyone is offering their condolences. Southend Council's registrar was next. Not wishing to run up Aunty Netty's phone bill I had taken a run out to Helensborough on business and sat in the car watching the rain driving across the Clyde as I listened patiently on my mobile phone to music which no longer invited performing rights fees on the council website. The registrar chappy was friendly as well as offering his condolences. He said it might be possible to register my mother's death without making an appointment to visit him but that I should check with the care home first to make sure they had not started the process. I did so and they had not but I could no longer get back to the chirpy registrar but instead was lost in a world of musak and pre-recorded options.
So I emailed them requesting an appointment. A day later the email was answered with the advice that I phone them. Meanwhile the receptionist at my mother's GP, after offering her condolences, asked whether she was to be buried or cremated.
'Cremated.'
That could be set in train her end once the GP had issued a death certificate.
'But surely that was already carried out at the home?'

'I'm afraid, Mr Durham, that was a confirmation of death. A death certificate can only be issued by a GP who has seen the patient alive.'

The presentation of a corpse being no guarantee that it once lived, must, I supposed, rule out the Frankenstein factor. The requirement to have known the cadaver had once breathed God's air, was the only acceptable confirmation it was one of God's creatures.

2 November

Today, back in Essex, I collected the 'Medical certificate of Cause of Death,' from the GP's surgery. The two young receptionists were chattering within the well-lit, well-heated, job-for-life, brand-spanking new NHS 'primary care' building, the shadow of death a long way off.

It was an elderly woman behind them who noticed me, Father Time's assistant, trying to attract attention and immediately, as though she'd been waiting almost, put her hand on the file.

It was sealed, but outside I tore it open.

'End Stage Vascular Dementia,' a scrawled and printed entry oddly in capitals from a Dr Muhammad Daud.

Of all the doctors at the surgery and of all the doctors who had attended my mother during her illness I had never heard of Doctor Daud.

If he had known her when she was breathing, it was news to me.

My mother was dead. That was that. She was 92 years, five months, one day and sixteen hours old. And that was five days ago. Each day passed and I was yet further away from her. On the other side of her being. I was drawing away from a black hole. I thought of it genuinely as a relief for her and as an escape for me and yet from this sense of being on a line moving further and further away I felt a sea change within me. A sadness that had been waiting, that waits for all of us. A sadness that makes us complete. And from this I knew that love is memory.

Yet I couldn't help wonder what actually happened at 'End Stage Vascular Dementia'? How did anyone KNOW it was 'End Stage Vascular Dementia'? I mean was that it? Did all that time just get written off as a hunch? If Doctor Daud had known her when she was breathing why didn't he find out exactly what made her stop?

I re-sealed the certificate and drove to the brutalist, concrete, 1960s designed 'Civic Centre' in Southend-on-Sea, HQ of the local council. Here it was I'd been 'matched' with my spouse in the registry office, here it was my Mother would be 'despatched.'

I welcomed the solemn approach of the female registrar, with sensible, as opposed to fashionable, cropped hair, who took me into an ante-room and entered details on a large screen computer.

The death had to be registered, I discovered, so that no-one can become my Mother, so that her body is disposed of properly: for public health reasons the funeral director has to report back to the registrar that this is the case; and to confirm she hasn't been murdered. Murderers don't register their successes.

She opened the certificate.

'If you haven't already seen this,' she said politely ignoring the tear in the seal, 'do you agree with it?'

'Well I wondered about the cause. I wasn't sure if there would be a post mortem?'

'If you are not happy with the cause of death then this can be conveyed to the coroner who could order one,' she said.

But of course it was academic. I just wanted my Mother to have died from something else. Something cosier than dementia. What was wrong with 'natural causes'? Or 'old age'?

'No don't worry,' I said, abandoning a sense of diminished responsibility.

On the advice of the registrar I purchased five death certificates at £4 each, using my Mother's credit card to pay and drove to the Co-op funeral parlour.

Charlotte's predilection for neo-punkism could not be completely countered by her smart navy blue corporate uniform. It didn't cover the tattoo on her forearm, the razor-cut, dyed black hair or the five stud piercings in her right ear-lobe.

'Ninety-two?' she said sweetly as she saw the death certificate, ' a good age.'

'True. But the last six would not be years you'd choose to exist through.'

'Oh,' she said, still trying to gauge me. Was I a sobber, or a callous bastard?

'Do you want your mother embalmed?'

I thought of a horizontal Stalin being a corpse for all time.

'Not really,' I said, but asked what was involved and why a person who was going to be cremated would be embalmed.

She told me the blood was replaced with a 'fluid' and asked if I wanted to see my mother. I confirmed I did and that I'd like to see her now.

Charlotte stalled, she said she wouldn't recommend it.

'Why is she naked then?' I asked.

'No she's in the clothes she came here in.'

But I guessed from her hesitation that she was right maybe it would be too shocking. I guessed this was why they suggested embalming. So I agreed to it.

Charlotte, now more relaxed, back on an even keel, not having to lead me into the morgue, said: 'We give her a facial,' and I briefly regretted my decision. But, like the thought of a post mortem I was defending a corpse. It was pointless what they did now.

I let it pass. She would have a facial. Briefly she would lie in state like Stalin.

Did I want my Mother dressed in her own clothes? I did. Then I remembered I'd told the home to distribute them among the needy residents. They were good clothes. New from Marks and Sparks each Christmas and birthday and hardly used.

It was OK they had gowns. 'White or pink?'

'White, I think. What do you think?'

'Definitely white.'

Did my Mother have any jewellery? Was a pace-maker fitted? This girl with the metal earrings asked, because the crematoria can sustain damage.

Did she have any infections?

Why did the funeral folks need a death certificate? I asked out of curiosity.

'To make sure there's been no foul play, you know, that you're not one of your classic Harold Shipman's,' she grinned, 'I mean obviously you're not,' she added, still not quite sure if I would sob or shout. How can she tell?

Was my Mother religious?

'No.'

Did we want music?

'No. I'm just going to say a few words.'

'You're very brave.'

'It's just that anything which smacks of phoneyness makes me gag and my Mother would hate it, too.'

But Charlotte recommended a 'piece' leading the mourners in and another leading them out. This seemed like a good idea.

'They've got a remarkable choice,' she said brightly warming to my agreement, 'They've had anything from The Lion King to The Final Countdown.'

With overt subtlety, Charlotte then left me to leaf through a brightly coloured brochure of coffins, which started with one called The Last Supper at £1,005.

I'm afraid my eye was immediately focused on one made of cardboard. Did I have the nerve to order?

When Charlotte returned I questioned this.

'Most people say: "Oh just give me a cardboard coffin" What they don't realise is that it has to be lined. I mean you imagine it if it got wet and they dropped out?'

I could.

'That's the last thing you want.'

It was. I went with the Maple version.

3 November

I returned to Westcliff Lodge to collect Ma's personal belongings: a few second-hand Rupert books, photos, CDs and a postcard with a Los Angeles date stamp. It was from Katie my eldest daughter:

'Dear Grandma,

Callum and I are now in Hollywood where there are constant reminders and tributes from the stars who you would have grown up with. We are staying in an hotel which is apparently haunted by Marilyn Monroe, we haven't seen her yet!

'Hope you are well, lots of love Katie Durham (Your granddaughter).'

It had arrived the day Ma died.

I mentioned to Kerry, the new manager, how it already seemed strange not having to design my day to fit around a visit to the lodge.

'Well you can always call in just for old time's sake,' she said and we hugged. I then hugged Janine, Riza and Jackie. Jackie said: 'Nancy will always be remembered. And you came and you spoke and you always said what you were doing, where you had been, what was going on, over and over and yet…,' she tailed off empathising with the fact I had missed being there on the last day.

I asked if Room 9 was occupied and if not whether I could take a last look.

'Of course,' said Kerry.

I walked up the deep pile, carpeted stairs for the umpteenth time, pulled open the fire door, for the umpteenth time, passed Room 8, for the umpteenth time. It was never occupied, the door was always open and a pair of men's shoes was always stashed in a bedside cabinet. It was all the same.

Room 9 was locked.

I returned downstairs.

'It doesn't matter, don't worry,' I said.

'No, no. We have the key,' Kerry insisted. The janitor was called, a key produced and I ascended the stairs once more. The room was still peaceful, and, oddly, still Ma's, even though the chest of drawers were open in staggered formation so each could be seen to be empty. Even though the wardrobe doors were ajar for the same reason.

Even though the sides of the 'trough' bed were lowered, perhaps to evacuate their occupant, still it seemed like Ma's room.

I walked to the door and looked round for the last time. It was then that I realised her framed squares of embroidery, almost merged with the magnolia wallpaper, almost becoming an assumption of institution, were still hanging there.

Magnolia, the non-colour, the non-risk, the non-statement for people who like to stay that way. Magnolia goes with anything because it goes unnoticed. It is a non-option, almost a camouflage for not having made a choice.

Perhaps mistaken for modesty, the magnolia environment is in fact an act of self-effacement, of apology for existence, a natural enough emotion growing up in the shadow of First World War decimation.

And the opacity of dementia, itself a state of magnolia, was the last shroud thrown over her life.

The End

35212012R00190

Printed in Poland
by Amazon Fulfillment
Poland Sp. z o.o., Wrocław